Iliazd

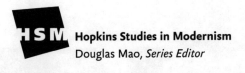

Hopkins Studies in Modernism
Douglas Mao, *Series Editor*

Iliazd

A Meta-Biography

of a Modernist

Johanna Drucker

Johns Hopkins University Press
Baltimore

Johns Hopkins University Press
2715 North Charles Street
Baltimore, Maryland 21218-4363
www.press.jhu.edu

Library of Congress Cataloging-in-Publication Data

Names: Drucker, Johanna, 1952- author.
Title: Iliazd : a meta-biography of a modernist / Johanna Drucker.
Description: Baltimore : Johns Hopkins University Press, 2020. |
    Series: Hopkins studies in modernism | Includes bibliographical
    references and index.
Identifiers: LCCN 2020019939 | ISBN 9781421439631 (hardcover ;
    acid-free paper) | ISBN 9781421439648 (paperback ; acid-free
    paper) | ISBN 9781421439655 (ebook)
Subjects: LCSH: Iliazd, 1894-1975. | Authors, Georgian—20th
    century—Biography. | Literature, Experimental—20th century—
    History and criticism. | Modernism (Literature) | Futurism
    (Literary movement)
Classification: LCC PG3476.I45 Z58 2020 | DDC 891.73/42
    [B]—dc23
LC record available at https://lccn.loc.gov/2020019939

A catalog record for this book is available from the British Library.

Frontispiece: Hélène Douard (later Zdanevich) with Iliazd in Venice
in 1962. Courtesy of François Mairé and the Fonds Iliazd.

*Special discounts are available for bulk purchases of this book. For more
information, please contact Special Sales at specialsales@press.jhu.edu.*

Johns Hopkins University Press uses environmentally friendly book
materials, including recycled text paper that is composed of at least
30 percent post-consumer waste, whenever possible.

Contents

Preface

Ilia Zdanevich, known professionally by the contracted version of his name, Iliazd (pronounced il-ee-ahzd), was a writer and publisher whose career began with the early twentieth-century Russian avant-garde and ended in late-century European modernism. Iliazd's creative work in modern art had a unique focus on the book format—as a poet, typographic artist, designer, and printer, as well as a publisher—and my interest in Iliazd was fostered by my own experience making books. In 1985, when this project began, I was in my early thirties and had been printing letterpress work for more than a decade. I felt an affinity with Iliazd since I had been a writer-artist working in the print shop, at the type case, and within the networks of relationships required for bringing a book into being.

I came to know Iliazd and his work through the research described here. I finished an initial draft of this biography in the early 1990s, and the project was scheduled for publication, but economic shifts caused changes in the publisher's lists.[1] Though already under contract, the book was canceled. The project lay fallow for many years, with intermittent revivals of interest on my part and that of others. But only in winter 2019, in the quiet afforded by a Beinecke Fellowship and the isolation of a New Haven winter, did the opportunity arise to pay attention to the work again—this time with a reflection on biography as part of the framework.

Iliazd is not unknown. In 2019, his work was the subject of multiple exhibitions. Among them was one curated by Boris Fridman, *Iliazd: The 20th Century of Ilia Zdanevich,* at Moscow's Pushkin Museum of Fine Arts. Another was in Málaga, Spain, and another at Columbia University's Rare Book & Manuscript Library.[2] Earlier exhibits of his work, with detailed catalogues and bibliographical study, took place in Paris at the Musée d'Art Moderne (1976) and at the Centre Georges Pompidou (1978), at the Université de

Montréal (1984), and at the Museum of Modern Art (1987) in New York.³
His books are well known among bibliophiles, curators, and collectors. He
is neither obscure nor unduly prominent within the history of the twentieth-
century avant-garde, and his recognition does not depend upon my contribution. At this point in the early twenty-first century, his work belongs to a
particular historical moment, formulated within the frameworks of twentieth-
century modern art, within which he worked. This is well-worked territory,
known, charted, and disputed. But our relationships with these periods and
their characterizations are always changing. I see modernism very differently
now than when I started this research more than thirty years ago, as will be
clear as the account unfolds.

But methods and approaches to scholarship also change. For decades, I
have written about artists' books, visual poetry, letterpress aesthetics, and
related topics in the history of art and literature of the modern period. But
I can no longer simply write about *things*, whether they are historical events,
objects, or aesthetic positions, as if they exist independently of the processes by which they are *assumed to exist as things*, events, objects, or positions. The attention to the meta-level of knowledge permeates my thinking.
At this point, having a chance to pay systematic attention to how biography
produces its supposed subject, as well as a chance to reflect on the events
of what is now another historical period, the 1980s in which the research
began, is what motivated me to return to this work. But above all, it is the
encounter with Iliazd through that research that is the focus of this study.

In its current form, this project mixes meta-reflections, descriptive biography, and accounts of how I came to know Iliazd through the documents,
conversations, and people I encountered. The sections on Iliazd's life and
work progress chronologically, as is the expectation in a biography. The
commentaries on the process of writing a biography do not map directly
to this chronology. They introduce issues that are present throughout the
project, part of its intellectual infrastructure at every point, though more
vividly evident at some moments than others. Anecdotes and stories are
intermittent, linked to appropriate points in the narrative.

The privilege of access to the Iliazd archive remains one of the unique
experiences of my life as a scholar, and for this I am indebted to the generosity of Iliazd's widow, Madame Hélène Zdanevich. I am grateful for her
faith in me and willingness to engage my naïveté as well as my sincerity at
the outset. We worked side by side for many hours in her living space in the

rue Mazarine. Those days of shared work built a respect and affection that remains, though she passed away in 1992.

The original biography was drawn on materials assembled between 1985 and 1989. Scholarship on Iliazd's *zaum* (an invented language based in sound symbolism), futurist poetics, and related topics produced in the past thirty years is assembled in an appendix and also finds its way into my notes. If I were beginning this project now, I would survey every scholarly work that includes a reference to Iliazd. I have included everything that feels compellingly relevant, but my bibliography is not exhaustive with regard to current scholarship. All research is a moving target, and the interest in Iliazd will continue to unfold dimensions of his work that were not known decades ago or even as I reworked this text. The *Carnets of the Iliazd Club*, edited in the past thirty years through the efforts of the family (first Hélène, then her brother, Henri Douard, then her son, François Mairé) with the work of many scholars, most notably and consistently Régis Gayraud, are an invaluable resource. André Markowicz has shown incredible dedication to translating Iliazd's poetry and other texts from Russian into French.[4] Thomas Kitson's English translation of *Rapture* (2017), new work assembled by Boris Fridman in an anthology of critical essays published in 2019, and catalogues for exhibits that now appear regularly are among the most conspicuous and important contributions. But in recent years, various scholars with an interest in Iliazd have convinced me that this biographical study still has a role to play. I had access to people and materials that have vanished. This project has a retrospective aspect to it, but also a fresh outlook as a memoir of that original biographical project. *Iliazd* provides insight into the work of a talented and unique figure, but it is also a reflection on the intersection of scholarship, relationships, and memory.

Note on Spelling

Orthography of Russian and Georgian personal and place names has been standardized to be consistent throughout, even though this introduces some anachronisms. Tiflis is spelled Tbilisi, for instance, just for the sake of consistency, though the former spelling was used in the brief period of Georgian independence. The titles of Iliazd's books, which I came to know through French, whether they were translations from Russian or originally French, are all given in English with French or Russian transliterations in parentheses.

A few exceptions: Olga Djordjadze is the spelling of the name of a Georgian scholar who wrote about Iliazd. This spelling was used in her English-language obituary and is used in the French-language essays where she is identified. I have kept this spelling for bibliographical reasons. Iliazd wrote an essay on Niko Pirosmani, the Georgian naïve painter, titled *Pirosmanach-vili 1914*. If properly transcribed in English conventions, the name would be spelled Pirosmanashvili. In the title used by Iliazd, I respect his spelling. In references to the painter, I use the short form, Pirosmani. Finally, Iliazd's friend, Mikhail Ledentu, has a name transcribed according to various conventions. I have opted to keep to the simplest: Ledentu. All other transcriptions from Russian or Georgian into English have been done, as closely as possible, in accord with the Library of Congress Name Authority File. Where an individual does not appear in that file, I have relied on search engines in English to supply the orthography through which their identity and work would be found. A special note of thanks to Peter Fletcher, colleague in the library at the University of California, Los Angeles, for assistance in this matter.

Iliazd

1 Encountering Iliazd
The Biographical Project

Beginning: The rue Mazarine, Winter 1985

The winter of 1984–85 was bitter cold in Paris. The extreme temperatures called forth apocalyptic mutterings from members of the French press who compared it to the dreadful season three decades earlier in which the Algerian War of Independence had begun. Struggling with the isolation of daily research in the somber chill of the Bibliothèque Nationale's domed reading room and the awkward silence of the Bibliothèque Jacques Doucet, I found a welcome distraction when I met someone with the exotic-sounding name of Madame Iliazd. She was the widow of Ilia Zdanevich. But who was he?

Though I was doing research on Dada and futurist typography from the 1910s, I had never heard of Iliazd. A young blond graduate student, whose surfer look made sense when I found out he was from Santa Barbara, had been sitting across the table from me in the hushed reading room of the Bibliothèque Jacques Doucet. Though the protocols of discreet behavior prohibit (or did in those days in France) any direct discussion among scholars about their work, I finally asked him what he was doing flipping through the pages of deluxe editions. While he signaled to me that no relationship was going to develop between *us*, he still tolerated a brief exchange in which he introduced me to the work of Ilia Zdanevich. Not only had Zdanevich been the creative force behind some beautifully designed *livres d'artistes* (artists' books), but he had been active in the Russian avant-garde and had produced, apparently, some typographic marvels. This was all new to me. Intrigued by the researcher's suggestion, I contacted Madame, who, he assured me, was always willing to engage scholars in conversations about her late husband and encourage attention to his work. The Californian went back to breezing through fine press books, and I set out to track this mysterious figure, Iliazd, who was barely mentioned in the accounts of early twentieth-century typography or broader histories of the period.[1]

To contact Madame in 1985 required a visit to a post office to consult a directory to locate her address, then write what I hoped was a polite note of introduction and inquiry, and then wait for a response. This took some time and had to be followed up by fixing the details for the rendezvous. At last, on Madame's invitation, I found my way to 35 rue Mazarine in the fading light of an icy afternoon and pulled the heavy door latch that let me into the small courtyard off the bright, bustling street. The gloomy scene in that sheltered yard, with its bald paving stones and windows in need of paint, belonged to an era long before the sixth arrondissement had become the trendy quarter of brightly lit boutiques and chic cafes that it was in the affluent 1980s. With some uncertainty, I found what I believed to be the correct staircase at the back of the courtyard. I went through its narrow entry to a small, twisting stairway and climbed to the third-floor landing. A dim light had come on when I had pressed the switch at ground level, but the timer yielded to its frugal impulse while I was still waiting for a response to my knock. I stood in the frigid darkness a moment before I heard footsteps approach and a voice query me through a well-worn door.

The lock turned and I was greeted by Hélène Zdanevich, a tall, striking woman with steel-grey hair swept up and back from her wide, strong forehead. Her features and manner had grandness and dignity, and the vigor of her step belied her age. Though I was still a stranger, she welcomed me with a gracious gesture and led me through a narrow passage to a chamber beyond. The low-ceilinged room was lit only by a fire in the gas grate, ineffectual against the extreme chill even in that confined space. The room had a bed against one wall, made up for daytime with an arrangement of pillows so it could double as a couch. A modest table with space for two small wooden chairs had been placed under the casement window, whose cramped courtyard view provided little light, even on the brightest days. A desk against the wall opposite and the armchair in which Madame sat close to the fire made up the rest of the furnishings. My hostess pulled one of the small chairs close to the grate and invited me to sit, then sank back into the shelter of the armchair, her handsome features barely visible.

The gas flames flickered and cast long shadows onto the walls. Slowly, in that dim light, I realized that I was surrounded by artworks of major modern masters. The chill that rippled through me with that realization was not cold but excitement tinged with disbelief. I was sitting in the midst of history, touching its living legacy in a room that had been inhabited by someone who had been an active participant in modern art. Earth tones and geometric forms of early twentieth-century abstraction were juxtaposed with the elegant lines of suggestively figurative work. Traces of cubism, futurism, surrealism, and other movements rose like phantoms in the crepuscular atmosphere. Modernism, in all its many dimensions, human and artistic, filled the room with tangible presences. Tea and conversation, awkward at first, gradually introduced warmth into the air. We huddled next to the heater and began a dialogue that would open up a world for me—the world of the fascinating and little-known modern master Ilia Zdanevich.

Names and references floated into the air—Goncharova, Larionov, Giacometti, Marinetti, Kruchenykh, Picasso. The room filled with ghosts, and the combination of that mysterious lighting and the invocation of days past charged the atmosphere with excitement. Was I grasping the spirits of persons who had passed through that room, who had sat with Iliazd in these very chairs? Madame Iliazd was forthcoming, spinning out her responses to my questions so that a pastiche of recalled information began to take shape. Whatever confused impressions I carried out from that initial interview, in which my enthusiasm raced ahead of my ability to keep track of all that was said, I grasped the basic outlines of Iliazd's life. Tbilisi, St. Petersburg, Moscow, Paris—the names were familiar, but uttered by Madame Iliazd they had an air of antiquity and mystery about them. And all the while, my eyes were peering through the darkness to decipher the treasures hung casually on the walls. The paintings in the background of my view registered intensely as the stream of conversation wove its own set of references into and out of their frames.

My grasp of Iliazd's life and work was still vague when I rose to go. I had spent several hours in Madame Iliazd's company, and I was late for another appointment by the time I left, my head spinning and my mind cluttered with its first glimpses of this fantastic world. Iliazd had known Viktor Shklovsky. He had worked with Max Ernst and Joan Miró. He had been part of a vibrant milieu and put himself at the cutting edge of innovative poetics. But above all, he had made books—incredible, luxurious, intelligent books whose formal properties and artistic vision were unlike those of any other editor or writer. As I would come to know in fine detail, he had explored the book form as an aesthetic instrument of modern art. He did not, in the contemporary sense, make simply *livres d'artistes*, as will become clear, but a hybrid form.

That night, of course, I knew very little of those details. I had gotten just a glimpse of this rare milieu and of the possibilities for a project. Madame mentioned something about a biography of Iliazd, but only in passing and in relation to a lost text. She had just made my acquaintance. My relative youth probably did not inspire confidence. But in the flickering light and among the many shadows, a suggestion hung suspended. I knew I wanted to explore what this approach to research—intimate, personal, entangled in lives and people—might offer that was different from that of the reading rooms and formal environments in which I was working. I left promising to return.

Time Travel

That first encounter let me over the threshold to time travel and offered a chance to reenter the world of modernism in the era of its full vitality. Modernism was already gone in 1985, eclipsed, passing out of unqualified acceptance of the canonical figures and artistic precepts. The postmodern critical reflection on the claims of modern art was emerging. Modernism's own formulations—aspirations of utopian social transformation through aesthetic means, the radical innovations justified by revolutionary rhetoric, the notion that a universal language of form could be articulated like a grammar— were all concepts that seemed like past tense. That characterization, formulated within modernism's own ideology, had shifted to one in which the global reach of colonial agendas, the unexamined biases in the concept of primitivism, the masculinist tone, and gender-normative practices, particularly within the "movements" of futurism, Dada, and surrealism, were all being scrutinized and rethought.

But the idea that I might, however briefly, visit that vanishing world motivated this project, as if the apartment, with all of its material details and richness, might serve as a portal into that period before it was gone entirely. I entered Iliazd's space, this cabinet of memories and memorabilia, without any idea of his persona. In a very clear and distinct sense, it was Madame's Iliazd I came to know. Ultimately, that recognition broke through my own illusions. But that comes later in the dual chronology of events in the life of Iliazd and the unfolding narrative of my encounter with the documents and people who provided the materials for the biographical study.

The Missing Manuscript

On my second visit, Madame Iliazd returned to the topic of the missing manuscript of a biography of Iliazd. The draft had been written by a youngish man named Christopher, she said, then paused.[2] She dropped her voice, then said he had died. We moved on quickly. She was certain the manuscript existed, and she gave me the name of a Mrs. Wilson who lived outside London. Other business was taking me to that city, so I began making arrangements to see what I could track down. Projects have their own momentum. I had no idea how consuming this one would become. Setting out in search of the manuscript draft, my hope was that it could be secured and that filling in the gaps or finishing it up would be a minor matter.

This was the first of many charges given to me by Madame Iliazd, and at first I followed her urgings out of curiosity, not yet fully committed to the work she wanted me to do. I would soon find out how tenacious she could be in the service of her late husband. Her admiration for his accomplishments, combined with a conviction that he had not had his due, created a driving force. A retired teacher with experience in business who had competed in athletic events for seniors, she had considerable physical as well as intellectual energy. She was determined that Iliazd should be more widely recognized, in part through a biographical study.

Mrs. Wilson lived in Harrow, near the renowned school. Once again, I went through the protocols—a formal inquiry letter, polite request, and a date set in advance with an estimated time of arrival. The woman, a stranger, met me at the train station in a large old-fashioned sedan, a very grown-up seeming car, and took me to her house. A midday hush prevailed in the well-appointed bungalow with its tidy front garden and orderly rooms. The sound of boys on a playing field came from a distance. Her husband was associated with the school. The community and their lives were oriented around its activities. I could sense from the way she listened to the rising and falling sounds in the distance that their rhythm organized her days.

She fed me lunch, coquilles St. Jacques, which struck me as incredibly elegant. With circumspect politeness, she did her own assessment of me, sorting out my credibility before releasing the slim folder of papers into my care. She had no claim on them, she said, and no intention where they were concerned, but they were the only copies of the project. The fact that I was simply taking them to Madame Iliazd was likely what convinced her to turn them over. Our exchange was awkward. Manners prevailed. No small talk softened the formal atmosphere. I observed the china, the settings, the tables with delicate legs and sofas upholstered in flowered chintz. All accorded with my idea of the well-bred, middle-class British home. She wore a twinset and a tweed wool skirt. The scene felt old-fashioned by virtue of its conformity to conventions, and compared to my student life in Paris (a sixth-floor walk-up attic sublet above the place d'Italie), the whole situation felt time-shifted into another era and even generation. She was kind, but perfunctory enough to let me know this would be the full extent of her relation to the project. Who had Christopher been to her? Unclear, just that the connection was not familial.

The manuscript was a disappointment. I despaired as I read through it on the train back to London. A few false starts, some framing sentences followed by a few unformed and unfinished paragraphs. No arc of a life, no structured chapters, no study of materials, no bibliography, citations, or primary sources were even hinted at in the draft, which, as I recall, was less than two dozen pages. I was bringing nothing to Madame, and I knew it, which meant I would have to decide whether to take up the research or abandon the project.

Back in Paris, sitting with Madame in the tiny apartment in the rue Mazarine, I felt the decision was largely made for me. I handed her the inadequate sheaf of papers with their sketched beginning and notes. Her disappointment at the text, the meagerness of which she immediately grasped, was only deepened by my description of its inadequate contents. What to do? she asked, shrugging in despair, looking at me. She wanted the biography. I was there. What to do?

I tiptoed toward that expectation. I said I could begin, do a little work, write at least a short study, pull a basic biography together. I had no idea what I was doing or the work I was undertaking. I am not even clear what purpose she saw at that moment for the project except to map Iliazd's work and life in a coherent way. I didn't know, entering into this, about the existence of other scholars working on Iliazd. They all had prior claim and work underway, as I would find, though none was writing the biography that Madame wanted. I was naïve, but the prospect of an archival project, and a biographical one, was seductive by contrast to the work I was doing with published journals and printed ephemera in the libraries.

Work Routines

So we began. Still awkward at the prospect of working so closely with Madame, I came to the apartment. I was shy in her presence, unsure of my role or authority. She must have been in her mid-seventies at that point, tall, with imposing stature and posture. She wore a small glass orb on a silver chain, a gift from Iliazd, in which metal flakes moved around in a liquid. The image of that adornment stuck with me, along with the memory of the graceful gesture of her arm reaching around her neck to adjust its chain. The physicality of presence breeds knowledge. We would come to know each other well.

Madame and I entered quickly into a routine of collaboration, and the contact provided companionship and succor through the long dark days of that persistently cold (and for me, personally rather difficult) winter of 1985. She became Hélène, though I always addressed her with the formal *vous* and she addressed me as *tu*, acknowledging my youth and our familiarity. There our relationship stabilized. Hours spent in her company, though focused entirely on our work and the subject at hand, supplied a gentle foundation of emotional support. The continuity of shared activity created an awareness of moods, perceptions of those changes and shifts in tone that subtly communicate understanding. She was a woman of great dignity and generosity, more than forty years my senior, and the uniqueness of that aspect of our relationship gave me a rare and precious insight into the vitality of age. Once trust was established, her kindness was boundless. So was her confidence that I would finish the project.

My study of Ilia Zdanevich and his work is thus intimately bound to my friendship with Hélène. She offered her time, her personal memories, and her archival files with openness and generosity. She gave me the introductions I needed to talk with others who had been part of Iliazd's elaborate book productions. Through her I met the other people who were attracted to the Iliazd flame: Régis Gayraud, the serious, then still junior scholar working on the Paris conferences of Iliazd from the early 1920s, André Markowicz, the talented young poet and translator, Françoise Le Gris (then -Bergmann) who had produced a retrospective exhibition in Montréal in 1984, accompanied by an insightful catalogue to which we referred endlessly for details and references. Some had known Iliazd directly, such as Herta Hausmann, who had been a friend and companion to Iliazd in earlier days, or Michel Guino, who entertained us in a magnificent fashion one fantastical afternoon. Along with many others, they figure in this history as witnesses and resources, each a distinct personality encountered in particular circumstances, the observation of which added yet another dimension to the complex encounter with Iliazd.

But above all, I spent many hours with Madame Iliazd, not in that small room that served her, as it had her late husband, as bedroom, dining room, and study, but in the glass-walled studio reached by a half step and tiny

Iliazd at his desk, working on book design, probably 1960s. Courtesy of François Mairé and the Fonds Iliazd

passage off to its side. The atelier contained a large work table, the one at which Iliazd had spent many hours carefully drafting his designs—calculating word spaces on graph paper and making dummies from the different papers he used over the years—the silky Japon, the thicker Chine, the encrusted *dragée* papers (sheets used in wrapping packages in French shops) that he favored as endsheets, and scraps of the rough-cut vellum he favored as exterior wrappings. The touch of each was a call to sensual awareness, to an appreciation of decisions about design made through knowledge of materials. We perched at one end of its expanse, near shelves that held file boxes, the personal documents of his life.[3]

At first I went to Madame's two afternoons a week, after my mornings in the reading room at the Bibliothèque Nationale or the Bibliothèque Jacques Doucet, where I was continuing research for my dissertation. But soon I was going there almost every afternoon, swept up in enthusiasm for the project and sobered by the scale of the undertaking on which we had embarked. I brought cookies most days, stopping along my walking route from either the BN on the rue Richelieu or from the much closer Jacques Doucet at the place de Panthéon. My small paper-wrapped parcel in hand, I would push open that heavy street door, cross the courtyard with the increasing confidence of a habituée, and mount the dark staircase. The age of the building and the sense of history in its structure and on its surfaces never left me.

I made my ritual ascent to the apartment in the rue Mazarine, to that place that Iliazd had moved into in the 1930s and in which he had lived for decades. Every day's visit was tinged by the feeling of touching the past, a longer past than Iliazd's occupancy, to be sure, but still these were his rooms. As they became familiar, they revealed more and more. I got to know the objects on those walls and on the mantel. His death mask leaned against the wall above the fireplace. I could hardly look at it: the somber cast felt much too intimate to examine, and I deferred to its presence rather than engage. But the portrait of Iliazd as an "angel" drawn by Natalia Goncharova in elegant black and white forms, the portrait by Robert Delaunay, and the energetic line drawings by Giacometti were vivid presences.

The room's walls were, indeed, covered with evidence of a life lived among these artist friends who were major figures of modern art: Pablo Picasso, Sonia Delaunay, Max Ernst, and the many others whose names figure in his list of collaborators. The boxes stored in the atelier contained all the artifacts that documented his personal history. The production notes for his books (including dummies, mock-ups, business correspondence, and so on) had been acquired by the Bibliothèque Nationale, where they were waiting to be catalogued. Hélène had kept the personal materials, not wanting to part with them for her own sentimental reasons, but also because she had hoped that someone might appear who might realize her dream of a biographical study. We worked in the barely heated studio, where most of our illumination came from the large glass windows.

The cookies I had brought would ensure us of tea at some point in the afternoon, hence their purpose beyond the simple act of politeness that French manners required. After the first few visits, I came to know how the cold would sink in as we worked, coming through the studio skylights with their splendid view of nearby rooftops, slate and copper, and the varied building fronts that reflected the shifting sun as it slowly sank. We were often chilled to the bone before we broke in the late afternoon for tea, made in the small nook of a kitchen tucked into a niche, closet-like, off the narrow

Drawing of Iliazd, known as "the angel," by Natalia Goncharova, 1913. Courtesy of François Mairé and the Fonds Iliazd

front hall. Some days we had visitors. André might appear, his knock delicate but precise, and sit with us long enough to translate a few pages of indecipherable *zaum*. Other days Régis might show up, his leather jacket smelling of cigarettes, shock of hair over his forehead, to talk of the "conferences" or other details related to Iliazd's poetic theories and works. Once in a while Hélène's niece, a lively pretty woman also named Hélène, filled the space with her exuberance—and recollections of the Liberation of Paris and gifts of chocolate bars from American soldiers to the children. But most days Hélène and I worked alone together, knitting the clues from one set of

Drawing of Iiazd by Robert Delaunay, 1923. Collection of the Bibliothèque Nationale, Paris. Image courtesy of Pracusa Artisticas SA, Barcelona. Copyright © Robert
Delaunay; all rights reserved

documents to another, expanding the timelines of events that constituted
the study of Iliazd's life.

    Short winter days gave way to spring's softer light. The reflection of the
setting sun in the windows of buildings opposite those of the atelier grew
richer and deeper as the weeks passed. My notes piled up as the time left
for work shrank and the season edged toward summer and my departure
date, determined by the end of my fellowship support.[4]

Chronologies and Evidence

The working method Hélène and I used was simple. We began with chronological lists of the events of Iliazd's life that she had compiled for a catalogue accompanying an exhibition at the Centre Pompidou in 1978. From these lists we worked back into the file folders and boxes, tracing every reference until we found its source in a letter or paper, a journal or notebook, or in one of the typed transcripts of Iliazd's own lectures or accounts.

Initially Hélène would take the "chemise," or folder, for the year in which we were working and open it to the chronology. I would copy the list of events, and she would begin to pull the evidence from the boxes. The trails that led from each reference often got tangled in the confusion of file folders over which Madame presided. As trust grew and the process broadened, she sometimes made copies for me, so in some rare instances I have photocopied versions of her original notes or documents in Iliazd's hand. I did not touch the file boxes, and simply waited as she pulled them down, went through them, and extracted whatever piece of evidence matched the reference. Every time something emerged from the boxes—photograph, report card, mother's notes transcribed from her journal in Russian, translated into French for me to retranscribe into English—I had the same feeling of anticipation, excitement. Each piece of evidence added a detail to the text. This was hardly an efficient method of research (we never organized the materials systematically), but the protocol left her in charge and built a buffer of privacy between me and the materials. They were hers. These papers were the closest thing to the man himself, his traces, and her intimacy with them was not to be violated, even by the work of compiling his biographical information.

We worked quasi-systematically, taking the yearly chronologies in order. The materials we associated with the individual events came from all periods of Iliazd's life. But because he wrote about futurism later in his life, or his connections with other artists and events crossed time periods, a reference might lead to a text from the 1960s as well as another from the 1920s. Much depended on Hélène's own recollections, and her ability to link a particular passage to a source in the files. Had I been more professional or experienced, I might have suggested that we organize the archive or at least go through it in an orderly fashion. That felt intrusive, and disrespectful, especially since we were sitting in the studio where Iliazd had spent so many

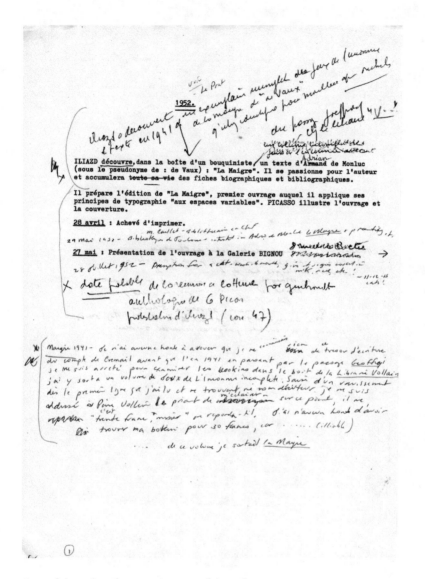

Page of chronology for 1952. Courtesy of the author

hours. In spite of the fact that this had been Iliazd's workspace, I never felt a
haunting presence. The archives had been organized by Hélène. Both rooms,
the living area and the studio, felt like spaces of recollection and repository,
more like a time capsule than a haunted sepulcher. But I felt acutely that I

ILIA ZDANEVITCH : Documents for the first section of the Biography

1894 : Dates, family background etc.
Journal of Valentina Zdanevitch from 1902-1903 (Olga Djordzaze)
"Ilia Zdanevitch et le Futurisme Russe" Olga Djordzaze from Beauborg Cat.
1911 Chronology
1911 -- Letter to Soffici 1962 on Futurism
1912 Chronology
Notes for a Biography of Ledentu
1912 - Account of Visit to Moscow, unpublished notes
Notes from Kyril Zdanevitch's Niko Pirosmani
Notes of Iliazd on discovery of Pirosmani (unpublished)
Ilia's Journal 1913 on Portrait by Pirosmani (In K.Z.'s Piros.)
Article on Pirosmani by Zdanevitch from Vostok 1914 from A.Robel's trans.
1913 Chronology
1914 Chronology
Letter from Soffici, 1964, on Marinetti's visit to Moscow in 1914
1914, Introduction by Ledentu on Toutisme
Iliazd's notes on Marinetti's 1914 visit (from 1968)
Melita Rafalovitch's meeting with Ilia Z. in 1914
1915 Chronology
1916 Chronology
Paoustovski on the Zdanevitch household
Notes on exhibition of Pirosmani's work in Tiflis, K.Z. and Paous.
First Rose poster, 1916
Letter to Markov notes on "Yanko" production 1916
Notes on Yanko, Olga Djor. and Terentiev
Iliazd's notes on Mane-Katz re Yanko production 1916
1917 Chronology
Price's letter to Iliazd
Section from Price's 1918 book on War and Rev. in Asiatic Russia
First Letter to Price, 1929, I.Z.   Extracts dealing with expedition
Notes to Director of Inst. of Georgian Art on pub.of Expd.
1917 Letter from Dimitri... friend on Expedition of 1917
Letter to Soffici on "zaoum" and Russian Futurism (1962)
Youri Annenkoff, Journal of Encounters, notes on Iliazd and Futurists
Notes on Opening of Cabaret Fantastique in 1917
Notes from the Journal of 41 Degrees (Melita Rafalovitz)
Terentiev on Dras of Zdanevitch
1918 Chronology
Manifesto of 41 Degrees
1919 Chronology
1919 Terentiev's Tender Record
1920 Chronology
Declaration to Arts Commission of Georgian Assembly 1920 I.Z.
Notes from Letters to Price on Constantinople I.Z.
Attestations of Iliazd's value as employee 1920
Opening of Philosophia, I.Z.'s novel from 20's
1921 Chronology
Serge Rafalovitch's presentataion of I.Z. to Paris Public 1921
Raymond Cogniat's University of 41 Degrees, Nov. 1921Comoedia
1922 Text of I.Z. on arrival in Paris
Nov. 1922 conference at studio of Olenine d'Alheim
1921 New Schools of Russian Poetry conference at Olenine d'Alheim
Feb. 1922, Forty-One Degrees Synapsed I.Z.

Texts of 1920 projects for a lecture at the Black Rose in Constantinople

List of Conferences given by 41° 1917, 1918, 1919

Why we Paint our Faces
Larionov / Gontcharova catalogue
Certificat of Maturity
Nuke on Oeil affair (1912)

Kyrill Zdanevitch, Nikos Pirosmani
Mane Katz article from ARTS
Paoustovski notes 'Incursion dans le Sud'

Document list for the first section of the biography. Courtesy of the author

was in a personal domain. Hélène lived there the way a lover lives inside the coat of a departed loved one, to be wrapped in it, surrounded by the intimacies of odor, traces, the subway ticket in the pocket, a scribbled laundry list—the ephemera that remind one of a living person.

We also worked unsystematically, following associations. We developed a private code of keywords—events, place names, people—as our own language of the archive. The chronologies gave rise to document lists that were my way of keeping track of the odd bits of paper, notebook entries, letters, and jottings in order to account for them. I never knew how complete this list was in relation to the contents of the boxes—or even how many boxes there were. Was it a dozen? Bankers boxes? File boxes? I only remember Hélène climbing up to pull them down, opening them, then pulling out a folder with a definitive statement: "*Voilà*," and then, handing it over, "*Ici, regards.*" The equivalent in English would have been, "This is what you need." And so it went: I read, transcribed, translated on the fly, creating my own shadow archive of materials. We rarely photocopied anything directly. Xerox was expensive, and not readily accessible, and taking the materials from the room felt wrong, as if they were too vulnerable to leave the secure environment.

From the first, I was fascinated with the gap between reference and evidence. A statement like "1912 At Batumi with friends" had to be substantiated. A photograph surfaced, showing a young Iliazd in company of his friend Mikhail Ledentu—whose importance to Iliazd I would come to recognize through the research—and others. The photograph is blurred, remediated many times, but the flush of summer on young faces and the presence of heads wreathed in leaves and flowers are fully legible. Suddenly the image poses the question of how to read this as evidence. What can be said? What narrative can be created beyond a statement of location and date? The image portrays youthful camaraderie and summer pleasures. Iliazd was eighteen and we have no other information to describe the image but what it contains. The gap between evidence and narrative is not enormous; it is unfathomable. It cannot be measured. Every narrative that fills it is part speculation, part fiction.

This mechanical process of carefully linking each chronological reference to an artifact was addictive and magical. Interestingly, at that stage I had little feeling for the man. The textual project was the satisfying activity. Working until the tightly constructed field of references wove an account in themselves was the goal. At first, I considered making the biography out

Young Zdanevich at Batumi in company with Mikhail Ledentu and others, August 28, 1912. Courtesy of François Mairé and the Fonds Iliazd

of evidence without commentary, excerpts and citations put into sequence and juxtaposition. But I realized that these materials were not self-evident; they did not simply speak by their presence. Narrative was needed as well as information from other sources and scholarship. Hélène told me tales, and so did others who had known him. A desire to describe a life began to emerge, but the methodological issues were daunting and the liabilities many.

Iliazd's Books

The books were the justification for the undertaking, the corpus on which Iliazd's identity and his historical value were based. Their appearance and production punctuated the chronology. They were not the only milestones, however, and this was a biography, not merely a critical study. If there was a boundary between the study of the books and the description of the life, I walked back and forth over that line, drawing the portrait across the materials that indexed the conditions in which the books were conceived and produced. I knew from experience how deeply entangled artistic projects were with living relationships as well as realities of production costs and constraints. Books are complex artifacts, made across a long span from conception to execution and distribution, with reception as an unpredictable afterlife following a major expenditure of resources. Such work was not separate from the life—it formed the life, and the books arose from those conditions.

In the course of our afternoons, Hélène would sometimes bring one of Iliazd's monumental printed works out from a concealed spot under draped tables in the atelier, unwrapping it from the protective layers of fabric or paper in which it had been swathed. The books were another order of experience, their dramatic effects staged like theatrical events that moved from cover to interior to text and image with the precision and impact of a play unfolding. Iliazd's concept of the *dras,* or plays, that had been his first book productions in the 1910s remained a guiding metaphor for the theatrical staging of all of his books. Each book was different, and each fresh encounter with them was a revelation. The elaborately folded *Poetry of Unknown Words (Poésie de Mots Inconnus,* 1949) was intimate, dense, complex. The variations in scale and styles of inscription in *Maximiliana* (1964) were without parallel in any other project. The perfectly calibrated mathematical symmetry of *Skinnybones (La Maigre,* 1952) was echoed but not repeated in the many volumes he designed. Each production was distinct, though the works were immediately recognizable as Iliazd's by their approaches to materials, composition, and structure as well as their typography. Starting in 1952, Iliazd used only one typeface, Gill Sans (*Gil* in French), for all of his editions.

Iliazd's work also belonged to the era of modern art. He had brought the same concerns with attention to the formal, physical properties of book construction that abstract painters and avant-garde writers had brought to their work, foregrounding attention to materials. But he also made them expressions of his poetic and artistic interests and research so that they embodied his personal point of view. The slightly more than two dozen books he produced across the six decades of his working life are remarkable as an oeuvre, a vision in its entirety, even more than as individual works. Their design makes an argument for books as complex aesthetic objects in which every element of typography, layout, content, imagery, printing, and printmaking is integrated into a finely articulated system of relations. But if their formal beauty rewards the eye and mind, it is still mute in another respect, unable to take on the task of telling the stories of their conception and making.

The contemporary artist's book that had surfaced in the 1960s in conceptual and photographic publications was still not broadly known in the 1980s and was far from the world of deluxe editions Iliazd produced. The idea of artists' books would be retrospectively applied to earlier avant-garde productions, particularly those of the Russian futurists. But artists had made books for centuries before the term "artist's book" was coined to designate a specific form of mechanically produced object that eschewed the crafts of handmade work and claimed to be "democratic multiples" within a conceptual practice. Whether Iliazd's books fit any particular definition of artist's books was far less important than attending to the way his unique combination of skills and sensibilities produced modern works of art in the book format.

The biographical research was meant to re-situate the works, rather than see them as autonomous objects. Iliazd's colophons detail the edition and production history, with respectful recognition of the contributions of his fellow artisans. But to appreciate the poignant resonance of their histories, we have to put in place the many points of reference against which this remarkable artist created his life's work.

The Biographical Project

I never knew Iliazd and I would not presume to say I came to know him. I did not. I had an encounter with the materials from which to produce a biographical study—with many caveats in mind. Reflecting on the process has become a crucial part of that study, a set of observations to the reader along the way here, comments on the organization and the structure of the presentation, not just the content and details.

Writing a biography is a curious business. The one element always missing is the central figure. Iliazd had died ten years earlier, on Christmas Day, in 1975. I had no living relation to him, no connection to him as a person. Hélène was the person I got to know. My understanding of Iliazd was filtered through her admiration and her longing. Every piece of information I had about Iliazd merely refined the ever more detailed absence at the center of my knowledge—a process like creating an outline around a silhouette. The darkness at the center remained, as points on the edge accumulated. That defining absence drives the effort at recreating presence. The many motivations for this activity are as varied as the figures on whom biographical works focus their attention: revenge, justification, redemption, anger, love, respect, adulation, celebration, and any number of other human sentiments hidden under the polite surface of a smoothly articulated narrative. At first, I had no agenda—how could I? I knew nothing of Iliazd.

I still had to wrestle with expectations, mine and Madame's. The study of his work mattered to her, but she wanted more, the living fiction of the past existence in its rich human dimensions and multiplicity of experiences. She wanted to be able to dwell in those recreated scenes, to inhabit the shared space of connection. She wanted the portrait to be vivid, to come alive, to recreate not only the past personage she had known, but also the events she had never been able to share with him. She wanted to be able to walk into the narrative of the life, to live it with him.

Hélène was Iliazd's third wife, and the details of their connection and marriage came to light only slowly. But she had not been part of the early Russian period, nor of the initial arrival in Paris, nor the beginnings of the editions and their publications. She had known him for many years before their marriage, since 1948, when he came to the Midi, where she was living. But their marriage was a late event for both of them, taking place in 1968. I did not understand the full significance of this at first.

Slowly I became aware of the impact Iliazd had had on Hélène and the affective force with which he had connected with her. Husband, lover, friend, and companion, he had been a major part of her life. In his death she became the widow making sure the monument to his memory would be built. I was to be the instrument of that making, and I entered willingly, eagerly, into the task, feeling a great sense of purpose in this connection to the past and to a legacy I would help perpetuate.

Inevitably, anyone who writes a biography finds themselves in a relationship with the figure who is the focus of their research. And, as in any relationship, the terms of intimacy reveal all kinds of dimensions to a person's character, some of which are more surprising than others. But of course the revelations are part of the construct, the projection, the woven-together statements that cover the absence to make it feel like a presence, replete and alive. Praise for a well-received biography arises from the strength of the simulacrum, the believability of the existence of the character, as if the task of the biographer were to "breathe life" into the portrait, a mythic Pygmalion transforming a statue into blushing flesh. Suspension of disbelief still reigns supreme in biography, triumphing over critical skepticism and suspicion of illusion.

Biography is a treacherous business on other counts, and these are the obvious ones. To write of another human being is presumptuous. Who grants the right to characterization, delineation, even in the most judicious terms? To write anything about their inner life and feelings or thoughts is pure hubris—and fiction. To make any judgment or assessment risks offense to the living as well as disrespect to the dead. Revelations have consequences: betrayals from the past, long buried, surface with vengeful effects. Basic ethical, moral, and intellectual problems arise at every turn in relation to ownership of personal information and depiction. Luckily, Iliazd's life contained no dark mysteries.

The seduction of the archive produces its own fascination. Handling the artifacts of the past—personal correspondence, journals, letters, ledgers—produces auratic effect. You believe, holding these artifacts in hand, that they transfer information about their owner. The slope of handwriting, changing over time and in different circumstances, may be an index of age or infirmity, or only of haste or even exuberance. A soiled envelope, kept for years, signals—what? Only its age, its preciousness? Or passive, accidental preservation? No explanation is attached, no caption floats into view, and all such statements are mere speculation. We have only the evidence, physical, literal, able to be described and put in relation to other evidence. What remains is partial, incidental, randomly preserved. What is missing is infinitely unaccountable. We cannot gauge absence in its general scale any more than in its particulars. Whole chapters of a life might be left out, occulted, shielded from view. Denial can become a more comfortable option than admission. You don't know what is missing. You read across these remains, comparing, looking for affirmation and contradiction. Or you read between the bits and pieces, extrapolating according to a probabilistic narrative calculus. Later you find whole chapters of the life were not revealed—not through design, but simply by circumstance. Witnesses vanish. Texts in Russian were indecipherable to me. Relationships that had come and gone in the past did not always leave a trace.[5]

Finally, biography is not a general proposition, but a specific one. The project is always about this person, this individual, and that about-ness becomes the technique of research and description from which the modeled figure appears. I walked into the project of writing about Iliazd without any preparation, naively pursuing a chronological narrative strung together by accounts of his books and work. The obligation to write *the life* only became apparent as the conditions from which his books arose seemed to warrant description. The books persist. They can be encountered, handled, read, entered into in all their physical actuality. But the contexts? And the man? Never again. And as the number of persons who had direct acquaintance with him diminished—he died nearly half a century ago—even the chance of contradiction or alternative explanation diminishes as well. Who among the living will protest a mischaracterization? Great care has been taken in this project to avoid all statements of projection, to eschew analysis of motivation or response except where they are warranted by Iliazd's own writing. As much as possible, I use his words or those of others. Even then, we know, the text out of context is only part of a more nuanced discourse.

The passage of time for a project also has an effect, and the reification of the past as it recedes fixes some of its qualities in ways that turn the whole into another kind of fiction—one's own imagination of the research experience and its motivations. *Iliazd* is not a story about me. I have kept my personal history out of this picture, though I am aware of how completely my viewpoint and voice are present at every moment in the narrative. My debt to Hélène remains unpaid until I finish this work. My appreciation for my colleagues and their generosity, especially that of Régis Gayraud and André Markowicz, who now seem like mythic figures from my youth, continues unabated. My respect for the family, its allegiance to Iliazd, and their desire to see his contributions recognized and memory honored is always in mind as well. My appreciation of the generosity of François Mairé in supporting this project is profound. I also have deep respect for the work of other scholars, some of whom I know and others whose work I have relied on. Many have made contributions on which I have drawn heavily and which I do not have the skills to replicate. And though I cannot recover that period of time, between 1985 and about 1989, when I paid regular visits to Paris, spent long afternoons in Hélène's apartment in the rue Mazarine, going through the files and working away, this profile of the process is an attempt to do just that—to bring that experience to life as its own simulacrum, a small opening into the theater of memory in which past events are still vivid, alive, in their own right, on the stage of our imagination.

1894–1916

Childhood and Formative Years

Initial Encounters with the Evidence

The working method Hélène and I developed began with chronologies, typed lists of dates with statements.[1] After the year of Iliazd's birth, 1894, the notes skipped to 1911, and only after 1913 were there a significant number of entries.

A basic challenge in any biographical project is periodization. Decades matter less than phases of life. Childhood in the family home, departures for university, activities as a young adult—these define periods. Other aspects of life—connections to family, parents, returns to places and habitations in new ones—offer different milestones and periods, many of which overlap.

I initially thought the first period of Iliazd's life finished when he arrived in Paris. The first document list compiled for this section of the project consisted of about sixty-plus references dating from 1902 to 1922. As the research deepened my understanding, I realized this range of time elided youth and early adulthood, the Georgian and Russian locations, as well as Iliazd's significant experience en route to Paris by way of Constantinople in 1921–22. The first section needed to include some mentions of childhood and adolescence, but it focused mainly on early engagements with avant-garde activity, including futurism and collaborations with Natalia Goncharova and Mikhail Larionov, as well as the discovery of Niko Pirosmani, through 1916. Iliazd traveled between Tbilisi and St. Petersburg in 1916–17, but after the October Revolution of 1917 he never again returned to the north. In Tbilisi his commitment to avant-garde innovation continued, the early influences fully absorbed.

Therefore, his work as a poet and typographic designer and publisher in Tbilisi between 1917 and 1920 will be treated as its own next section, following this formative period. By 1920, when Iliazd left Georgia for Paris, he was twenty-seven years old and the futurist movement was already in eclipse, if not decline. The rise of constructivism and establishment of the Moscow art school, Vkhutemas, as well as other Soviet initiatives in the arts, signaled a major change in the relation between the avant-garde and state agendas. While these specific changes did not affect Iliazd directly, sorting out the shape of his life, rather than defining it by external events, took time. Sometimes events that loomed large in global politics or local artistic circles factored very little into his work or life choices, and other times they had significant impacts. He did not engage with the ideas of surrealism, whose principles were crucial for many modern artists, in spite of collaborating with Ernst and Miró. He wrote an unpublished poem on the Spanish Civil War, but he made no other comments on those political events. However, in the 1940s, the provocations of Isidore Isou, founder of Lettrism, changed the course of Iliazd's creative life.

Another challenge of biographical research was to build from fragments into a coherent whole. Many parts of the story had no evidence or contemporary witnesses. For instance, the critical frameworks of reception in which futurism was understood mainly appeared in later scholarship, not in the archives. The desire to keep as close as possible to the evidence in the archive was always in tension with the need to find secondary sources with which to interpret that evidence.

The final challenge was to address the objections that Iliazd had expressed to the writing of biography. Though throughout his life he was quick to rectify misrepresentations of historical events in which he had participated, this passage from a letter written in 1962 to the futurist Ardengo Soffici makes his attitude toward biography clear:

> I was born in Tbilisi in—look at me beginning a biography in the typical mode of our times. Every painting exhibition these days is accompanied by the biography of the painter obligingly placed in front of the visitor or made available on a folded pamphlet. Prefaces for a heroic epic, passing into common usage—not surprisingly, considering the impoverishment and vulgarity of contemporary criticism. . . . But certainly it is obvious that this style is German and has come to us by way of the Swiss and is the inheritance of the Nazis with their racial prejudices. Every artistic or literary work has to be accompanied by a curriculum vitae and especially if it includes the phrase, "I am a Jew. . . ." Another country where they insist on the c.v. is the United States, where they have a horror of communists—

which is just the other side of the same coin . . . therefore I will omit my age, my origins, the position of my parents, the site of my studies . . . which are only of interest to a police mentality.[2]

I went on, in spite of objections Iliazd might have had. Materials from the archive combined with research to create the "as if" of biographical narrative. In the first phase of work, implicit but articulate emphasis came from Hélène. An exclamation, or a tone in her voice as she brought something forward, tapped a sheet, and pointed to a passage, a photograph, or a bit of paper from decades earlier, indicated what she thought was valuable. That web of affective commentary cannot be recaptured, but it remains in this narrative, the imprint of her judgment.

Apocryphal Tales

Writing childhood as if it were the explanatory foundation for an adult life is a typical trap for biographers. The bits of evidence come forward like postcards from another era, messages whose context has to be construed. The evidence that remains from the childhood of Ilia Zdanevich is meager: a few photographs, some pages from his mother's diary, a visitor's description of the family home. In addition, Iliazd contributed a few recollections of his own, casting his early years in an origin myth that suited his later identity.

For example, one of the only photographs from Iliazd's childhood shows the nursery with a cherubic-looking Ilia in the corner of a well-appointed and brightly lit room. He is just a toddler, seated firmly on a child's diminutive wooden chair, and surrounded by stuffed animals and other toys appropriate to the nursery. His older brother Kirill is sitting on the floor nearby, behind a wagon filled with wooden blocks. He gazes at the camera more seriously, a touch of anxiety on his sharper, more angular features. But the scene is idyllic. Sun casts a shadow through the shelves of bric-a-brac onto the papered wall of the room. The detritus of childhood litters the scene as if the brothers have broken off in the midst of play to pose for the photographer. Ilia's shiny hair falls in pretty curls to his shoulders, above the ruffled front of his outfit. He is still in skirts, his sturdy legs placed flat on the floor in front of him in black stockings and buttoned shoes. His eyes express a confident spirit and energetic attitude. All is calm and cheerful in this picture of well-ordered, securely middle-class life.

Excerpts from the diary of his mother, Valentina Kirillovna, give a glimpse

Ilia and Kirill Zdanevich in their nursery in Tbilisi around 1899. Courtesy of François Mairé and the Fonds Iliazd

of the domestic atmosphere at a slightly later date, when Iliazd would have been about seven:

October 1902
Kirill and Ilia have become very good children. They study hard and in general provide me with a great deal of pleasure. Kirill adores his drawing lessons and Ilia has great success with his arithmetic and takes so much pleasure in forming the numerals that he seems to be playing a game. Kirill never finishes his dinner since he is afraid he will be late for his drawing class. I suspect that this love of drawing will internalize itself in him and that certain aesthetic principles will form so solidly that they cannot help but bear fruit. Ilia is always joyful and sweet. He often plays on the piano to amuse himself . . .[3]

November 1902
Winter morning. The children's room is streaked with rays of bright winter sun. It is warm and pleasant. The children have finished their morning ablutions—part of their routine; they've had their tea and are beginning their lessons. On the

chest are all sorts of tablets with paintings and drawings, cut and colored—these provide the artistic element. Also, near the window in the sun a small brindled cat is rolled up in a ball. Her presence pleases Kirill, who often pauses to caress her fluffy back (he loves all furry animals) or to lay his face against her side speaking mysterious words in her ear. The children are not very serious. As they work at their lessons they talk constantly, and the sound of their sonorous voices echoes without a moment of silence—like the chattering of small birds.[4]

Thus, children are differentiated. Are their characters constructed, perceived, or reinforced by the parental gaze? The following undated passage, written by the adult Iliazd, provides another perspective: "At night, my mother put my hair into curls with strips of paper which were taken, page by page, from the gradually diminishing library of my grandfather. Pushkin, Griboyedov, Gogol all disappeared bit by bit. I spent the night with these books hanging around my head, and sure enough, little by little, I became a poet."[5] The apocryphal tale is presented to confirm events it supposedly foretold. We can imagine the baby Ilia as a veritable scrapbook of Russian literature, tossing nightly on his pillow amid the crunch and rustle of words he was presumably too young to read or recognize. Along with the influence of those literary snippets, Iliazd claimed that his mother, disappointed he was not a daughter, dressed him in skirts (it was the fashion of the day) while he was a toddler. Iliazd used this history to justify the creation of the character Lilia as the central figure of his cycle of futurist plays. She bore a feminized version of his name, signaling her identity as an alter ego or surrogate. Self-mythologizing is the privilege of those who write their own history.

Life in the Zdanevich household in the Georgian capital was comfortable if not luxurious. Father Zdanevich taught French and pursued his avid interest in cycling; his mother had musical talent and had studied with Tchaikovsky. A glimpse of the household comes through in this vivid sketch by a family friend, Konstantin Paustovsky. Published in English in 1964, this reference was not in the original list of documents we compiled, but Hélène knew of its existence and I found the book later in my university library:

The Zdaneviches lived in an old house with large terraces and chestnut trees which gave onto a courtyard. The rooms were cool and a bit dark, with faded Persian rugs and a mass of miscellaneous furniture coming apart from dryness and old age. The steps that led up to the terrace trembled under foot without disturbing the house in the least. The notes of a piano being played, songs, declamations and conversation seemed to pour off the walls. There were pigeons on the terraces and in the eaves. From the early hours of the morning the sound of French verbs being conjugated aloud by the pupils of Father Zdanevich could be heard throughout the house.[6]

The parents' encouragement of their sons' talents is clear in the mother's journal. She divided the world between her sons, allocating each a domain:

January 1903

Two painter friends of G. B. Trifonov, the painter who lives in our house, came to visit during vacation. They painted like madmen in the studio, each doing my portrait in his own style, and the children spent hours watching. Ilia was laughing, skipping, twirling, saying all sorts of clever things and charming the entire group. Kira [Kirill] watched the process and the paintings very seriously. The painters praised his drawings and were surprised by the precision and detail of certain of them. I love watching Kira when he looks at a painting. It's clear that he understands far more than he can say. My aim in nourishing his artistic development has been to awaken in him vital interest—and my goal has been achieved. He's been exposed to masses of illustrated books, paintings, pictures, painters, exhibitions, lessons for the last three years, between the ages of 7 and 10. Now comes more serious problems: discipline, technique, and real supervision; how am I to resolve them?

Summer 1903

Ilia . . . also told the story of a lost book and told it in a striking manner, arranging the tale so as to communicate all kinds of information, ". . . suddenly I passed by a fort built in 1883 . . ." He exercises his prodigious memory with these facts, with foreign words and data, anything which he comes across he seems to be able to store in his mind as if he were playing a game.[7]

The social life of the Zdanevich household brought the brothers into contact with artists and intellectuals. Iliazd's first exposure to futurism came just as he was graduating with honors from the gymnasium in 1911, at about seventeen, an event recorded in a passage from his unpublished manuscripts: "Among my parents' friends there were quite a number of artists who had lived in Paris. One of these, the painter Boris Lopatinsky, came back from a trip to Paris in which he had made the acquaintance of the Futurist Marinetti. At the beginning of 1911 he had brought the manifestos of Marinetti back to Tbilisi with him in a suitcase. For me, this was the moment of conversion."[8] The scene is not hard to imagine—a family circle in the provincial

Ilia and Kirill Zdanevich in student uniforms, 1910. Courtesy of François Mairé and the Fonds Iliazd

capital, in a house where ideas about art circulated freely as the currency of the day, an interested teenager, poised for departure to take up studies in the Russian capital, St. Petersburg, aware that his older brother had inserted himself into vital artistic circles where staid academic traditions were being put aside.

Kirill had fulfilled his mother's hopes: he became a painter. Two years Ilia's senior, Kirill had connections in St. Petersburg and Moscow that would pave the way for entry into the active scene Iliazd encountered on arrival. Many of the poets and artists central to the Russian avant-garde had come from similarly solid bourgeois families. Nothing in the milieu of Iliazd's childhood predicts his turn to futurism. But the generation that formed the radical avant-garde was steeped in literary and fine art traditions, as well as middle-class mores, aware of precisely what they wished to reject as part of creating their inflammatory rhetoric. Until he was exposed to Marinetti's manifestos, Iliazd had considered himself a symbolist, which was the prevalent aesthetic style, with its mystical overtones and richly saturated imagery.

Elements of that earlier movement persist in Iliazd's *zaum*, as will be clear in some of his poetics and imagery. When Iliazd, still Ilia, left his parents' home to pursue his studies in law in St. Petersburg, his imagination was already inspired by Marinetti's rhetoric. He arrived in the Russian city ready to immerse himself in artistic scenes and to proclaim the doctrine of futurism.

Introduction to Futurism (1910s)

Iliazd's own documentation of his engagement with futurism included a handful of texts from the 1910s as well as later writings by himself, including a manuscript "Letter to Soffici / Fifty Years After," written in 1962.[9] Materials from 1912 to 1916 were sparse in the archive as were mentions of Iliazd in secondary materials dealing with the period. During the winter of 1985 I worked mainly with the documents Hélène handed to me. Correlation of events and counternarratives from published sources came later but are interwoven here within the narrative. Futurism was clearly formative *for* Iliazd, but in the years of his first exposure, his impact *on* the movement in Russia is more difficult to gauge: "I don't claim that the term 'Futurism' . . . was my invention, but I was incontestably the first to bring it to the street, the first to make it known in a public declaration."[10]

This statement appears in an undated letter written by Iliazd to Vladimir Markov, author of the first major study of Russian futurism (published in 1968), in response to a draft section of the manuscript.[11] The claim is grounded in verifiable events that took place in January 1912 when Iliazd climbed onto the stage of the Troitsky Theater in St. Petersburg and proclaimed the manifestos of Filippo Marinetti (who was not present). Iliazd was a few months short of his eighteenth birthday. A young cadet in the ranks of the avant-garde, he was just a year younger than Vladimir Mayakovsky, who would make his first public appearance on the same stage in November. But they were both almost half a generation younger than David Burliuk, Natalia Goncharova, Mikhail Larionov, and other figures whose activities had already begun to create a unique formal and theoretical language for a new art arising from Fauve and cubist sources combined with Russian stylistic elements.[12]

Iliazd had left Tbilisi for St. Petersburg in fall 1911 to study law. He enrolled in a course of study, but, like many college students, he seemed to find the allure of extracurricular activities at least as attractive as the academic discipline he was pursuing. His account in "Fifty Years After" provides a clear recollection of the scene into which he entered and the tide of events that would lead him into his futurist literary pursuits and innovative book productions. By the end of the decade, Iliazd would have created one of the most remarkable and sustained accomplishments of futurist literary typography. The scenes he describes on his arrival were well suited to galvanize his poetic imagination:

> I left for St. Petersburg to continue my studies. There I met the cubist painters Viktor Bart and Mikhail Ledentu who introduced me to avant-garde circles. I dreamed only of one thing during this period—to make Futurist ideas known. In the end of 1911 Futurism was known in Russia only by means of a few short letters written in *Apollon* from Italy by Paolo Buzzi. Mikhail Kuzmin had published an article about Futurism in the same review appended to Buzzi's letter, but there were no Futurists. There were the Burliuk brothers, David and Nikolai, Alexei Kruchenykh, and painters like Larionov and Goncharova who all formed the core of the group "The Union of Youth" in St. Petersburg that was hostile to the Symbolists as well as to the group of artists known by their association with the *World of Art* reviews like *Apollon* or *The Golden Fleece*. . . . Some pamphlets had already been printed, and there were exhibitions beginning, but the principal organ of the struggle was the public gatherings where the audience was haranged by orators in proposals in which there was absolutely no margin of tolerance. . . . In St. Petersburg there were gatherings at the Troitsky Theater or at the auditorium of the Tenishev school; in Moscow it was at the auditorium of the Polytechnic Institute.[13]

Accounts in the work of Vladimir Markov made clear that the work of Marinetti had been disseminated widely, but also that the term "futurist" had meanings in the Russian context not directly related to the Italian.[14] The initial publication of the Futurist Manifesto on the front page of the French newspaper *Le Figaro* in 1909 had created a publicity event possibly unparalleled in the history of visual arts. Marinetti's text was not a review of work published in the press; it was an original work using the press as its platform. Mass media were being pressed into the service of the avant-garde, and the impact had been immediate and international in scope. The call to break with tradition increased the pressure to create clear distinctions between contemporary trends and those that had been considered radical even a few years earlier. Impressionism, postimpressionism, and the arts and crafts movement were to be jettisoned.

Iliazd had yet to make any contribution to the life of arts and letters. His generational enthusiasm was quickly shaped by peers and those around him. The social life of art became a lived reality, and though he did complete his law studies in a timely manner, he was spending time in the company of vibrant artists directly involved in shaping the Russian avant-garde. Mikhail Larionov and Natalia Goncharova, though barely into their thirties, were "the acknowledged leaders of the new Russian art" at the time Iliazd met them in 1912.[15] Though attending the university in St. Petersburg, the young Iliazd went to Moscow to see the couple and began collaborating with them almost immediately:

> When I arrived in Moscow from St. Petersburg in 1912, Goncharova and Larionov were living in a little street called Trekhprudny. The entrances to their apartment and into the two rooms were crammed with paintings and books. It was that way every place they lived—everything was jammed together and it was difficult to move. Even in lifting one's feet up over various obstacles there was the problem of putting them down without breaking the glass in a frame or stepping through a canvas. I had trouble just clearing enough place to put down a door on which I slept while visiting them.[16]

Along with David and Nikolai Burliuk, Larionov and Goncharova had been crucial in fomenting the activities that came to be referred to as Russian futurism. In 1912, there was little cohesion or coordination among the many artists rushing to claim leadership in the rapidly shifting world of avant-garde art. Exhibitions and alternative spaces for performance in cabarets or in small theaters like the Troitsky helped establish visibility for these ambitious young artists eager to break with academic traditions. They were keen to define Russian work on terms distinct from that of European movements and combined radical innovation with political excitement and a certain nationalist fervor.[17] Small groups sprung up, partisan to their own position, with names attached to themselves or their exhibits. Larionov, originally associated with the symbolist-oriented Golden Fleece, had founded a group called the Jack of Diamonds in 1910. Within two years, he created an even more radical group, the Donkey's Tail, just about the time that he and Iliazd began their close association (donkeys figure prominently in Iliazd's *zaum* cycles composed after 1916). Iliazd could not have found himself in circumstances more ideal for the formulation of his own aesthetics.

Iliazd's friendship with Larionov and Goncharova grew rapidly. While continuing his law studies in St. Petersburg, he saw them frequently. In 1911, Larionov displayed an interest in neo-primitivism and abstraction. He began using sharp angles and a deliberately crude drawing style that signaled a striking shift in approach similar to the aggressively vernacular language in futurist poetry. The dreamlike miasmas and otherworldly tones of symbolism, with roots in the French writings of Charles Baudelaire and Arthur Rimbaud, vanished in the bright headlights of futurist rhetoric, with its speeding cyclists, car horns, and airplane motors, and motifs distilled into dynamic abstraction. Formal languages, not symbolic ones, were the new order of the day.

The young avant-garde writers drew their strength from spoken language and vernacular sources to create effrontery and scandal, as is clear from the title of the 1911 anthology of work by David Burliuk, Kruchenykh, Mayakovsky, and Khlebnikov, *A Slap in the Face of Public Taste*. Nuance and nicety were associated with the past, as outmoded as gaslight and candle flames, carriages and corsets. Books succeeded in being part of the avant-garde because they were considered a part of mass media and also because they were created with inexpensive and do-it-yourself methods far from the rarefied world of the atelier. Books had aesthetic vitality because they circulated more widely than art in galleries. Aesthetic changes registered not only in themes and methods of poetic composition, vocabulary, or rhyme structures, but as a shift in attitude about the relationship of art to mass-mediated culture.

If we pause to consider the graphical styles prevalent in Iliazd's youth, we can understand how radical was the break embodied in the futurist publications. The most visible early twentieth-century magazine was Sergei Diaghilev's *The World of Art* (*Mir Iskusstva*). It was published between 1899 and 1904, well before the publications of Russian futurists appeared. Its graphic style and lavish production methods were part of an international trend in turn-of-the-century publication. Chromolithographic covers or colored woodblock prints filled with garlands, floral patterns, organic letterforms wreathed in vines, images of white swans, dark forests, lithe women with long hair and naked limbs, and even mythical creatures were characteristic of the style shared by art nouveau, Jugendstil, Viennese secessionism, and other turn-of-the-century movements. The British arts and crafts movement had had a profound influence on book design after the mid-1890s, with elaborate borders and illustrations printed on handmade paper in many limited-edition (and commercial) works. Russian artists of the late nineteenth century had a strong affinity with these European stylistic trends and movements. When small Russian avant-garde books began to appear in the early 1910s in handmade, individually written or drawn, and inexpensively produced editions, they created a striking contrast by their physical format and their poetic tone. Iliazd's allegiance to futurist aesthetics, as we will see, was clearly marked in the design of small format works. These contained no elaborate borders, floral decorations, or anything extraneous to the text, and were made using techniques he could learn himself or access directly.

But the strongest influence on Iliazd in the 1910s came through his work with Goncharova and Larionov. Goncharova was charismatic, talented, well educated, and accomplished, with a distinguished artistic pedigree (she was a descendent of Aleksandr Pushkin). She had met Larionov at the Moscow Institute of Painting in 1900 and they become lifelong partners. Both artists were ambitious, driven by intellectual vision and professional aspirations for their painting but also their position of influence within Russian art. Goncharova was included in the 1906 Salon d'Automne exhibit organized by Sergei Diaghilev in Paris, and her work at that time was strongly influenced by French postimpressionism. By the 1910s, she had become part of the radical Jack of Diamonds group in Russia. In 1912, when Goncharova and Larionov met Iliazd, Larionov was hard at work organizing the only exhibition of the Donkey's Tail group, which took place that year. The work was far from the established *World of Art*, with its trappings and pageantry, which they deemed old-fashioned, or, in the term of the day, *passéiste*. Though they shared an interest in folkloric motifs or Russian themes, these younger avant-garde artists considered Diaghilev's Ballets Russes bourgeois spectacles, fit mainly for export aimed at popular audiences. The 1913 Paris debut of *The Rite of Spring* caused a sensation, but younger futurists, including Larionov, Mayakovsky, and Iliazd, were also eager to capture public attention—this time through irreverent shock and radical use of language.

Iliazd had less experience than either Larionov or Goncharova and was a good decade younger. His futurist proclamations were based on his direct readings of Marinetti's work in French in *Le Figaro* (he was fluent in both Russian and French). Russian translations of Marinetti's *Manifestos* only appeared in 1914, and thus for many of the Russian artists breaking new ground under the futurist banner, Marinetti was unimportant.[18] Their own innovative agendas drove their work. This was certainly the case for Larionov, whose theoretical investigations took more from cubism and the philosophy of Henri Bergson (his theories of perception in relation to matter and light were echoed in Larionov's Rayonnist theories) than from the Italians.[19] Marinetti had the glamor of a high-profile figure whose very mention brought a frisson of excitement to a public event even if the associations

Iliazd with Natalia Goncharova and Mikhail Larionov (note the paint on their faces),
1913. Courtesy of François Mairé and the Fonds Iliazd

were more for effect than substance. But Larionov was close at hand and
absorbed Iliazd directly into his orbit. Iliazd took ideas from both of them.

Photographs of Iliazd during that period display his enthusiasm. His eyes
glow with intensity and determination. One photograph shows him with
his mother, her hourglass shape still corseted, hair drawn up in the perfect
decorous style of the turn-of-the-century bourgeois matron. Iliazd stands
next to her, obedient and tender. But one senses already the young man
about to take flight into his own life. Another photo, probably taken in the
same session (the details of dress and setting, such as the floral arrangement
in his jacket pocket and his neatly arranged hair, are identical), depicts him
sitting demurely at a desk with a pen, his papers arranged in front of his
inkwell, hands neatly posed below the well-starched shirt cuffs. He assumes
the posture of the young law clerk, conscientiously attending to the business
of his tasks. A year later, in a photograph with Larionov and Goncharova, he
appears with his face painted with marks, leaning into the couple with all
the attentive engagement of an acolyte eager to show he is up to the challenge of their company.

His 1962 description of his entry into the public life of futurism reveals his conviction about the impact of his activities:

> It was at the Troitsky Theater, on the 18th of January in 1912, at a gathering sponsored by the Union of Youth, that I took the stage with a Futurist declaration. . . . The next day all the schools and groups of young artists suddenly became "Futurists."
>
> The only thing that had been missing to unite all these various factions in their struggle against the establishment art world was a word. All I did was to bring that word, "Futurism."
>
> With incredible rapidity this word obtained currency in Russia while the "World of Art" remained a phrase known mostly among aestheticians and specialists (with Aleksandr Benois at their head). But Futurism became a popular term. And just as "The Wanderers" got their name from their practice of going from village to village to display their work, the "Futurists" became itinerant to publicize their manifestos and going from village to village made this word a part of everyday Russian life. I am not claiming that Russian Futurism was based on complete ignorance of Italian Futurism, to which it was a sort of sorcerer's apprentice, but it is true that Russian Futurism had little in common with Italian. From the start, the aesthetic positions were completely different. Italian Futurism was the creation of F. T. Marinetti and his friends. Russian Futurism was the application of the word to a vaguely similar tendency which had evolved much earlier. Every school battled to be considered the real Futurism. . . . This tendency to call any and all new art Futurism meant that cubists, fauvists, and so forth were all included under that label. . . . It was only after the first enthusiasm began to fade that more specific terms like "constructivism" began to make their appearance.[20]

Iliazd took distinct pride in feeling he had helped bring Marinetti's ideas into the Russian sphere. When Marinetti visited in 1914, the event was of considerable importance for Iliazd. Again, the notes from 1962 give us Iliazd's version of events:

> F. T. Marinetti came to Russia at the beginning of 1914. It is amazing that this visit has such a small place in the archives of Futurism. We have no document, even a letter of his, as evidence of this trip. Or of any of the impressions Marinetti had of the journey to Moscow and St. Petersburg. It is only by the letters of his friends that we know he came and went from Russia. This lack of information has led a number of art historians to declare that Marinetti was in Russia several times and

that the first time was in 1911. I do not know if Marinetti came to Russia before 1910, but I know for a fact that he did not make a visit between 1910 and 1914. And the claim that he came to see what the Russians were up to in order to take his findings back and apply them in Italy is pure nonsense—an opinion expressed by M. Larionov, for instance—cooked up to assert Russian priority in the field of Futurist innovations. But I find something strange about his utter silence on the subject of his Russian voyage.[21]

The mystery of Marinetti's silence lifts when we consider the rest of Iliazd's account of the events in the same document (filtered through half a century of memory):

> True, the visit was not a success. I was in Moscow that week and attended his lecture at the Circle of Free Aesthetics. We had hoped he would rail against the old Russia and encourage us to destroy the Kremlin. But he was the perfect, polite foreigner and only spoke out against Rodin. That day he probably saved the Kremlin in Moscow.
>
> There were immediate protests from the Futurists . . . and there was a meeting the next day to make up an anti-Marinetti manifesto stating that Russian Futurism was entirely independent of the Italian, but I refused to sign. I wasn't concerned with what differentiated Russian and Italian Futurism, but with what they had in common—not politics, but aesthetics. . . . The internal quarrels provoked by Marinetti's visit gradually increased the squabbling among the Russians, and hadn't even died down when the war arrived."[22]

In the 1960s, Iliazd wondered whether any trace of the visit had remained in Marinetti's papers. This in part was what prompted his correspondence with Ardengo Soffici, who had been part of the Italian inner circle. Soffici suggested that Marinetti had come away with the impression that the young Russians had absorbed all the lessons of the *Manifestos* and took them very literally. In addition, he noted that they had decorated themselves outlandishly and behaved in a flamboyant manner full of disdain for the conventionalized arts of the past. Iliazd corroborated these details, noting: "At the lecture Mayakovsky wore his yellow blouse and I had drawings in India ink on the collar and cuffs of my shirt, as was then the fashion."[23] The pose of the well-trained law clerk had given way, and those same starched white surfaces that had signaled bourgeois decorum in his dress now served as a canvas for these crude markings.

In his 1964 reply, Soffici also suggested that Marinetti had actually felt himself "a bit passé and a bit of a provincial in comparison" to the Russians.[24] But in any case, the visit had more impact on Iliazd than on Marinetti, who was already an internationally renowned artist who apparently had little use for a bunch of fractious young Russians who were not ready to subscribe to his program. Iliazd recalled that at the banquet held at the studio of Nikolai Kulbin, Marinetti read from *Zang Tumb Tumb* and Benedikt Livshits picked quarrels with him in contests to outstrip each other in aesthetic radicalism. Marinetti countered by claiming that *zaum* was nothing more than *parole in liberta* ("words in liberty") in translation.

As Iliazd stated in his account of Marinetti's visit, a document declaring Marinetti's irrelevance to the Russian scene was actually drawn up by the young avant-gardists, and Iliazd refused to sign. This loyalty to Marinetti remained intact and even continued late in life. This says more about Iliazd's character than his aesthetics or politics. His poetic experiments and typographic work, as will be clear, owed more to the influence of Velimir Khlebnikov and Aleksei Kruchenykh than to Marinetti.[25] Nowhere in the writings or publications he produced between 1913 and 1923 did he invoke any of the vocabulary central to Marinetti's definitions of modernity: speed, velocity, industrial technology, machines, or media. None of the Italian's trademark phrases, like "words in liberty" or "wireless imagination," appear in Iliazd's writings, except when they are directly referencing Marinetti. Instead, Iliazd created a personal iconography that borrowed from folk motifs and Russian language and celebrated the work of a naïve and anti-technological painter, Pirosmani, who provided him with the model of what an artist's life and identity could be outside of conventional frameworks.

Marinetti inspired Iliazd's passion for art and radical aesthetics. But his work with Mikhail Larionov and Natalia Goncharova provided a more direct apprenticeship for the young poet. Iliazd was fortunate in having these collaborator-mentors beginning in 1912.

Formal and Personal Exchanges

In the time I spent with Hélène, I learned how profoundly a formal relationship could develop personal dimensions without ever lapsing from its protocols. We were respectful with each other and I took my social cues entirely from her. We spoke of topics related to the project, or work, or sometimes the day's weather, but the process of revealing personal information was slow. She gleaned the basics of my circumstances from a few exchanges, and my status as a student made the generational gap easy to negotiate. She had been a teacher, and the role suited her. The mentoring she offered was subtle. She gave me pointers on how to act with persons with whom we came in contact or about whom we spoke. Her tone and her judicious way of situating someone with respect to our undertaking or her knowledge about their lives were always respectful. Sometimes, of course, she avoided saying much. Of Goncharova, for instance, she once said something highly sympathetic, but which indicated an unhappy late chapter. I could sense in this brief mention an epic of historical dimensions—of Hélène's recognition of the many vicissitudes of life for a figure whose experience had been so varied and whose life circumstances so complex, mixed with her own loyalty to Iliazd and his version of events. Hélène merely raised her eyebrows and shook her head with an expression that communicated volumes: "At the end, it was difficult." Little else was said, or needed to be.

The archives in the studio held some materials relevant to the futurist period in Russia and in Tbilisi, but much of that had to be extended and supplemented by what I could find in secondary sources I gradually discovered.[26] As we made our way through the many folders and pages, documents and materials, the basic outlines of events and activities came into view. In each exchange, Hélène's hands reached and sorted. As she gave me the folder or paper, my eyes followed her motions. On her left hand the broad wedding band was always in view. That sign, so ritually charged, so solid, so present, was part of each transfer of papers. I was always aware of her place in a network of history and identity—her role as wife, her life with Iliazd, her widowhood—and her trust in handing me the documents. The repetition of these gestures created its own bonds. I had been let into the connection as witness and scribe, a permission by which I always felt honored.

I never pried and she never questioned me much about my personal life. But little by little, we offered information. I would mention a letter from my sister, or an account of an event not directly related to the work. These were small acknowledgments that the larger lives we were living were also connected by this shared space of regular activity and combined effort.

Larionov and Goncharova

Among the treasures I recall on the walls of the rue Mazarine was a black and white portrait of Iliazd made in 1913 by Goncharova. Her elegant abstraction depicted him with wings, a pen in hand, flooded with inspirational light. He received from her the nickname "the angel" with no indication of irony. Though relations among Goncharova, Larionov, and Iliazd apparently deteriorated in the later phase of Iliazd's life in Paris, the early connection and work it produced remained very important to him.[27]

Beyond the passage already cited about Iliazd's visit to Larionov and Goncharova's flat in Moscow, little evidence of their personal connection remained. But Iliazd wrote three significant pieces in connection with Larionov and Goncharova. They show his transition from acolyte to independent spirit. The first was a catalogue essay of their work, published in 1913. The second piece was jointly authored with Larionov, "Why We Paint Our Faces," also published in 1913. The third, a text now lost, was Iliazd's proclamation of "Everythingism" in 1914, of which we have the preface by his close friend, Mikhail Ledentu.[28]

Iliazd's essay for the exhibition catalogue—the first comprehensive study of their work—contains evidence of extensive collaboration. He remained very sensitive to the issue of authorship of the catalogue, and wanted it clear that he had written it, a point he stressed repeatedly. This was particularly necessary because it had been published under the pseudonym Eli Eganbyuri. An undated, unpublished note in his papers clarified this identity:

> I was Eli Eganbyuri. It is curious to realize that Larionov always hid the identity of the author of this text, which he used several times to supplement the prefaces for his exhibition. Meeting Mr. Waldemar George recently at an opening for Czobel at the Zak Gallery, I was obliged to respond to his question, "By the way, do you know who the Caucasian was who wrote in 1913 . . ." "It was me!"—which left Mr. George a bit surprised to say the least. Meeting him again later I was gratified to hear him refer to the book as "The one you claim you are the author of . . ." Fortunately the pseudonym Eli Eganbyuri, which I used until 1919, the year I took the name Iliazd, was a pseudonym à clé. It's a French reading of the dative form in Russian of my name, Zdanevich, and was the reading given to the name on my father's mail by the Parisian postman.[29]

Iliazd wrote the text, but reading through the text, one senses the influence of his collaborators. Many of the ideas in the piece came directly from Larionov, including theories of Rayonnism, which he had begun to articulate as early as 1910. These theories do not make any subsequent appearance in work by Iliazd, whose poetics stressed the materials (sound and graphical forms) of language, as well as eroticism and psychological melodrama, not Rayonnist notions of perception. Working closely with the artists, Iliazd crafted the presentation of their careers and positions within the recent history of Russian art, demonstrating knowledge of the crosscurrents of European and Russian influences in the preceding years.

Vladimir Markov summarized the contents of the essay:

> He gives an interesting survey of Russian art with a touch of neo-Slavophilism. He praises the Tartar yoke in Russia for its beneficent influence on native art, and accuses Peter the Great of practically destroying national tradition and splitting Russian culture between the city and the country through his reforms. Zdanevich does not condemn Western influences as such, however, and notices that the Western influence on Russia in the field of poetry was, on the whole, good. . . . In painting, however, the results were disastrous; and the Russian countryside, superior in its culture to the city, could never be properly approached by Russian painters because they lacked the taste and craftsmanship. Awakened by French artists at the turn of the century, Larionov and Goncharova finally reversed the situation and discovered the true Russian art. At the end of the book there is an announcement of a forthcoming edition of a collection of Rayonnist poetry, which never appeared.[30]

Questions of national traditions and their relation to art were central to the avant-garde. Like others, Iliazd wanted to define a unique identity for Russian poetics.[31] But he did not want his work, or that of those he admired, to be considered significant only on these grounds. Writing about Goncharova, he showed his understanding of the sources of her themes as well as his appreciation of her drawing style and its basis in folk sources. He characterized her adoption of this mode as "gestural drawing," one that crudely displayed its making in an energetic and vigorous line. He also noted the influence of Byzantine mosaics, the profile form taken from icons, and the decorative motifs from religious art. He commented on the rough, primitive quality of the images and her interest in *lubki* or woodblock books (which would have an enormous impact on futurist book designs). He took great care in his description, attending to the literal aspects of representation, the formal, tactile quality of marks and lines. Goncharova's preference for what she termed "the Orient" over the Occident, for the spiritual over the secular and urbane, for the ostensibly primitive over the visibly sophisticated and mannered, were all noted and praised in his assessment. In his final observations he commented on her books, and in this moment we can sense him rehearsing a critical profile of his own work to come: "And finally she has illustrated a number of works by young poets; she makes use of a whole new attitude about the rapport between the appearance of the exterior of a book and its content, and these books represent the beginning of a whole new era in Russian illustration."[32] In fact, Goncharova was more than an "illustrator," and her visual work was created in active dialogue with texts—as a complement and response. This might have had an influence on Iliazd's understanding of the book as a site of intertextual play, rather than as a static presentation. These insights would be at the center of his book productions, along with those of Larionov, Kirill Zdanevich, Olga Rozanova, and Kruchenykh.[33] This design sensibility would bear fruit in the editions of Forty-One Degrees, once Iliazd established the imprint in Tbilisi after 1917.

When he discussed the work of Larionov, Iliazd took a very different tone. His writing became charged with excitement in a way that never appeared in the evenhanded treatment of Goncharova. Though he conscientiously allocated the same amount of space in his essay to their individual work, the difference was striking: "A force was needed that could break like a storm on the stagnant water of Russian painting. . . . What was required was a man capable of analytic reflection. This man appeared in the person of Mikhail Fedorovich Larionov. . . ."[34] This celebratory tone communicated Iliazd's boundless admiration of Larionov and his work. Even if this praise had been prompted by Larionov, the admiration was not feigned. The details of Larionov's development had paralleled those of Goncharova, with his early style very much in the postimpressionist mode. At the moment in the essay where Iliazd noted the break with European influences and the creation of a new mode of abstraction, he shifted to a detailed description of the paintings. Rayonnism clearly excited his interest, and Iliazd listed the pigments and colors and elaborated the textural qualities of surface effects and brush treatments with a painter's knowledge. Attention to making—the *faktura*, or *made-ness*, of works of art—that was a central theme for early twentieth-century modernism shows in this critical approach:

> Everything is painted with tenderness, with a profound understanding of the Russian provincial spirit, which, until our times, has been the object of derision to cultivated city dwellers. The colors in his canvases are the opposite of those in his earlier Impressionist paintings; they are thick, strong, bold, covering the entire surface of the canvas. The dominant tones are ultra-marine, ivory, white, burnt and raw sienna, a deep dark green made from a blend of ochre, ultra-marine, and Indian red. Sometimes he uses a different spectrum—from vermillion to emerald green, with Veronese green or cadmium, or even a speckled lacquer with ivory

white and light ochre. He has also begun to incorporate writing in his compositions as if by accident, bits of inscription, like those one finds on walls, then later
the inscriptions become more carefully chosen, ornamenting the painting with
letters. The rendering of these works is distinguished by its diversity, by the love
of creating and recreating surfaces. He uses all kinds of techniques, not only those
used by other painters—such as brilliant, matte, rough, or impasto surfaces—and
processes generally found on poster such as sponged or granular effects, but one
also finds new surfaces, invented by Larionov, which are lacy, velvety, etc. These
processes, combined with somber colors and national themes, created a completely special effect enhanced by the fact that the painter applies several techniques on the same painting.[35]

Iliazd delighted in the scraps of writing in the canvases, and clearly lingered over the letterforms and inscriptions. Rayonnism was paving the way
for a completely new, modern aesthetic in Russia. The catalogue continued:
"In this manner, the extermination of ancient art is achieved completely,
without the necessity of resorting to fire or the destruction of galleries and
museums, because . . . the infinite, traversed by the rays springing from
rayonnist works, creates new, free forms, independent of the existing three
dimensions which up until now marked the limits of painting."[36]

Parallels with cubism were evident in the concern Rayonnism had with
the perception of multiple dimensions, in this case, the rays of light. Larionov's essay, "Rayonnist Painting," published the same year as this catalogue
essay, outlined the basic precepts. Described in the pseudoscientific jargon
that was popular at the time, it centered on the process by which light is
refracted from objects. The job of the painter was to represent these "rays."
Here are Larionov's words from 1913:

> Luminosity owes its existence to reflected light (between objects in space this
> forms a kind of colored dust).
>
> The doctrine of luminosity.
>
> Radioactive rays. Ultraviolet rays. Reflectivity.
>
> We do not sense the object with our eye, as it is depicted conventionally in
> pictures and as a result of following this or that device; in fact, we do not sense
> the object as such. We perceive a sum of rays proceeding from a source of light;
> these are reflected from the object and enter our field of vision.
>
> Consequently, if we wish to paint literally what we see, then we must paint
> the sum of rays reflected from the object. But in order to receive the total sum
> of rays from the desired object, we must select them deliberately—because to-

gether with the rays of the object being perceived, there also fall into our range of vision reflected rays belonging to other nearby objects. Now, if we wish to depict an object exactly as we see it, then we must depict also these reflex rays belonging to other objects—and then we will depict literally what we see.[37]

The phrasing used by Iliazd was very close in every detail: "We know that the object becomes visible owing to the rays which . . . are returned by the object and reach the retina. In fact, we never see the object itself, but the sum of rays which reach our eye . . . if we developed these facts and wish to render that which really exists, we must paint, not the object, but that which exists between us and the object, that is, the sum of intermediate rays."[38]

The influence was clear, and such links between painters and poets were strong throughout the Russian avant-garde, as Olga Djordjadze made clear in her recollections of Iliazd:[39] "It is interesting to realize that at this moment in time, painting, because of its experiments, laid the groundwork for the development of the Futurist aesthetic in literature. Poets like Kruchenykh, with whom Iliazd was closely linked, as well as Mayakovsky and David Burliuk, were painters. Pasternak was the son of a painter, Khlebnikov an amateur painter. This link between the two disciplines explains to some extent why the literature of the avant-garde was so frequently conceived in terms of pictorial terminology and ideas. . . ."[40]

Iliazd played a greater role in the next jointly authored work, "Why We Paint Our Faces," published in 1913 in the newly established middle-brow journal *Argus*.[41] The exclamatory and hyperbolic text was placed across from an article about the tango, and the graphic juxtaposition added a bit of flair to an already flamboyant tone:

> We have joined art to life. After the long isolation of artists, we have loudly summoned life and life has invaded art; it is time for art to invade life. The painting of our faces is the beginning of the invasion. That is why our hearts are beating so.
>
> We do not aspire to a single form of aesthetics. Art is not only a monarchy, but also a newsman and a decorator. We value both print and news. The synthesis of decoration and illustration is the basis of our self-painting. We decorate life and preach—that's why we paint ourselves.
>
> Tattooing doesn't interest us. People tattoo themselves once and for always. We paint ourselves for an hour, and a change of experience calls for a change of painting, just as picture devours picture, when, on the other side of a car wind-

shield shop windows flash by running into each other; that's our faces. Tattooing is beautiful but it says little—only about one's tribe and exploits. Our painting is the journalist.[42]

Iliazd, Larionov, Ledentu, Goncharova, Burliuk, and others painted their faces to signal this blurred boundary between art and life. The artists made themselves into a surface on which designs could be painted, putting elaborate decorations on their cheeks and foreheads, sometimes on collars and cuffs of their clothes, to carry out the tenets of this manifesto.

In 1984, Régis Gayraud recorded a curious recollection about this practice provided by Melita Rafalovich, who had been Iliazd's childhood friend.[43] She was so impressed by face painting as a sign of avant-garde credentials that when she heard Iliazd was passing by train through a town where she was taking a rest cure, she painted her face and stationed herself on the platform where he would see her. She stood with another young friend, a painter, and apparently though Iliazd saw the friend and waved, to the poor girl's dismay he ignored her completely.[44]

The final document from these collaborations was the manifesto of "Everythingism," which had its first public pronouncement in St. Petersburg in 1914. The text, a proclamation of the tenets of the new movement, was lost. But a record of its contents was preserved in a preface written by Mikhail Ledentu, a copy of which was in Iliazd's possession:

By carefully comparing the forms of art which have flourished in various times we find, despite vastly different cultural conditions—which only influenced the external appearance of works of art—a great similarity.

The unity of everything which is artistic is determined by analyzing the method used to create the forms. In possession of a sufficient amount of artistic culture . . . it is not necessary to employ some conventional method of analysis to evaluate a work of art. We can arrive at a method of pictorial construction, however, of which we will speak later. We can begin by saying that the presence of this construction and its perfection is the one condition indispensable to the achievement of a work of art. This method has nothing to do with either subject or style, as the idiot theoreticians of the "art world" would have us believe, but with an analysis of the essential content of the painting or sculpture, the study of the language of its lines or colors, which can be established according to the invariable and indispensable criteria used in turn to determine the artistic level of the work. . . . Everythingism affirms the value of artistic works and gives us the possibility of creating a contemporary art which has some rapport with the reality we have learned about from studying the art which has flourished in all cultures. The Futurist who is afraid to look into the past thinking that he will lose sight of what is going on at the moment is in error—because in so doing he reinforces the influence of the historians who are the most obtuse, the historians of art. We must seize the forms of art that reveal that which has an immutable essence in art! By taking this point of view we have the right to assert that everything that was created by the artists before us, even long before us, is contemporary and assimilable—as our perception insists![45]

Olga Djordjadze commented that Everythingism was Iliazd's "reaction against the fanatical narrowness of many Futurists."[46] The manifesto-like tone of Ledentu's introduction resonates with the other works jointly authored by Larionov and Iliazd, but the insistence on eclecticism echoed sentiments expressed by Goncharova. Through his connections with these two artists, and the active circles of poets and painters in which they moved, the young poet had absorbed the lessons and language of the avant-garde.

Pirosmani

Another fortuitous circumstance in Iliazd's artistic development began in the summer of 1912, when he was in Tbilisi on vacation in the company of his brother and the painter Mikhail Ledentu. The three wandered in the region around the Zdanevich home and were struck by the appearance of a number of naïve paintings they found in inconspicuous haunts or on hand-painted signs for local businesses. These were the work of a Georgian painter, Niko Pirosmani, and the three young men became enthused about their authentic primitive quality.[47] Pirosmani, they asserted, was a painter of indigenous style, naïve and untainted by academic training or the trends of modern art. This style clearly resonated with the neo-primitive works that Iliazd had seen appearing among the avant-garde.

Pirosmani was about fifty years old at the time they met him. He had had a difficult life, struggling to survive, and such difficulties had taken their toll. He appeared as a venerable but neglected man in Iliazd's young eyes, an artist whose remarkable accomplishments had been overlooked. He often traded his work for food or drink, and his paintings appeared on tavern walls and storefronts in the region.

Iliazd first met the painter in person a few months later, in December 1912, a meeting he recalled in the preface to the 1972 publication *Pirosmanachvili*: "Sixty years have passed since the afternoon when we met Pi-

Iliazd in his cadet uniform. Courtesy of François Mairé and the Fonds Iliazd

rosmani. . . . This meeting occurred thanks to the fact that he was working out of doors under a lantern and followed several months of searching for the paintings of this elusive artist. He was already well known as a popular painter in the neighborhood of Tbilisi."[48] Later in this winter vacation Iliazd commissioned a portrait from Pirosmani and kept a detailed diary about its progress.

January 27, 1913
I went to Niko's. He was in the process of working on my portrait. The canvas was

Iliazd as painted by Pirosmani, 1913. Courtesy of François Mairé and the Fonds Iliazd

only sketched out. *The Stag,* another picture I had commissioned from him, was already finished except for the background. It was a splendid painting.

January 28, 1913

I went to Niko's in the morning. He had added a tree stump to my portrait and *The Stag* had grass on it. . . . Before lunch I went to Bego Iaksiev where I bought a still life of Niko's for a rouble and fifty kopeks. Then I went back to the tavern. The proprietor told me that he wouldn't have paid fifty kopecks [about fifty cents] for the painting I was carrying, He kept on talking and told me, "Niko wanted to paint a tree stump in your portrait and pose you with your hand on it holding a book. I told him to put in a table. It was *The Stag* that needed that tree trunk so that the beast could lean on it." I told him that I wanted Niko to paint the portrait as he pleased and that I wouldn't think of telling him how to do it.

January 29, 1913
I promised Niko that I would do an article on him that would appear published in a magazine.

January 31, 1913
I went back to pose this morning. The portrait is almost finished. The sky of *The Stag* is done. I went to the editorial offices of *The Transcaucasus Herald* to see if the open letter I had written about the painter had been accepted for publication. They told me it would be in the paper the next day.

February 1, 1913
This morning I went to Niko's. The portrait was finished. . . . At night I went back with G., the painter, and A., the journalist. We looked at the paintings. The painter, G, told me, "These paintings resemble Persian paintings with the difference that they are much cruder, have less color, and in general, have very little to recommend them." In general his reactions to the work are indifferent. For the most part, the intellectuals of Tbilisi consider Pirosmani a joke.[49]

When they first saw the paintings of Pirosmani in the tavern in Tbilisi, Ledentu reportedly said to the Zdanevich brothers, "He is the Georgian Giotto of today."[50] In the summer of 1912, which they recall as extremely hot, they scoured the countryside looking for other work by the painter. By summer's end, Ledentu had acquired two paintings, *A Girl of Ortachala* and *A Festival of Kurds*.[51] These were displayed with the others at a small reception at the Zdanevich home. On their way back to St. Petersburg in the fall, the three stopped off in Moscow and gave an informal lecture on Pirosmani. They displayed the paintings to Larionov, among others, and convinced him to exhibit the works in an exhibit the following year. In 1968, Iliazd reflected:

> The discovery of Pirosmani is not something for which a small group of us can claim exclusive credit. Pirosmani was discovered in the context of the Russian Futurist movement. Mikhail Ledentu . . . and Kirill Zdanevich, the painter, saw one of his paintings in the cellar of a tavern. It was Larionov who agreed to display some of his canvases in an exhibition in Moscow in 1913 (and also 1914). It was I

who actually found the painter himself and attempted to relieve somewhat the miserable situation in which he was living. We had already been fighting against academic art and that of the *World of Art*. As for the intellectual circles of Tbilisi, as far as they were concerned, the whole "Affair Pirosmani" was the story of a drunken bum promoted to the status of an artist as the prank of a group of students. It was only after the war, with the independence of Georgia and the movement of local culture, that artists and poets of the region were recognized. Unfortunately, Pirosmani was no longer there.[52]

In February of 1913, Iliazd published a critical essay on Pirosmani in the Tbilisi paper, *Zakavkazskaia Retch*. The piece was greeted with disdain and disbelief by the public. In 1914, Iliazd published a second article in *Vostok*, another local paper, and its tone had a mordant edge:[53]

Tbilisi—a jackal that feeds on the corpse of the European marketplace. The salty earth, strewn with the wreckage of the past, can still swell the heart of a pilgrim guarding the work that Pirosmani painted on a morsel of oilcloth.

The name of this artist has remained unknown and it has never occurred to you that the true domain of art might not be found in the theaters or deluxe editions. You praise the rejects of impressionism and call the reheated coffee served to you daily by the bloated denizens of the café "poetry," but in the damp cellars where the itinerant with bloodshot eyes comes to drink, squalling and carrying on, in the taverns on the outskirts of town . . . in the shops of hairdressers, bakers, and other shopkeepers there are the paintings of a master who is the honor of the nation whose work demonstrates research into the furthest limits of contemporary art. However, this old painter frequently takes refuge in drink, cursing the destiny that has forced him to wander from tavern to tavern giving away the incredible works of his marvellous talent for pennies or a bit of food or a glass of wine. Your poets, your artists, your musicians and your critics of art and professors, young and old leftover imitators of Europe, aren't worth a single centimeter of his canvases. It is already two years since we brought Pirosmani to your attention and asked for your assistance and you have remained silent. You have closed your eyes to a crowning treasure. . . . Your laziness and your ignorance are unpardonable. In refusing to recognize this artist you have lost a huge portion of your heritage—five centuries of art on which you turn your backs.[54]

Iliazd described Pirosmani as the son of a gardener who had moved to Tbilisi at the age of twelve, acquired a box of watercolors, and begun to paint. Later he bought a dairy and covered its walls with paintings, generally prospering until various misfortunes made him attempt to live from his work: "But his paintings only sold with difficulty and his existence became that of a vagabond always searching for a place to sleep and a bit of bread. He began to drink and by 1912 when the Futurist painters Zdanevich and Ledentu found him he was already a wreck. . . . The old man bemoaned his horrible poverty . . . begged for our aid, for some paints and a room and said, 'I will still paint some beautiful things.'"[55]

Iliazd continued:

At last there is justice and recognition of the glory and immortality of a work whose plastic qualities and formal perfection have no need to be emphasized . . . not that we attach any importance to the historical assessment of critics who laud the most mediocre work as the classics of their generation . . . more than any of his contemporaries he knows how to invoke the tenor and tone of his time . . . the work of Pirosmanachvili serves as example for all of the painters of a new generation. Our proposition is not to revive the historical criticism in order to save things that are worthless. The value of artistic monuments does not come to them by their ability to revive the past. But it happens that the vital forces of a country can be concentrated in the work of an artist, and in forcing some recognition of this, the works demonstrate their intensity and value. It is in this intensity that exceptional art gets its value. Pirosmani understood how to find the style appropriate to his era and he was the only one to do so in the sense that it would be impossible to render his era in any way other than the way in which he has done so.[56]

When he turned to description of the canvases, his language became even more vivid:

. . . frenetic musicians with eyes like cherries, servants with their eyelids swelled from insomnia, fighters with flat stomachs and prostitutes with old sagging breasts, lions, sheep, deer, giraffes, and bears, animals and fantastic birds, still lifes and signs—the artist renders everything in a classic style not just by his choices of subject but also by his manner of interpretation.

. . . His primitivism is that of life itself and the success of Pirosmani is to have communicated in his art the characteristic traits without which perfection is inaccessible, those which are the interpretation of primitive culture. But what makes Pirosmani particularly valuable to us is that even though he is an Oriental artist, he inserts himself into the Oriental/Occidental debate in a manner which preserves the traditions of the Orient in such a way that he should be looked to as an inspiration for young artists.[57]

Iliazd and his brother became collectors of Pirosmani's canvases. By the summer of 1915, when Iliazd and Kirill (who had been drafted into the Russian army the year before, mobilized, wounded, and sent home to Tbilisi) were together, their parents' apartment had taken on the appearance of a "veritable museum of Pirosmani's work:"[58] "More than fifty drawings and paintings had been acquired at different times and covered the walls of several rooms from floor to ceiling. It was an astonishing, unforgettable site. At the end of 1916, Ilia organized, at Tbilisi, a one-day exhibition of these works of Pirosmani. The invitations were printed, distributed by hand to the homes of the guests, an announcement was even printed in a journal, so that an important crowd assembled. The rooms were crammed with people seriously discussing the work of Pirosmani."[59]

The large collection was in the Zdanevich family at the time of Iliazd's departure for Paris in 1920. When Konstantin Paustovsky (whose earlier recollections had given us a glimpse of the Zdanevich household) visited again in the 1920s, he was overwhelmed: "Barely over the threshold, I stood amazed. All the walls of the bedrooms, the corridors, the terraces and even the entryways of the bathrooms were covered, from floor to ceiling, with paintings remarkable by their color and design. Many of them that had not found a place on the walls had been rolled up and leaned in the corners. They were the work of a single painter, though one hardly ever found the name of Niko Pirosmani appearing on the canvases themselves."[60]

Iliazd formed an identification with Pirosmani that would last throughout his life. The 1914 essay he published about the painter formed the text of one of his last books in the 1970s. The values he perceived in Pirosmani would govern his life and work, particularly the belief that an artist should never compromise their artistic vision:

February 2, 1913 I took home the portrait and *The Stag*. Niko insisted, "Don't pay me anything for *The Stag*, but if there is a commission from Moscow, let me know." I told him that the paintings would be in an exhibition in Moscow, which made him very happy. I bid him a fond farewell and went directly to the train station. As the train left town, I saw a man seated by a mass of glowing embers, a man with an anguished expression, a solitary wanderer, a great painter. He made a profound impression on me—the moment I met Pirosmani was the moment I knew what life really was.[61]

Who Is Iliazd? Evidence and Absence

In the earliest period of Iliazd's life he was little Ilia, younger brother of Kirill, born in a bourgeois family in Tbilisi while Georgia was part of Tsarist Russia. The scant evidence of that era had a double quality of remoteness about it. So little remained, and what there was—the photograph of the children in the nursery, a report card, the mother's journal, and that passage of a visitor's reminiscence—seemed of a much different time. Unlike the letters and ephemera associated with the Paris period, or references that could still, almost, be checked with a living witness, these pieces had the air of relics. How were they to be interpreted? For instance, the statements made by Ilia's mother about his identity as a poet in contrast to his brother, whose aptitude for the visual arts had stamped him for an artist—were these really the seeds of a teleological unfolding, inevitably shaping the children's adult lives? The evidence was all being read retrospectively, as if it foretold later developments. But all reading of childhood material should be anti-teleological. No destiny is so fixed and determined. And the absent material? The infinitude of gaps divides between marked absences—things missing about which something is known—and unmarked ones so vanished they left no trace to follow. What unfulfilled possibilities are missing in these accounts?

Iliazd's books are what matter, what remains, what has value. But to understand them fully, the conditions of production have to be described. The narrative of a life does not explain the work, only situates it, exposes the intellectual and artistic lineages that are manifest in text, type, format, and design. What made the attitudes toward publishing in the Russian futurist era distinct was that artist-writers engaged with making books themselves. With only a handful of notable exceptions—William Blake and William Morris, for instance, in the nineteenth century—this hands-on engagement was unprecedented. Few artists or authors had made books; they made images or texts and craftsmen made them into printed volumes. But as Iliazd was maturing in the circles of artistic activity in Moscow and St. Petersburg in the 1910s, he was surrounded by artists producing books. This created a conceptual foundation for later work. The idea that books were not vehicles for distribution, but unique forms of expression, became a central tenet of his approach.

In the 1980s and even early 1990s, before Internet access, I was not able to fill in the background on references and contexts without going to the library at Pompidou and tracking materials in their stacks. These resources could not answer the question of "who" Iliazd was, or how he should be understood. I was in the position of trying to sort out whether this was a formal portrait, or an intimate one, an image of an artist, a figure, a mind, a bourgeois man, or a bohemian. I soon realized that one does not write "the" biography but "a" biography—that is actually "*my*" biography—imprinting an identity and projecting it at the same time.

Hélène always spoke of Iliazd with hushed praise, respect. Her tone cast the aura. That was to be expected. I moved forward into that charged space—a void that was also a plentitude. From the beginning, the profile of Iliazd was filled with expectations and associations, even if it was empty, for me, of a referent. Everything had to be constructed, which was a benefit and a liability. I had no way to check Hélène's statements or her assessments. Was Iliazd responsible for the origin of Rayonnism or merely a conduit for Larionov's vision? Only later did I come to understand how I had become just an aspect of how the process unfolded. I was the instrument of her desires, and my role was to realize a project she could not do herself.

My impulses and training put me at odds with the concept of a "great man." Non-artists are often overawed by creative talent. Within a limited view, exhibits, publications, events, and public attention—the general rule for artists—are taken for exceptions by family members unacquainted with this milieu. Given the relative absence of reception history for his work, particularly in the early periods, the question of scale arose as well. Mentions of Iliazd were present, but few and far between in the standard accounts of Russian futurism. He had a place in the works on Russian artists' books. But was this absence a historical oversight? Had his contributions been forgotten? By what instruments and metrics could importance be gauged?

The basic issues of biography arose frequently. At the outset I wasn't clear if I was pursuing a description of an individual or trying to understand the values and vision that guided Iliazd's work. If this individuation, this fingerprint-specific persona like no other is assumed at the outset, then how does that shape the research? In asking "who is X," do I already lead with an identity to which I work to make the evidence conform? Like an old-fashioned sleuth matching boots to the footprints in the garden, did I use the remains of a life to reconstruct the lost figure? If the imprint of the persona is already present, do the details of actual information merely get poured into a mold to fill out the substance of the form? How else might a figure emerge from the details, be made, not in small shifts and nuances, but as an effect of research? The question of "who" is being constructed—understood as a question of ontological identity—always haunts a biography. This is an existential haunting, filled with the problem of constructing and imagining an identity of a once real person. Does the identity exist before, outside of, in spite of a biography? Does a biographical subject have an autonomous existence? If we say yes, then we condemn biography to inadequacy, and if we say no, then we charge it with fictitious surrogacy. Without some projected specificity, the project feels unjustified. But if every piece of evidence is checked against the presumption of an already extant identity, then where is that entity embodied? Where is it *person*-ified?

If a biography sidesteps the issue of unique identity and focuses on "the work," on the accomplishments of Iliazd, then what kind of supporting roles does the information about the life play? Is the idea to create a scenario for vicarious identification? As a child, I read the biographies of the young Queen Elizabeth I and shuddered with her in the dark, waiting to be whisked off in the night for safekeeping by her partisan supporters. Iliazd's life was not sensational or scandalous, and he was not a celebrity. He had lived, he had made books, he had been part of artistic circles, activities, and struggles. He was not Colette or Lord Byron, for whom the creation of a life was an artistic project in its own right. Again, a case could be made to simply describe the books. But the books were entangled in his life—describing one without the other gives only a partial profile.

In the process of doing the research, I was seduced by the material engagement and the conversations and relationships it engendered. Curiously, the one person I never interviewed directly was Hélène. Our exchange of information was mediated through documents, artifacts, other social connections. She would offer her thoughts about the testimony of other witnesses and of the materials of the archive, but no details were ever communicated about her marriage, the longer courtship, or any of their private life.

Whether a biography is motivated by the pursuit of a *person* or an *identity*, an imagined essence or a social construct, it exists in a condition of profound and fundamental incompleteness. Only later would I realize—and have to come to terms with—some of the implications of this fact.

3 1916–1920

Futurist Poetics

The Creation of Forty-One Degrees

Having been exposed to futurism, and having aligned himself with
Marinetti, collaborated with two highly visible and prominent artists—
Goncharova and Larionov—and publicized the "discovery" of an authentic
Georgian painter, the young Zdanevich had to contend with the impact of
political events on his geographical circumstances. Though he had kept intermittent connections with the Russian capitals, Moscow and St. Petersburg, his activity from 1916 to 1920 was centered in Tbilisi. Here he established the Fantastic Cabaret and fostered the activities of his own group,
Forty-One Degrees. During this time, and in collaboration with Igor Terentiev and Aleksei Kruchenykh, he articulated his theories of poetics. In particular, he developed a distinct approach to the innovative language of *zaum*.
This included the critical concept of *sdvig,* or shift, as a dynamic transformation in aesthetic form, and the features of orchestral verse that structured his
typographic scoring in his own plays, the *dras* of his Aslaablitchia cycle. He
established the imprint of Forty-One Degrees and produced numerous editions (he noted around twenty publications), only a few of which remain.[1]

I relied heavily on secondary sources in this phase of the research, as did
Hélène, for whom this was a period of Iliazd's history she had not shared
directly. Descriptions of childhood and formative years seemed accessible,
describable, because they referenced experience. But poetics are rooted in
language and texts have to be read, seen, and heard to be understood. A
handful of published works, such as Benedikt Livshits's *One and a Half-Eyed
Archer,* a memoir originally published in 1933, Vladimir Markov's comprehensive *Russian Futurism,* published in 1968, and Viktor Shklovsky's *Mayakovsky and His Circle,* first published in English in 1975, were crucial refer-

ences.[2] *The Look of Russian Literature* (1984), by Gerald Janecek, and Susan
Compton's *Worldbackwards* (1978) on Russian avant-garde books were also
extremely helpful.[3] But except for Janecek, these mainly provided discussions of artists and ideas that surrounded Iliazd, so that his early work could
be placed in relation to that of others. But precisely how his work was to be
read, or how it had been received, was mainly a matter of speculation. No
living witnesses remained from this period of Iliazd's activity to share recollections of events that had taken place seventy years earlier in Tbilisi, and
only a tiny smattering of records about reception of his work. A disjunct
existed between our fragmentary evidence and any critical discussion we
borrowed from another source.

Iliazd's commitment to *zaum* only complicated things more, as this work
was suggestive and affective, creating effects from sound and pattern rather
than conventional meaning. The plays were steeped in a combination of
personal symbolism (Iliazd's own psychic mythologies) and references that
tapped into Russian folklore in an oblique way. These I could only understand
secondhand. Even if I could have read Russian, the cultural specificity of these
works would have remained elusive, their resonances embedded in lost time
and lived culture, like other details of a life. The semiotics of a haircut, an
outfit, the name of a school or location—these are not readily recaptured any
more than passing references to current events. The double remove of language and cultural references increased reliance on secondary sources.

The *zaum* work of Iliazd, which carried over into his work in Paris in the
decades ahead, drew on work by others. Benefiting from dialogues with
Kruchenykh and Terentiev, who were in Tbilisi with him, Iliazd's *zaum* was
a unique idiolect. On hearing him read one of the texts in 1919, the poet
Sergei Spassky wrote, "I never encountered a nihilism so complete. The
poem was formed of onomatopoeia and one could hear the rumbling of
motors and the explosion of bombs."[4] Possibly the reference was to Iliazd's
poem for Roland Garros, composed around 1914, which was more like Marinetti's *Zang Tumb Tumb* than any of the *zaum* texts, but the comment gives
some idea of the foreignness of such work even to Russian speakers.[5]

Tbilisi

The chronology for 1915 contains several statements that make clear
that Iliazd was back in Georgia. In August he took a journey with his father
to the Western Caucasus.[6] Hélène suggested that his parents had requested
he return to Tbilisi on account of the war. Georgia was a part of the Russian

Empire, and after Iliazd's brother, Kirill, was wounded in the war, he was sent back to Tbilisi later in 1915.

In 1915 and 1916, Iliazd worked as a war correspondent for the Petersburg/ Petrograd paper *Retch*. As recorded in one of his letters to the British journalist Morgan Philips Price, whom he met during the period, they were both present at the brutal Turkish defeat at Sarikamish in January 1915. The chronologies of these years through early 1917 are filled with references to journalism, mountaineering expeditions, and continued art activities. His 1916 ascent of one summit near Tbilisi was recorded in a Russian Geographical Society publication in 1917.[7]

Other statements in the chronology show his ongoing involvement with the Russian avant-garde:

> October: Returns to Petrograd and is given permission by the Union of Poets to found a "University" for young poets . . . called "The First Rose."
>
> Iliazd begins this project with Vera Ermolaeva, Le Dentu, and Le Dentu's fiancée, Olga Lechkova and Lapchine. They publish a cyclostyle journal called "Murder without the Flow of Blood."[8]
>
> This group put on a production of Iliazd's first play, *Yanko, King of the Albanians*, on December 3, 1916.[9]

In the letter to Soffici (1962), Iliazd provided more details about activities in the beginning of 1917 and the demarcation he himself perceived:

> On the eve of the upheaval of February 1917, the activity of the Futurists which had been brushed aside during the war began to reawaken in a new form; the manifestos were finished, as were the theories and the discoveries, and the work took plastic form. I stopped doing poetry in the style of *Words in Liberty*, like my poem for Roland Garros, and did nothing but transmental verse.[10] The *zaum* language existed long before the invention of Lettrism.[11] Let me explain clearly. For the word *zaum* "the other side of intelligence" is the closest translation because the expression "an intelligent man" corresponds precisely to the Russian word "oum-nyi" and in the expression "beyond reason" the Russian word to use is *Zazoum*. The translation "transmental," the first translation I used, is less close because "mental" in Russian is "myslennyi." But this was not my translation, it was Khlebnikov's. At first I avoided using this word and my play *Yanko* (the first of the dramas), as stated in the prologue, was written in "Albanian." Khlebnikov never constructed abstract phonetic words in that way. All his writings, beginning with "Smekhatchi" published in 1911, are composed in words produced by the games

in which roots are transformed by the use of particular prefixes. The sense of the word therefore may be far from being readily grasped by the intelligence in any precise way, but more immediately available to the emotions, a product of charm and sorcery.[12]

Kruchenykh created phonemes like the famous "Dyr bul shchyl" embedded in popular language the way Antonin Artaud did in French, whereas I created a phonetic language which worked on the emotions both by its sonority and by the associations it produced in relation to current language—which was far from the sense of the words of Kruchenykh.[13]

. . . It wasn't until 1919, in Tbilisi, after the founding of the 41 Degrees with Aleksei Kruchenykh and Igor Terentiev that I began to make use of the term *zaum* to describe the character of our creations and mine in particular.[14]

The founding of the "university" of Forty-One Degrees took place in Tbilisi. These years were very fertile for Iliazd's engagement with poetics and theoretical discussions of language, particularly with Terentiev and Kruchenykh. This aesthetic activity took place against the complex and changing ground of much larger events.

Here, in a manuscript from 1968, is Iliazd's account of personal events set against political circumstances:

The day of the revolution of February 27th [1917], I went to the Duma where I was placed in juridical post, having received my university degree a few weeks earlier. But I refused all other official positions offered to me at the time. I battled with the Academy of Arts and in public meetings against the project of the minister of arts to bring Serge Diaghilev back to the country to take his post. But in May, with my degree in my pocket, I decided to go and see my parents and I left Petrograd—to which, alas, I was never to return.

I committed an error that changed the course of my life. To satisfy a friend of my father's, a professor, and to continue the dream conceived during childhood vacations passed among the ruins of ancient convents, I, the Futurist poet, took part in an archaeological expedition to Turkey. Afterwards I carried this period like a ball and chain through my life and it caused me to lose I don't know how many years in useless experience only to arrive at the conclusion, centuries after Agrippa, that erudition is vanity and poetry is eternal.[15]

The trip, between July and October 1917, in the company of the Georgian archaeologist Ekvtime Takaishvili, did have an effect on the course of Iliazd's future, though in retrospect it is hard to cast the event as an error.

However, when he returned to Tbilisi, he found himself trapped in Georgia. "Between myself and Moscow had arisen the frontier between the Reds and the Whites."[16] He was still in Turkey, near Erzerum, when he learned that his friend Mikhail Ledentu had been killed in an accident in July. As an homage, he traveled to the Caucasus, made a solitary ascent, and named a hitherto unnamed peak for his friend.[17] His enthusiasm for mountain climbing and for Byzantine architecture would remain throughout his life, but, as we shall see, the only direct record of concern about politics was written in the later 1920s, recollecting his experience in Constantinople between 1920 and 1921.[18] In 1917, his immediate focus was on the work of Forty-One Degrees.

Activities of Forty-One Degrees

Filippo Marinetti appears like a cutout in the account of Iliazd's life, a flat figure without dimension. For Hélène, the connection conferred importance. She held Marinetti in awe and assessed Iliazd's currency by the value of association. I had to negotiate between her understanding and critical assessments of scholars whose work she did not always know. Marinetti was best left as a name put in play, rather than a subject of investigation. Making an explanation, apology, or argument for or against Iliazd's association with any known individual merely clouded evidence with inflections that would themselves be subject to confusion. After all, on what terms— those of 1914, 1922, 1962, or later—should Iliazd's conception of Marinetti be assessed? What remains are his communications and tone.

In a 1922 letter, written after his arrival in Paris, Iliazd addressed the futurist in honorific terms. This letter is relevant for the details it provides about the establishment of Forty-One Degrees, but it also raises the obvious questions of self-narrativization. No counterwitness or corroborator exists. We read Iliazd's account, mainly a list of factual statements, as a record of events past, even as we have to consider his desire to connect with Marinetti. Was he seeking affirmation, collaboration, ongoing critical engagement? Marinetti had an established profile in 1922, though futurism was already fading from its prewar position. But Iliazd had not previously referred to him as a teacher. The letter provides insights into the events beginning in 1916:

> My dearly esteemed teacher, Marinetti:
> I have come to Paris and I would like to have the honor of reminding you of our meeting in Moscow eight years ago. This is what has happened to us in the inter-

vening period. We have taken up again the work which was interrupted by the war. In 1916 we opened a theater in Petrograd which was called "Murder Without the Flow of Blood" where my first play was performed, composed in orchestral verse, "Yanko, King of the Albanians"—a play which was quickly prohibited by the censor.

I would have liked to be in continual communication with you. The last few years have so devastated the artistic culture of Europe that exceptional cooperation among the militants of art will be necessary for our interrupted work to continue.

In the company of two of the best contemporary Russian poets, Kruchenykh and Terentiev, I founded the 41 Degrees Group and during two years we published two magazines in which we printed our research and our work.

41 Degrees had published about twenty works while in the North poetry had degenerated.

I am sending you, dear teacher, all of the publications I was able to bring to Paris, and I think that you have received the almanac of the "Fantastic Cabaret," in the special care of Mr. Constan Machin [sic].[19]

I am sending you the first edition of this comedy. Our creation was "The University of Poetry" for the propagation of our research and our numerous poetic inventions. At the end of 1917 we moved this "University" to the mountains of the Caucasus where the conditions were more favorable to the continuation of our work.[20]

The capital city, Tbilisi (then Tiflis), provided a refuge for artists and writers following the February 1917 revolution, when Georgia was part of a short-lived Transcaucasian Democratic Federative Republic that included Azerbaijan and Armenia.[21] Forty-One Degrees was just one of several groups that formed for the purpose of critical discussion of aesthetics, informal reading, and exchange of ideas. Prominent among the venues for these gatherings was the Fantastic Cabaret, its name betraying the air of unreality in which poets and artists realized they were living. An eyewitness account noted: "Tbilisi had become a fantastic city. A fantastic city needed a fantastic corner, and on one fine day, at No. 12 Rustaveli, in the courtyard, poets and artists opened a Fantastic Cabaret which consisted of a small room, meant for 10 to 15, but which, by some miracle, had about 50 people in it, more women than men. Phantasmagorias decorated the walls of the room. Virtually every evening the Inn was open and poets and writers read their poems and lectures."[22]

A typical evening at the Fantastic Cabaret was described as follows: "The opening of the evening began with declarations about the 'metalogical language' by the poets Kruchenykh, Zdanevich, and Kara Darvish. They then read poems in this language. The effect was unexpected and new. There followed a recital of exotic verse by S. Koron, the actress Melnikova, and Degen. Thus two camps were formed and they joined 'battle'; the audience was delighted and encouraged them as best it could."[23]

Other firsthand descriptions of events expand this view, emphasizing the impact of poetry recitations of futurist verse that, as Kruchenykh explained, was meant for a listening audience. "He shouted out words full of juicy dullness and brought the listeners to the verge of fainting with his monotonous construction of sentences."[24]

The work of Forty-One Degrees had begun "officially" after Iliazd applied to the Union of Youth to start a "Futuruniversity" for young writers. Forty-One Degrees was unequivocally Iliazd's, though he had considerable support from Kruchenykh and the newly emerging *zaum* poet, Igor Terentiev. In addition, Mikhail Ledentu, Kirill Zdanevich, Olga Lechkova, Vera Ermolaeva, and others formed active members of this scene. In a comment published later (1921) in Paris, Iliazd explained the symbolism of the designation: "Most of our great cities and centers of learning are on the 41 degree latitude. Jesus was in the desert forty days. Zarathustra likewise. It was on the 41st day they emerged, strengthened in spirit. It is also the temperature at which fever turns into delirium. Forty-one is a symbolic number."[25]

The manifesto of Forty-One Degrees summarized the general program of the group. Some of the terms that occur in this treatise are directly relevant to Iliazd's *dras* (the term used for the *zaum* dramas), such as "verbal mass" and "global itinerary," that were specific *sdvig* (shift, an act of aesthetic transformation) operations, as will be discussed below. But the full text of this manifesto is worth attention:[26]

> The Society for the elaboration and exploitation of poetic ideas of the entire world: Peking-Samarcand-Tbilisi-Constantinople-Rome-Madrid-New York. With sections in Paris, London, Berlin, Moscow, Tokyo, Los Angeles, Teheran, and Calcutta.
>
> Universities, publishers, journals, theaters, and farms for the use and treatment of literate idiots.
>
> Forty-One Degrees is the most powerful organization of the avant-garde in the realm of poetic industry. The organization originated in the first decade of this

century when thanks to its collaborators and pioneers, diverse parts of the globe were found to contain the rich and unexplored domains of language. At the present moment, Forty-One Degrees embraces more than sixty linguistic systems with new territory and new capital being included each year.

Forty-One Degrees has destroyed the monopoly of sense on words by putting their *zaum* content foremost.

Forty-One Degrees has discovered the existence of *sdvigs* in words and defined their creative role.

Forty-One Degrees has discovered the autonomy of the laws of poetic language and liberated poetry from the authority of ordinary language.

Forty-One Degrees has discovered the existence of sonorous associations and demonstrated their dominant role in poetic construction.

Forty-One Degrees has discovered the direct relation between sound and emotion and demonstrated the limits of the possibilities imposed by sense.

Forty-One Degrees has demonstrated the objectivism of sound by comparison with the non-objectives of *zaum* content and has synthesized the abstract tendencies in poetry on a utilitarian basis.

Forty-One Degrees has defined poetry as the art of content.

Forty-One Degrees has destroyed the hypocrisy of its predecessors and dissected the constructs of indecency and injury.

Forty-One Degrees has shown the uselessness of the ideas of talent and ability by comparison to the role of chance and autonomous construction.

Forty-One Degrees has delivered creativity from all the constraints of moralism and all practices thereof.

Forty-One Degrees puts first and foremost the idea of the treatment of the verbal mass.

Forty-One Degrees has discovered the significance of contrast and global itinerary.

Forty-One Degrees promotes the role of voice in poetry.

Forty-One Degrees discovered the synthetic sound and orchestral poetry.

Forty-One Degrees defined the fragmentation of sense and of content insofar as the indissoluble essence of things shows the incommensurability of volume and content.

Forty-One Degrees refused the concept of destruction and embraces renovation based on the principle of an imaginary tradition.

Forty-One Degrees has the firmest base of any poetic school in the world.

Discoveries, inventions, revelations, perfections.

The president of the Paris (France) section of 41 Degrees—Ilia Zdanevich. Send your address to this central bureau of 41 Degrees and you will receive invaluable information free of charge.[27]

Traces of his earlier Everythingist attitude, charged with enthusiastic eclecticism and irreverence for established culture, are clear in the manifesto, alongside the commitment to their poetic language.

Poetics

Kruchenykh's presence in Tbilisi galvanized Iliazd's commitment to experimentation with graphical treatments of poetic works. Kruchenykh's earlier poems had been produced calligraphically, and the freedom of handwriting allowed for much invention.[28] Iliazd's typographic compositions introduced a different sensibility as he began to engage directly with letterpress production, exploring the graphical specificity of metal type.

Iliazd's aesthetic positions matured in this context. He gave lectures and organized events, made posters and designed publications. The Fantastic Cabaret was one center of this activity, though other venues were also used for these events, which probably had an informal and rather raucous atmosphere. The list of lectures offered by the group between 1917 and 1919 is impressive.[29] There are more than forty separate events, of which most are lectures by either Iliazd or Kruchenykh on *zaum*, futurism, poetry, and art. Among the more colorful titles are these by Kruchenykh from spring and summer 1918: "The Apocalypse and the Creatures of Language," "The Maccabee Poet, Blok," "Luminous Letters of Electric Books," "The Flying Restaurant in Yamoudie," and "The Hidden Vices of Academicians."[30] Iliazd also touched on a wide variety of topics: "The Eyeglasses of Dody [*sic*] Burliuk," "Kruchenykh and the Soul of His Nose," "The Magnetism of Letters," and "A propos of the Stammering of Tioutchev and Brioussov [*sic*]."[31] Aside from the list of titles, very little remains of the lectures from 1917 to 1919. Iliazd's Paris lectures from the early 1920s, when he was struggling to bring new Russian poetics to a fresh audience, have to be relied on to give some idea of the concepts the Tbilisi group developed.

As Iliazd wrote in a letter to Marinetti in 1922, "Our creation was a 'university' for the development of the art of poetry and for the propagation of our poetic inventions and discoveries."[32] The discoveries were as real as the inventions, but a ludic spirit prevailed, continuing that which had accompanied their initial performances in 1916 as the group "Murder Without the Flow of Blood" in St. Petersburg, where Iliazd had been cited for his "beautiful mezzo-soprano voice" as "part of a sextet for clothing hanger, gramophone, and three mezzo-sopranos on all fours and oboes."

The commitment to poetics was charged with theoretical substance, as is clear in this description by Olga Djordjadze:

> The fundamental attitude of 41 Degrees can be explained as follows: human language does not represent a motivated expression on the part of mankind, it is only the result of certain emotive excitations. The act of expressing the logical operation of thought has ended up by bringing language to the atrophied condition which is characteristic of our times and of nineteenth century Europe. There are several exceptions to this which represent the assertion of primitive poetry in a growing reaction to utilitarian language. 41 Degrees incarnates this reaction against the utilitarian spirit through the use of the method of *sdvig*. *Sdvig* destroys ordinary language in the form of the totally abstract *zaum*. Everythingism moves towards orchestral poetry.
>
> The elaboration of principles of 41 Degrees appeared in the program of seminars devoted to their elaboration.
>
> 1. the theory of poetic deformation: *sdvig*, orchestral poetry;
> 2. the theory of language; of sound, of texture, of orthography;
> 3. the history of poetry and knowledge of contemporary literature.[33]

An earlier iteration of these ideas had appeared as an accompaniment to the 1916 exhibit "The First Rose," that announced the creation of "The Faculty of Pastry" by Ledentu and Iliazd:

> The procedure of 41 Degrees is one in which the grains of language are transformed into grains of poetry and habitual logic is not necessarily the best way to prepare the dough. With the aid of a *sdvig* machine, the paste can be made directly with the grains avoiding the intermediary stages. The superiority of this

dough is so great that the grain keeps all its precious qualities—sound, structure, readability. No residue should be lost and any fragments should be re-milled. The best bread, of which we offer you several sorts—orchestral, *zaum,* everythingist, and Futurist—is always served fresh, and the choice is yours. Here you can learn to make it yourself, at home, without too much work, milling or grain, by following the system of 41 degrees.[34]

In this context, language is conceived of as material, capable of manipulation, transformation, and reformulation just as surely as any other solid matter. By referring to the dough of language and considering its qualities apart from any act of meaning production, Iliazd emphasized the basis of his *zaum* poetics.

Iliazd and Kruchenykh published a single number of a *Journal of 41 Degrees* in 1919.[35] The cover stated its credo: "The company 41 Degrees unites left-bank Futurism and confirms metalogical language as the obligatory form for the realization of art. The task of 41 Degrees is to use all the great discoveries of its collaborators and to set up the world on a new axis. The newspaper will be a haven for events in the life of the company and a cause of continuous disturbance. We are rolling up our sleeves."[36]

Other articles in the "newspaper"—which promoted itself as a "weekly gazette" but appeared only once in this single number—included a piece on Khlebnikov by Kruchenykh, a review by Terentiev of "an evening of dances by the school of Ginna Matignoni," and general gossip about figures in the Tbilisi avant-garde.[37] The poets were clearly keeping busy.

Publications

The journal that had appeared in 1916, as part of the program *Murder Without the Flow of Blood* in St. Petersburg, was created on a cyclograph machine, an inexpensive stencil method of duplication. This was common practice among the avant-garde artists, whose preference for readily available, do-it-yourself technology also set them apart from earlier writers and later publishers. As a way of getting outrageous and irreverent works into print, such techniques worked very well. But when Iliazd returned to Tbilisi in 1917, he entered a new level of commitment by gaining direct experience in a print shop. Iliazd was never a professional printer, but he learned typesetting and composition to expand his own artistic vision: "I placed myself as an apprentice with the Journeymen Printers of the Caucasus and, a year later, I composed and published a little orange book in phonetic orthography."[38]

Cover of *Yanko, King of the Albanians* (Tbilisi: Forty-One Degrees, 1918). Courtesy of François Mairé and the Fonds Iliazd

That "little orange book" was *Yanko: King of the Albanians* (1918), the first full-length *zaum* play designed and hand-set by Iliazd. This experience began a lifelong engagement with hands-on typesetting as an aspect of Iliazd's design work and distinguished it from the freehand calligraphy that characterized many other avant-garde Russian books. The decision had an immediate effect on the publications associated with Forty-One Degrees. His firsthand acquaintance with these techniques gave him intimate knowledge of the technical constraints of letterpress—which has to conform to rigid rules of production. Learning to set, justify, and print the pages of type that he created for his own work as well as that of Kruchenykh and Terentiev (as well as for the posters and anthologies of the group) meant that he understood the language of the type case and the forms required for the press. A type case is laid out in small compartments arranged according to the frequency of letters, rather than alphabetic order. Familiarity with its organization, like the ability to combine the hand-set in lines into a single form to print on the press, only comes with direct experience. Iliazd's appreciation of cast metal and the physical limitations imposed by letters designed for strict linear arrangement were key to the experiments he devised in these years and later in his life. His skill allowed him to push the letterpress medium to great limits without violating its integrity.

The term "letterpress" refers to relief printing from movable type, the technology invented by Johannes Gutenberg in the mid-fifteenth century. Though some features of automation had changed the technology in the nineteenth century, many print shops still used hand-set type (put letter by letter into a composing stick from a wooden case holding the individual metal letters) through the early part of the twentieth century. Even though printing presses were driven by electricity, typesetting, particularly for ephemera like posters or invitations, remained the work of compositors. One of the basic features of letterpress is known as "quadrature," or the quality of squareness, because all letters are cast on rectangular metal bodies that have to fit into lines (usually the same point size) and forms (the assemblage of these lines into the format of a page) in order to be printed. Straight horizontal lines are characteristic of the mechanical disposition of letterpress (letters are set between thin pieces of metal known as leads—because they are cast in that metal). Deviating from conventions of same-sized letters or straight lines requires considerable extra effort—and imagination. Precedents for this innovative work existed mainly in advertisements, not literary works, and Iliazd's typographic imagination in the editions in Tbilisi was remarkable. He wanted to score his texts as if they were orchestral pieces for simultaneous voices, and he also wanted to combine multiple fonts and sizes on his pages. Iliazd did not merely learn the skills of letterpress composition; he pushed them past their conventional limits in the service of a poetic project.[39]

His self-conscious reflections on the inherent qualities of the printed form bring his work sharply in line with the attention to formal properties of media that were characteristic of modern art. Just as abstract painting called attention to the flat surface of the canvas, patterned poetics focused on the sound values of language. Iliazd complemented these through his engagement with (and push against) the property of quadrature (square-ness) that is the essential physical constraint of letterpress. Thus, as early as 1917, we see Iliazd begin the meticulous work that extended through his lifetime as a book artist and printer.

He designed and oversaw the production of all the publications that appeared under the Forty-One Degrees imprint between 1917 and 1920 in Tbilisi. He said that he worked with the printer Andrei Chernov "in the capacity of a client" and that Chernov "executed, according to our instructions, the composition of all the editions of 41 Degrees."[40] Janecek cites a firsthand account of Iliazd setting type in the print shop in 1918 when he was composing the forms for the production of *Yanko,* and then hiring someone to complete the work on his instructions.[41] The impact was noticeable, as Markov observed: "Similar books had been published by Kruchenykh before, but he had never displayed so much imagination or variety in his use of print. Both were missing however, when he later reprinted some of his Caucasian poetry in Moscow. Obviously, the printing houses in Tbilisi were both more cooperative and more patient. The idea itself surely came from Ilia Zdanevich, who was a past master in matters of typographical art."[42] In fact, Iliazd was not quite a "past master" in 1917-18, but he was becoming a skilled designer and typographer through the work he did on the Forty-One Degrees publications. Iliazd supplied more than ideas. He supplied labor and direct application of his skills. Perhaps most importantly, he began to *think* and *write* with an understanding of letterpress, and this approach would distinguish him from other editor-publishers—and poets—in the decades ahead.

Iliazd also engineered the substantive publication *For Sofia Georgievna Melnikova, the Fantastic Tavern, Tiflis, 1917, 1918, 1919,* an anthology of works in Russian, Georgian, and Armenian by poets who frequented the cabaret.[43] The volume was created as an homage to their muse, the actress for whom Iliazd had a strong affection. He bore the financial costs for the elaborate collection and also saw to its design. The volume was splendidly produced, on high-quality paper, and described by Tatiana Nikolskaya as "in a great variety of typefaces" and "a model of polygraphic art."[44] Each piece was given a distinctive treatment according to its tone and themes. Iliazd contributed a section from his new play, *Donkey for Rent,* with a subtitle "Zokna and her suitors." The foldout sheet is a remarkable piece of typographic

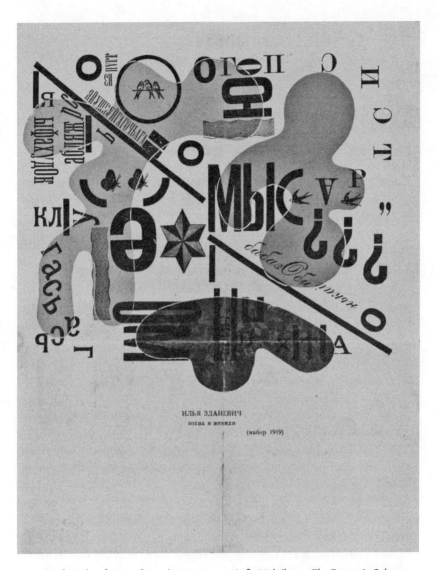

Page of *Donkey for Rent* from the Homage to Sofia Melnikova, *The Fantastic Cabaret* (Tbilisi: Forty-One Degrees, 1919). Courtesy of François Mairé and the Fonds Iliazd

work, with letters placed on their sides, aligned on a diagonal, inverted, and so on, so that they create the effect of the state of mind of a young man infatuated to the point of confusion. These effects are more varied than the ones he would use in printing his plays, but the piece was clearly meant to call attention to itself—and to distinguish him in the eyes of the actress.

Amid this cacophony of letters and youthful high jinks, the tools of poetic deformation continued to receive careful articulation. These provided a framework for Iliazd's typographic compositions as well as for his poetics. Four basic techniques were central to his work: *sdvig* (shift), *faktura* (texture), *zaum* (transrational language), and orchestral verse. These concepts had their origins in the broader context of Russian avant-garde activities. *Faktura* was shared by visual and verbal disciplines. Originally applied to painting as a term designating the treatment of a surface to create texture, it was expanded to refer to the effects of making in any highly self-conscious way.

The three poets of Forty-One Degrees, Iliazd, Kruchenykh, and Terentiev, worked very closely during the years 1917 through 1920. They clearly pushed each other to a high level of performance and benefited from the contact to enhance their theoretical positions as well as their creative art. Kruchenykh's verses became more elaborate and his theories of *zaum* more expansive, as in this passage by the poet cited by Janecek:

> In this way one notes the emergence of new art from the dead end of pastness not into zero and not into clinical insanity.
>
> Earlier there was: sane and insane; we provided a third alternative—*zaum*—creatively transforming and overcoming them.
>
> *Zaum*, taking all the creative values from insanity (*bezumiya*) (which is why the words are almost the same), except for its helplessness—its sickness.[45]

Zaum

Zaum's extreme poetic invention was one of the distinguishing and unique features of Russian futurism. Experiments with *zaum* had been a part of its activities from about 1912. In that year Velimir Khlebnikov and Aleksei Kruchenykh's essay "The Word as Such" appeared, with its provocative suggestions about linguistic invention. In response, David Burliuk charged Kruchenykh with the task of writing "a whole poem of unknown words."[46] Kruchenykh wrote "Dyr Bul Shchyl" as a response to this instigation. Kruchenykh's engagement with *zaum* sprung from the conviction that conventional language could neither express nor embody thought—or sensation and emotion—in an adequate manner. His fragmentation of words into smaller units that were suggestive rather than explicitly meaningful was designed to produce emotion rather than name or describe it.[47]

Though Marinetti had called for involvement with the materials of language in the "Technical Manifesto of Literature" of 1912, vast differences arose in the approaches of Russian and Italian poets. Marinetti's decision to replace punctuation with mathematical symbols, eliminating conjugations and other nuances, made the Italian approach reductive and (deliberately) mechanistic. By contrast, Russians combined an interest in elemental abstraction and an emotional, affective language.[48]

Iliazd, Kruchenykh, and the young Terentiev took zaum innovation and experimentation as far as they could. Only Velimir Khlebnikov's work rivaled their efforts. Zaum was not nonsense, however, for all that it might partake of irrational impulses, and the fullness of its associative properties amplified the richness of language.

In his essay "On Madness in Art," delivered as a lecture on February 18, 1918, Kruchenykh wrote:

> It is impossible to write nonsense. There is more sense in nonsense than in anything else. If each letter has meaning, then any combination of letters has meaning. If somebody, in an attack of jealousy, spite, or love, starts to write words in an arbitrary assortment (as happens when people are aroused), then what he is really doing is to give a flow of words immediately (without his reason controlling them), words which reflect this feeling and which even outgrow it. Therefore, there are no completely irrational works. And in our day this is being proven by the fact that now, as never before, the work of savages, children, flagellants, and the mentally ill is being studied. And now we have the final conclusion—to leave reason aside and write in a language which has not yet congealed and which has not been labeled with concepts—to write in a metalogical language! Let it be absurd, incomprehensible, monstrous![49]

An example of Kruchenykh's zaum verse gives a sense of the suggestive feel of his language even in translation. An excerpt from "Lacquered Tights," written at the same time as his contributions to the Melnikova anthology, was cited by Janecek:

Ayebit
Is the sack of marten
Threddle

Fatesourge washed off
incarry ins
swallowed beads
wheelless,
I lie—horrible—
LIKE A WHITE GALOSH
without milk[50]

In his extensive studies of *zaum* and its typography, Janecek notes that in this verse there are word fragments, compounds, and coinages, alongside syntactic dislocations and other transformations.[51] Kruchenykh became very systematic, "trying to establish different kinds of sound texture in words: tender, heavy, coarse, muted, dry or moist."[52] Hints of synaesthesia lurk in this description, with its keen attention to the physical properties and analog sensations. But Kruchenykh also identified a wide variety of textures in verse, from "syllabic, rhythmic, semantic, syntactic" to "graphic, colorific, and lectorial."[53] Iliazd would try to exploit the graphical qualities of type to similar ends, extending the notion of *faktura* to the entire material format of a book.

Sdvig was defined as the sum total of devices that could be put at the service of transformation. Markov characterized it as "all conscious violations and distortions of traditional aesthetics," but he also points out the way it worked with specific characteristics of Russian language. The ends of words and beginnings of the next could often be elided to produce a second meaning, an effect used by futurists to produce obscene or comic effects. Kruchenykh used the approach to develop suggestive traces of anal eroticism throughout his writings. Iliazd adopted similar techniques and themes throughout his cycle of *zaum* plays. But *sdvig* was not limited to these instances of manipulation. It became a larger mode of operation for Iliazd, who used various metaphoric images—like that of the pastry with its grains and textures—to describe the activity of transformation to which the material of language could be subjected. Thus *sdvig* came to stand for any and all of the many contortions, distortions, and reformulations central to *zaum* practice.

Many Russian poets used *zaum* to enrich their poetic work. But Iliazd took it as the very substance and core of his work. The general spirit and tone of his *zaum* was close to that of Kruchenykh, and, not surprisingly, their third companion of this period, Terentiev, whose playful and erotic *Seventeen Tools of Nonsense* Iliazd also printed in a typographically elaborated

manner. These qualities distinguished the work of these Tbilisi poets from
that of Khlebnikov, whose *zaum* verse was serious and mystical. Among the
Forty-One Degrees group there is rarely a hint of transcendent experience,
sentiment, or mysticism. They do not search for universal "truth," and
though concerned with escaping the censorial taboos of the conscious
mind, expressing in sound the traditionally inexpressible depths and breadth
of sexual and emotional experience, they are consistently irreverent in their
approach.

   Zaum verse must have begun to pall in its appeal. Markov says that
Kruchenykh's work became dull—and that particularly on the page "dullness reigns . . . despite his efforts to shock the reader."[54] By contrast he
notes that:

> Zdanevich is to be praised for the purity and excellence of his *zaum*, which was
> never used before or after him in a major work of such proportions or on such a
> large scale. Kruchenykh's short exercises in *zaum* may have a forcefulness and an
> individuality of their own, but on the whole, they are a spotty affair, containing
> only a few hits and oh so many misses, based, as they were, on pure accident.
> Zdanevich never subscribed to the aleatory theories of his colleagues; he was a
> classicist of *zaum*, which he constructed and balanced in an elaborate manner. It
> is genuinely persuasive. Zdanevich displays in it unbelievable verbal imagination,
> and he never repeats himself. In a sense, it is a creation of genius . . .[55]

Clearly Iliazd's *zaum* was his own synthesis, and it gave him the opportunity
to pull together the many strands of his futurist development. He inves-
tigated the properties of language in accord with the notions of *sdvig* and
faktura, and then, when it came time to give his *zaum* a graphical form, invented the treatment he termed orchestral verse. This technique of scoring
lines of text was a hybrid of musical piece and theatrical work. These lines
were to be read simultaneously by several readers with a cacophonous effect. Iliazd's themes drew on folkloric motifs in ways he had learned from
Goncharova and Pirosmani. He worked with direct, expressive emotionality
and borrowed the scatological and erotic humor of Kruchenykh while em-
ploying the nonsensical and playful tone of Terentiev's *Tools*. He added other
elements that were uniquely his own: the exploration of infantilism and
attention to representation—realism and abstraction—as themes. Finally, he
made a sustained demonstration of the relations between visual and verbal
domains in his exploration of design elements and typographic methods.

   The outstanding accomplishment of this period of his life was the cycle

of five plays, four of which were printed in Tbilisi, that constitute the cycle
of *dras*, to which we can now turn our attention, fully prepared with an understanding of the conditions from which they sprung into being.

How We Came to Know about *Zaum*

Hélène and I had been able to track events in the early years of Iliazd's
life using the evidence in the archive, or sources referenced in the chronologies. But to address the work of the five *dras* and the properties of Russian
futurist poetics we needed assistance. The language and concepts were embedded in linguistic contexts too difficult to untangle without more knowledge. Hélène said she would invite André; he could help us. She paused for
a minute: and also, Régis. The isolation of our work environment was about
to be broken. So these two scholars, Régis Gayraud and André Markowicz,
both came to lend their expertise to assist in our understanding.

They were distinct in their talents, interests, and personalities. Régis
Gayraud was working on his thesis on the Paris Conferences of Iliazd between 1921 and 1923, the lectures given to extend the work of the Forty-
One Degrees. Gayraud was at an early stage of his career, though his project
was well developed, and he had invested considerable energy in translating
the Russian texts into French and making them the core of his thesis. Régis
arrived in his leather jacket and jeans, thick dark hair falling on one side and
over his pale forehead. He smelled of cigarettes and his fingers were stained
with tobacco. He was absorptive and cautious, his willingness to share this
work understandably tempered by questions of priority in his research connection to Iliazd—and ownership of the labor he had already done. Who
was I, after all, suddenly present, in the atelier, having my tea and cookies
with Hélène on a regular basis? Generosity prevailed, and Régis shared his
translations of the lectures Iliazd delivered in Paris between 1921 and 1923.
He also shared his thesis, with its scholarly apparatus. He did not visit often
but would come if asked, and help clarify points of historical, linguistic, and
poetic confusion. His manner was slightly reserved. He offered insights and
interpretation, but was not expansive, though his work on the lectures delivered in Paris was a gold mine of information.[56] The texts in Russian had
not been previously translated, and Régis was generous in explaining how
these lectures had expressed Iliazd's poetics.

If Régis was reserved and scholarly, André was effulgent, luminous and
poetic. Cursed with wretched physical health and some childhood misfor-
tune that suggested developmental issues that had affected his bones, André

was delicate and moved with enough difficulty that it seemed painful. But his beatific head, shiny hair, and brilliant eyes filled the room with his presence. André had gifts and a poetic imagination with which he made the *zaum* writings come alive. André was an angelic spirit, endowed with vitality, and he brought a living presence to our project. They were both invaluable to our work.

We saw André rarely, but visits from him infused our afternoons with wonder at his capacity to invoke the spirit of Iliazd's poetry. He would knock lightly at the outer door. We would have been listening, but even so, his touch was delicate. He would come in, his slight figure hardly filling the small corridor. He came into the studio, where we gave him a wooden armchair softened with cushions that was still almost too large for him. Even without speaking, his presence emanated through the space. He settled into the room, but always with the air of a visitor, perched as if he might leave at any moment. We were quiet, trying, I think, to seduce him into staying by concentrating our attention.

The incredible good fortune of being able to consult with these two men was never lost on me. The work here that concerns *zaum*, futurism, Forty-One Degrees, and the early cycle of *dras* produced between 1918 and 1923 is deeply indebted to them both. They were clearly attached to Hélène, but she was respectful of their time, their own work and projects, and their differences. We usually saw them alone, for they had very different investments in their connection to Iliazd, and they sometimes seemed uneasy in each other's presence—and Hélène was sensitive to that fact. We had more contact with Régis, and he integrated more often into our afternoons, while a visit from André was a rare gift. When it was planned or hoped that either of them might arrive, our day was charged with restlessness. We would barely settle into our tasks, so keenly tuned were our ears and attention to await their knock.

Russian Futurism and Artists' Books

The publications Iliazd produced in Tbilisi (1917-21) extend the remarkable futurist publications of the earlier 1910s. The Russians, more than those of the other avant-gardes, embraced the mobility and flexibility of small, intimate, and innovatively made book works. Books were a mass medium and these artists wanted to have their work out in the world, but they rejected the rules of fine printing that had come to dominate the illustrated books of the later nineteenth century. The avant-gardists looked on such luxurious and decorative productions as another expression of bourgeois taste. They were as keen on inventing irreverent forms of books as they were in making art that caught in the craw of their elders.

One of the earliest of the Russian artists' publications in this brash mode was *A Trap for Judges*, produced in April 1912.[57] This collaborative effort between Khlebnikov and Vasily Kamensky was printed on the reverse side of wallpaper. This made it cheap to produce, but also wallpaper is a quintessentially bourgeois product and using its inverse was a way to signal the relation between the avant-garde and the culture to which it was reacting. *Old Fashioned Love* and *Game in Hell*, both produced in 1912, contained images by Larionov and Goncharova respectively, with texts by Kruchenykh and, in the latter book, collaborations with Khlebnikov. Larionov's Rayonnist motifs, drawn in thick, bold lines, reproduced well in lithographic methods, even using affordable paper printing plates. The expensive *World of Art* productions, with their elaborate, highly decorative illustration, were at a great remove from the black and white outlines and primitive folk motifs drawn by Goncharova. Other artists, such as Olga Rozanova and Kazimir Malevich, collaborated with Khlebnikov and Kruchenykh on *Te li li* (1914) and the second edition of *A Game in Hell* (1914). The books were small in format, about half the size of a sheet of office paper, and often bound with staples or a bit of glue. The ideal book had been displaced by a new idea of the book as a rapidly made expression of nearly spontaneous graphical form.

The production values of the avant-garde books varied but tended toward inexpensive methods of production, making use of readily available means. In a manner unprecedented before that time, these artists took production into their own hands. They sat at kitchen tables and assembled books with rubber stamps. They drew on lithographic transfer paper and went to their local printers to have pages printed in a version of twentieth-century quick and inexpensive printing. Or they cut linoleum blocks, or used wallpaper, or even hand-drew their small editions. Office duplicators, stencils, and individually made collages were all methods taken up by the artists and writers for whom books were a major form of poetic expression. Books circulated. They had currency. And they were the perfect medium for imaginatively hybrid visual-verbal works.

While many futurist artists made books, only a handful of typographic experiments preceded the work of Iliazd. Most notable are the poems of Vasily Kamensky, for which he appropriated the term "ferro-concrete." Reinforced concrete, a material that made modern architecture possible by its combination of strength and flexibility, was an apt metaphor for the visual-verbal play Kamensky introduced to the page. Kamensky's *Tango with Cows*, also printed on multicolored wallpaper in 1914, used letterpress to create a dense page of variably sized fonts packed into surprising relations with each other. Different fonts are juxtaposed in an affront to the rules of good taste and decorum. The poems focus on modern media, the telephone, and the gramophone, but also the contrasts of urban and rural life, and the onomatopoetic notations produce imitations of sounds and codes for dialing that are part of the contemporary experience.

The excitement of putting books together and sending them into circulation as small missives launched into the public sphere showed in the speed with which they were assembled. These books were not destined for rare collections or meant to take their place in a case near a Fabergé egg or other precious artifact. They were meant to live in the hands of readers, to be taken up after a performance, passed on or used as a script from which to read aloud. They appeared quickly and often disappeared quickly as well. They were printed on newsprint and machine-made papers whose life expectancy was notoriously short. Freed from the trappings of conventional book format, they were a means for immediate embodiment of radical texts and images.[58] These were the 'zines of the 1910s.

Iliazd tamed the impulsive approach of his peers and brought order and structure to the publications of Forty-One Degrees. Variety and invention continued to proliferate, but once Iliazd began to design books, a sense of consistency pervaded his approach. He saw the book as a whole, and its sequences as a dramatic unfolding of parts that were all related to each other. The five books in his *zaum* cycle are connected to each other thematically as well as graphically, and the evolution from the beginning to the end is as unpredictable as it is remarkable.

In 1917, Iliazd was twenty-three years old and had spent six formative years in the company of some of the most talented and energetic artists of the pre-revolutionary Russian avant-garde. His concept of poetics had been influenced by the futurists, the abstract language of Rayonnism, and the concrete visual forms of primitivism. He was ready to realize his individual vision of *zaum* poetry in typographic form.

The *Aslaablitchia* Cycle: The Five Plays (*Dras*)

Hélène possessed copies of all of the *dras* in the cycle of five plays, but she never offered them to view in a coherent group. Little by little, features of each of the works distinguished them one from another. My encounters were mainly graphic and material, since they were doubly removed by being in *zaum*. Hélène held them in memory and in her hands, like relics of a vanished poetics, which, indeed, they were—precious and indecipherable.

The main means of access to the contents of the plays was through the summaries that Olga Djordjadze had provided in the 1984 catalogue for the Montréal exhibition. Taken as a whole, the plays provide an insight into Iliazd's sense of language and its role in power, gender, and representation within the aesthetic discussions of the period.

Four of the five plays were produced in Tbilisi during the period from 1917 to 1919. With the exception of a handful of images that appear in *Donkey for Rent*, pasted into the pages, the books are exclusively typographic, printed simply, in black ink, and have none of the qualities of technological production that makes the work of the renowned Russian constructivist designers of the early 1920s so vivid. Iliazd did not use photographic techniques in this period—or, in fact, at any point in his long career. He stayed very close to the typographic form that his writing and poetics required. His work in Tbilisi, like the later work in Paris, respected texts as primary elements of a book, not simply material to be manipulated for gratuitous effect.

Régis shrugged at the esoteric opacity of the texts. But André provided a bit of gloss on a page or two or made a handful of comments. But none of this was systematic or sustained. In the intervening decades, substantial work has been done on *zaum*, in particular by Gerald Janecek, but Djordjadze's summaries remain undisputed. My description of the typographic and design progression follows, since having a sense of the action of the plays is essential. Here the dependencies built into scholarship are foregrounded. I trust these summaries of the Georgian scholar, but I remain, irrevocably, on the other side of a linguistic divide I cannot cross.

The cycle of five plays was grouped under the title *Aslaablitchia*. They weave together the story of a central figure who goes from infancy to adulthood and then in the final play has exchanges with the underworld in the afterlife. Djordjadze says, "If we deconstruct this word according to its phonetic orthography, we find 'asla' (of the donkey) and 'ablitchia' (traits) and we get 'traits of the donkey,' adding into this the fragment of the word 'slab' (weak) we undoubtedly end up with the donkey and all its weakness."[59] The five plays, in order, were *Yanko, King of the Albanians* (1918), *Donkey for Rent* (1919), *Easter Eyeland* (1919), *As Though Zga* (1920), and then the final production, *Ledentu as Beacon* (1923). The alter ego of Iliazd (Ilia), Lilia, is present throughout the first plays. *Yanko* is focused on issues of power, *Donkey* on thwarted courtship, *Easter Eyeland* on female sexuality and religion—but also themes of representation that will be taken up again—*Zga* on hermaphroditic sexuality, and *Ledentu* an extended engagement with the tensions between realism and abstraction in art.

Yanko was actually performed in St. Petersburg in December 1916, but according to Iliazd, "it could not be published until two years later . . . because the military censor saw in the piece a satire of the czar. . . ." In one recollection, Iliazd suggests the set was designed by Ledentu, and music by Mikhail Kuzmin accompanied the play.[60] Elsewhere Iliazd has recorded that the stage sets were by Lapchine and Olga Lechkova (Ledantu's fiancée at the time), and that the music by Kuzmin replicated "the sounds of the sea."[61] Iliazd played the Master while the other characters—brigands and the flea— were taken by others. Iliazd described the part taken by one of his friends, the painter Mané-Katz:[62] "To show you how much courage and good spirit he had, his willingness to sacrifice himself for his friends, let me cite for you the four lines he learned by heart for the part":

> Outoufpatam nzitimitit vitiriti fchitepiti
> Vrataj fatafututatap oriyjututatata
> Stipep rytimigegoutou matamzotol getepiti
> Tsytet doutounichatata tchabatatatata[63]

The rhythmic sequence of syllables, largely without identifiable meaning, could hardly have caused alarm to the censor even if they contained occasional scatological or sexual innuendo, but the plot could have caused some consternation in then Tsarist Russia. Markov notes that the *dras* used the conventions of puppet theater, or *vertex*, in which marionettes performed works that "mixed episodes from the Bible with comic scenes of everyday life."[64] In keeping with these traditions, Iliazd introduced a "Master" who narrated the action, pointing out the meaning of the play at the outset and at critical moments along the way.

Djordjadze tells us that Yanko is a sexless, or at least ungendered, flea who talks baby talk in an essential, elemental language throughout. Lilia, his alter ego and counterpart, is in a similar state. When forced to take the kingly role, Yanko simply responds like a baby wanting to be reunited with his mother. Somewhere in the play is a secret source that all the characters want to suck, but to which only Yanko has access. Yanko refuses power and language and falls back from the throne into an identification with his mother so that we watch him "pass from fearful babbling, whimpering when he feels his impotence, to a puerile affirmation of his will. . . ."[65] The other persons in the play are a bunch of brigands, as Terentiev notes: "The adventurer Yanko stumbles on some bandits who happen to be quarreling. As a complete outsider, without any interest, Yanko is forced to be their king. He is afraid. They stick him to his throne with fish-glue; Yanko tries to tear himself free and he is assisted by a German called Prenatal. They both shout out 'water' but there is no water and Yanko falls victim to the bandits' knives, emitting the sound 'yayyu.' That is all."[66]

The two brigands "express themselves by defiling the order of the Cyrillic alphabet" in a way that gives the impression of a shamanistic script.[67] Clearly power and language are magically connected. Yanko's baby talk, an essential, elemental language, appears both in response to the brigands and also as an act of refusing the authority they are pushing him to assume. The death turns out to be merely a symbolic murder, but in falling, stricken, he cries out for his mother in language that is bursting with vowels. Yanko dies on account of too great an attachment to power, manifest literally by his being glued to his throne. The symbolism of this work makes it easy to read as a study of infantile sexuality and the fear of the power of language.

In the second play, *Donkey for Rent*, the main character has advanced to the point of direct sexual engagement, and, according to Terentiev, the language of the play was "all tenderness and softness with the saliva of love in it."[68] Terentiev went on, pointing out the extent to which *Donkey* addresses the dilemmas faced by the main character Yanko at the end of the first play:

> There is no single "yo," not a drop of moisture . . . the poet has met the fate of his hero: he ran out of water. He had a temperature of 41 degrees and a hard nose. Zdanevich looks for emotional softness (the saliva of love): this was the formation of a call for anal eroticism! He gets ill with typhoid! He writes a new play, *An Ass for Hire*—a compress made of woman, which is reverently applied indiscriminately now to bridegroom A and now to bridegroom B and sometimes, by mistake, to the ass.
>
> All the indecent words in this ecstasy without causality go "yu," whoop and squawk, and produce more saliva than the extreme poet Velimir Khlebnikov . . . Zdanevich has won the record of tenderness and radiates satisfaction.[69]

An excerpt of the play, which was composed in 1918, was first published in the anthology dedicated to Melnikova. At the center of the drama is a sexual fantasy, by which Iliazd shows his willingness to suffer any form of humiliation to win the actress's affection. According to Djordjadze, anal eroticism permeated with the sounds and imagery of this play, with its poor suffering beast longing for love of any kind. Iliazd put himself into this drama and has the heroine Zokhna (a version of Sosna/Sofia for Melnikova that can also be read as "waking from a dream") address him at the end of the play. The Iliazd character has the nickname "Lo" or "Liou," a variation of the Russian "Liu(bit)" or "he loves," and Zokhna closes the play, saying "the lover weeps for the face which she does not see. I love my love, love me, Lo, I am Liou, Liou." Only by transforming himself into a donkey could he achieve his sexual desires even in this fantasy. Eroticism had its own transformative power, reshaping the language into suggestive sexual tones. But the image of the donkey points to the absurd condition brought on by infatuation.[70]

Terentiev described the third play, *Easter Eyeland*, as "a very cheerful drama" in which "everybody dies and everybody is resurrected—a monthly period."[71] In this *dra* the female character is a conflation of Ilia, Lilia, and also Melnikova. She has become an adult female, but the images of femininity are spread all over the characters in this play. We have no evidence that Iliazd had had a love affair or even a girlfriend at this stage of his life. We know that he had a crush on Melnikova, and paid her court (to no avail, as it turned out), but the sexual energy of his work has the potency of a young man's libido, sexualizing everyone and everything around him. While the title, according to Markov, referred to the actual Pacific island, Djordjadze suggests "it also stood for Tbilisi as an island of relative calm during the war, the 'harbor of Melnikova' and of her 'wisdom.'"[72] The tale of murder and resurrection plays with motifs of sexual desire and menstruation, though the blood is always symbolic and represented by cranberry juice—as in a puppet play.[73]

At the end of the play, a summary of the action is presented to the audience in succinct form, here in the translation by Nikolskaya:

Two-and-a-half stone women
they get out of their coffins
they die
the boss, the merchant Pryk, slams down
the lids of the coffins
a sculptor enters
boss, asks the sculptor

the sculptor
smashes the first coffin
smashes the second
smashes the third
the merchant runs in
the sculptor grabs the merchant
he stabs the merchant
the sculptor stabs him
the merchant dies
the sculptor sprinkles the blood on the women
the women are resurrected
the women in a chorus,
"Blockhead"
they beat the sculptor
they sprinkle the merchant with the sculptor's blood
the merchant comes to life
Easter
the women depart
leaving pools of blood
the boss
Easter is a negative indication of the death of menstruation
Easter gives the stone women their activity and the sculptor too
It sprinkles the blood of the women over the sculptor,
comes to life, runs
the boss[74]

The themes of violence, resurrection, repression of the women, and death will be reworked in *Ledentu*, but first, *As Though Zga* was written to complete the first phase of these compositions. The play is a "game of mirrors: a woman of a certain age looks at herself in the mirror and becomes a version of Zdanevich." She sees herself seeing herself and the whole play becomes a study in masks and doublings.[75] Iliazd claimed his own identification with *Zga,* the main character, and then stated in the play, "a girl become a boy that's also me—an old woman become a man—that's also me." Echoes of his childhood experience, at least in its apocryphal form, come back here. The story is full of mirror effects that serve the now familiar themes of death and resurrection. Djordjadze cited these remarks from unpublished notes by Iliazd:

Lilith, Lilia, that's me, Ilia-Liou, as I have been called and am still called. In my life I was a girl and then a boy. This gives me the possibility of fighting with myself and biting my tail, fighting while being a man with the woman in me and a woman with the man. Isn't this the goal of metamorphoses and wasn't I, at the beginning of my life, a woman? Zga? As though Zga? Isn't the problem resolved after the resurrection of the woman by the appearance of a new hermaphrodite?[76]

The action in *Zga* takes place in a state between waking and sleeping. Again, this is paraphrased from Djordjadze: Zga wakes up and looks into a mirror at a reflection that is, at first, the only other character in the play. The mirror comes to life, dances with Zga, and then the mirror character disappears, transformed into As-Though-Zga. The new character talks about Ilia who had become mute, attacked the mirror, broke it, and died while As-Though-Zga becomes Zga again and fell asleep. The feints of identity and transformation, cross-gendering, and play with reality and illusion are well distilled here, filled with the games of language and mirroring. What we know for sure is that at the time the play was written, Iliazd's parents were pressuring him to break off whatever relationship he had with Melnikova. This may also have played a part in his decision to go to Paris. The actress was older and married. But *Zga* ends in reconciliation—of Iliazd with his female identity—whether that resolution says anything about the status of his love for Melnikova or not.

Discussion of the final *dra*, *Ledentu*, will be taken up in the context of its publication in Paris in 1923.

Design Development in the *Dras*

The cover of *Yanko*, designed in 1918, is strong and stark. In the same font and size, the author's name, Ilia Zdanevich, and the title, broken into short lines, are printed in black Cyrillic letters on orange paper.[77] The effect is striking, but not innovative, except that it marks a break from the hand-drawn, lithographed, or stencil-printed aesthetics of the first phase of futurist books. The decision to use and explore typography gave these works authority as literary publications. The interior pages of *Yanko* are not typographically complex. Single lines of text make use of a bold font intermixed with a lighter one to provide sound emphasis.[78] The difference between this treatment and that in the subsequent play, *Donkey for Rent*, 1919, is marked. To begin, in a display of Iliazd's growing skill, the title text in an italic font is curved with dramatic flair around the cutout drawing of a donkey collaged

Cover of *Donkey for Rent* (Tbilisi: Forty-One Degrees, 1919). Courtesy of François Mairé and the Fonds Iliazd

into the page.[79] Interleaved with pages set in standard lines are double-page spreads that stack words and intersperse larger and smaller fonts. The resulting pages have great graphic contrast to them. These scored passages required considerable attention to design and execution—for the compositor the challenge is that each different size of letter requires different spacing material, and the gaps above and below smaller-font letters must be filled out with spacers to create a solid form (as if a stack of bricks were made in

Cover of *Easter Eyeland* (Tbilisi: Forty-One Degrees, 1919). Courtesy of François
Mairé and the Fonds Iliazd

which some were half the size of the others, the spaces between them would
need to be filled to make a stable structure). The technique became one of
Iliazd's signature design features up through the final book he produced, *The
Grotesque Courtesan* (1974).

The cover of *Easter Eyeland* consists of the author's name, inconspicu-
ously set in smaller (probably twelve-point) type, and the title pushed into
the center of the cover to form, appropriately enough, an island. The effect

raises questions about the production, since the letterforms are a modern Cyrillic, with the sharply differentiated thick and thin strokes, mechanically formed lines and curves (a contrast to the cover of *Yanko*, in type that had some resemblance to a Craw Clarendon, a mid-nineteenth-century display font). Though the "modern" font designs were from the late eighteenth and early nineteenth centuries, they were frequently used in French publishing as a sign of "contemporary" literature, distinguishing them from publication of classical texts in humanistic fonts. But the aesthetic import of the font is only part of the interest raised by the composition, which contains letters warped and distorted in ways that lead letters could not have been (they probably would have cracked or broken). In fact, these look like hand-drawn versions of a modern font, created with a ruling pen and compass (though there are no true circles in the image). The result is highly legible but also curiously unnerving—we don't quite know if this is a drawing or an impression of type, and the image creates a strong effect with minimal means.

As Though Zga was the fourth play in the cycle, the last one composed and printed in Tbilisi, where it appeared in 1920. The word *zga* is suggestive of darkness, difficulty seeing, and also, a hermaphrodite.[80] The title on the cover is a double impression, out of register, playing with this optical difficulty by creating a blurry, shimmering effect. The *A*'s in the title appear in a font about four times the size of the rest, which allows the words of the title to be nested into each other around the majuscules. In letterpress composition, this required careful justification (the insertion of spacing to stabilize the type) and inking (much larger letters require heavier ink to coat their surfaces completely). Again, what looks like a single, simple effect was achieved through highly skilled manipulation both of the materials and of the basic conceptual understanding of what the medium of letterpress could do.

The interior of *As Though Zga* made use of the typographic scoring technique Iliazd had already developed and incorporated into his designs and writing.[81] To this technique Iliazd added a material effect, interleaving colored veils of tissue paper between the printed sheets. The result reinforced the core themes of reality and illusion at the heart of the play. As the pages turn, the veils have to lift, and the sense of seeing and not seeing creates a dynamic moment of disorientation for the reader. The color of the interleaved tissue sheets darkens toward the center of the book, where the action is most dour, and then lightens again toward the end. Iliazd was creating a book as a dramatic physical object capable of producing emotional effect

As Though Zga, cover and interior (Tbilisi: Forty-One Degrees, 1919). Courtesy of François Mairé and the Fonds Iliazd

with material means. How much of the actual hands-on typesetting work Iliazd did in these projects is far less important than the demonstrated understanding of the aesthetic specificity of letterpress. In addition, his creative engagement with the spaces, sequence, and development of the book as a space of experience, a phenomenon in which effects were produced, not reproduced, was consolidated through the cycle of the *dras* and other productions made between 1917 and 1920.

The skills of dramatic type design he had acquired in Tbilisi all came into play when he arrived in Paris and composed the final *zaum* drama, *Ledentu*. In terms of thematics, that play is less concerned with infantilism, eroticism, language, and authority—the issues that bound the first four plays together—and more focused on art and representation. But its relation to the others will be clear and its identity as a termination to the cycle will be evident.

Reflections on Modernism and the Avant-Garde Book

My work on this period of Iliazd's life depended on secondary, even tertiary materials, the interpretations of others and translations or summaries of Russian texts. But one afternoon, as we were talking of the *dras* and of the period in Tbilisi, speaking of typography and print production, Hélène paused with a kind of purpose in her posture. The pause was long enough to build anticipation, though she said nothing, and simply moved to another part of the atelier. We usually focused our energies on one end of the table, next to the shelves where the files were stored, and so I never looked behind, never thought of what the other shadowed space and cloth-draped boxes might contain. Hélène pulled out a small packet from which she drew out a copy of the "little orange book." *Yanko*, the first of the *zaum* plays, printed in Tbilisi in 1918, was placed in my hand.

The living connection through the object to that moment of the past was profound. The astonishing little pamphlet was tiny—only about 4½ by 5½ inches. I had never seen a publication of Iliazd's from that period, and the modesty of the work combined with the innovative typography was immediately striking. Iliazd scored his *dras* and used the page as the theater of visually marked sound. Because of the combination of complex graphical rendering and the invented *zaum* language, Iliazd's *dras* have to be understood intuitively rather than literally. We came to have a sense of the sound of the plays through the interpretations offered to us by André.

This may have been a day when he appeared in the afternoon, his features alight with enthusiasm, to pore over the pages of the elaborately scored text, his thin wrists holding the edges of the book, shiny dark hair obscuring his eyes. He always read first to himself for a few moments, parsing the difficult typography and idiosyncratic spelling. Then, lifting his pale face, he began to intone in a musical voice. He warbled as if inspired, translating into French where he could, and simply pronouncing the *zaum* sounds where he could not, offering the rendering of the affective verse in an equally forceful vocalization.

His performances were remarkable. Spontaneous and incomplete, they left an indelible impression of Iliazd's languge. The characters came alive—such as the young Yanko, the central figure of the initial play, whose cries and whimpers were high pitched and whiney. Then a host of other characters followed—donkeys, statues, women, corpses, each of whom received their own enunciation. Hélène showed me each of the *dras*, dwelling on their graphic features, their varied papers and presentations. André did not perform all of them for us. But when we arrived at the final, most elaborately typographic work of all, *Ledentu*, André showed us a page taken up almost entirely by a single word. He opened his mouth and with all the breath of his

narrow chest exhaled an enormous "MaaaaaahhhhHHHHHHHHo-MMMM-
IIIIIEeeeeeeee." This was the sound of the main character crying for his
mother. André explained the scoring, deciphered morphemes and phonemes, played with the poetic structures, and let his voice dance around the
elements on those pages. The language was vivid. His engagement with
the impossible task was suffused with imaginative channeling that gave the
whole experience an otherworldly sense—for all that it was a very physical
poetic performance.

These moments of immediacy broke through the routines of archival
work. They made the poetry live in a very real sense, through the spoken
voice. My understanding of Iliazd was greatly expanded as a result. Even
if he did not—could not—appear before us as a living being, the work thus
voiced rose from the printed pages into a vivid presence.

Not all degrees of historical distance are the same.

1920–1921

Transition: Tbilisi, Constantinople, Paris

Displacement

Tracking Iliazd as he went from Tbilisi to Paris in 1920 was like watching the movements of a man through the wrong end of a telescope. While he was in Tbilisi, his activities seemed to be framed by the same assumptions and ambitions as those that had developed throughout the 1910s, but when he left his home city, and whatever platform had stabilized his circumstances within familiar contexts (however indistinct these were to me six decades later), his course across unknown territory created new challenges. He shrank in scale.

At first it seemed that until 1920 not a note in his archives or the sparse recollections of anyone else had suggested the material difficulties, and the hand-to-mouth existence, in which he found himself in Constantinople. A year in limbo is a long time, and for a vital, ambitious young poet-artist in his mid-twenties, it might have felt interminable, especially as it had not been anticipated. Here, again, the biographer faces the challenge of reading gaps for the essence, their particularities. Between one event at the Fantastic Cabaret and another, the spaces seem explicable, filled by planning, colleagues, the activities of a circle of artists engaged in their program. But the gaps between the events in 1920 to 1921 are illegible, filled with waiting, the challenges of subsistence, the vagaries of trying to sustain a sense of purpose in the void of personal and political uncertainties.

However, evidence for the period of Iliazd's life between his departure from Tbilisi and his arrival in Paris was supplied by a series of texts he composed in 1929 as if it were a series of "letters" to his former colleague, Philips Price.[1] By the time he wrote the texts, Iliazd had been in Paris for many years, but the impressions of travel were still vivid. They are, however, recollections, and the characterizations of moods, decisions, and events were shaped by distance and narrated retrospectively. Alongside these *Letters* a few other documents offered contemporary evidence about the transition from Tbilisi to Paris by way of Constantinople. Setting out from Georgia in fall 1920, Iliazd could not have imagined what lay ahead.

Iliazd filed a petition to the Arts Commission of the Georgian Assembly on October 5, 1920, stating his goals for travel, and here we see the political realities registering in relation to art:

> By this declaration I ask the Arts Commission to aid me in making a trip to France to continue my education. The evolution of contemporary artistic ideas requires a large exchange in every new and forming direction. Independent of the political changes, France and Paris continue to play a central role in the world of art since the 2nd Empire and contact with it seems necessary for all cultural groups. The brilliant speed with which the French artistic spirit has been reestablished after the war and the rhythm of art in the world, only further emphasizes the importance of the role of Paris.
>
> Moreover, not having had the possibility to make the trip during my student years (1911-16), and having returned to Georgia in 1917, I have lost all links with artistic centers and movements. Given the conditions of life in Georgia, I am now condemned, like any amateur, to slow decay and decline because of the refusal of Georgia to orient its culture towards the north. The link with the occident being even more insufficient for the moment, there is an even smaller import of artistic ideas. Thus a voyage to France is essential to the continuation of my artistic life. I am a poet. There is no tradition according to which young poets go abroad to study. Also, my affinity with the Russian school gives me no right to count on the material aid of the government. I can only count on myself. After two years of work in attempting to gain the money, I am certain that any hope of a solid financial base is in vain. For this reason I leave for Europe with extremely modest material resources and to smooth out some of the difficulties which may present themselves I ask your help in providing the following: 1) Authorization for my voyage and papers attesting to this; 2) a request for the French department to grant me a visa; 3) ask the Georgian representative in Paris to have the kindness to look for some work for me; this is especially important; 4) provide me with letters to Georgian representatives in Constantinople and Rome, points in my voyage; 5) ask of the Government Bank permission for me to exchange currency.
>
> Please accept in advance my thanks and appreciation.[2]

Iliazd's self-identification as a writer and artist is clear, as is his recognition that the Arts Commission of the newly independent state of Georgia might have other priorities than supporting the work of a poet whose orientation and formation had been within the Russian avant-garde. He does not mention his law degree; instead, he defines his identity by the projects he had undertaken in the futurist circles and carried on in Tbilisi. His concept of Paris as a center of artistic life is also evident (though mention of the Second Empire feels anachronistic). Paris would play out somewhat differently in his experience ahead than he might have anticipated. By the mid-1980s, when this material was surfacing in my research, Paris was more of a historical reference, rather than a center of contemporary art. Publishing, poetry, scholarship, cultural activity of all kinds were flourishing, but the prominence of the city had long been displaced by New York, Berlin, London, and other venues. Iliazd's attitudes were a reminder of the importance of the city in the early twentieth century and its magnetizing force in the period between World Wars I and II.

Iliazd's notes rarely contain any suggestion of regret, but the tone in which he characterized his departure from Tbilisi was charged with emotion. His ambivalence about the 1920 decision to leave was clearly with him when he composed this text in 1929. He described a period working as a barman, selling grain, petrol, and playing the stock market. He had witnessed the "retreat of the Russian army, the advance of the Turks, the occupation by the Germans, and the arrival" of the British:[3]

> It was no longer possible to subsist in Tbilisi as I had done during the two previous years. There was hardly room to breathe. It was necessary either to leave for the North or for the West, anything but stay in place.
>
> Should I reproach myself now for not having chosen to go North? If I had, a respectable occupation would have awaited me, perhaps some success, in any case, a full and respectable existence . . . but I renounced the life awaiting me in the North and chose instead the road to oblivion, forgetting, misery and disillusion.[4]

What that "respectable existence" was or might have been, is unclear—a position in civil service perhaps? The administrative circumstances for which Iliazd had trained with his law degree had changed radically, so it is hard to know how he would have been able to settle into a life imagined before the revolution when that world had vanished.

The material difficulties Iliazd experienced in beginning this transition are noted in detail in the *Letters* to Philips Price.[5] He dreamed of going to Paris, where his father and brother had traveled frequently before the war, bringing back "vertiginous tales" of the capital.[6] "Before leaving I had sold my books, my typewriter, my furnishings, my cufflinks. But this money was soon gone." He says a friend lent him the cash and he purchased a fourth-class ticket on a monstrous Italian vessel. The voyage was disturbing. The ship was filled with Turkish prisoners of war on the last stage of their homeward journey from Siberia: "The deck was filled with human beings to the point that the sailors, in the course of doing their duty, simply walked on the bodies and encountered a protest only when they accidentally stepped on someone's face. In addition, all of these people were dressed in sheep skins, perfect for Siberia, but filled with insects."[7] He noted the contrast to an earlier visit to the coast of the Black Sea in 1916 in the company of Price. The first of the *Letters* contained a detailed account of the expeditions into the Caucasus Mountains, the churches, their state of preservation, architecture, and their location. But it said little about his activity in the intervening four years—his journalism during the revolution, his brief involvement with the Bolsheviks, and the other upheavals that claimed his attention. In 1929, nothing of that remained. He felt that his imaginative life and his unconscious (the term that he used) remained "pre-1917" in their essence. He attributed the lack of impact to the fact that he had not witnessed the post-revolutionary events in Russia directly—and that while his friends in Moscow lived in abominable conditions, he had been "strolling without a coat in the warmth of Tbilisi."[8]

One through line of the *Letters* details a relationship Iliazd struck up with one of the Turkish prisoners being returned. Tall, blond, blue-eyed, the man had suffered years of imprisonment and separation from his family at the hands of the Russian army. The distinctive features and height of the man, even in his shabby garb and miserable state, made him recognizable—and Iliazd realized he had encountered and worked with him years earlier in his travels. He was later identified by other travelers as Moussa-Said, an imam of the Hagia Sophia.

The *Letters* contained considerable detail about the war, conjured in dialogue with this Turk, referred to always as "the blonde." Iliazd's anti-war sentiments came to the fore in these accounts. He had seen the ravages of the Russians during his expeditions into Asia Minor, and deplored the waste and destruction. As the ship approached the Bosporus, it passed White Russian general Pyotr Wrangel's fleet, which had been put to sea by the Bolsheviks:

> As we drew closer to this fleet of boats we could see not only the blue cross on the white field of the flag and also the flag of St. Andrew, but also the men on the deck, and I began to feel that attack of disgust mixed with anger which I had felt before at the sight of military massacre. I have described already the number of sheep and prisoners of war which our captain had crowded onto the deck of our ship, but now I saw that the discomfort I had experienced was only that of a spoiled man. We were stretched out one next to another on the deck, but at least we could lie down. On the boat we were approaching, the soldiers were standing in such a manner that they could neither sit nor lie down. For the first time, I saw that vulgar expression—like sardines in a can—truly applicable. We were in the Bosporus by then, and we were so close that I could distinguish the faces of the men on the other ship. I wanted to turn away, but could not, realizing that these men had been standing for days, without moving or eating, and that those among them who had died remained in the midst of those who had not yet had the wisdom to die. I looked without understanding how the sight of this incredible torment failed to make the very sea boil and the sky cry out in revolt.
>
> A week later, I arrived in Constantinople where I lived in misery for a year at which point another 4th class ticket allowed me to exchange the misery of Constantinople for Montparnasse.[9]

The *Letters* provide a detailed description of Iliazd's life in Constantinople. He lived by buying and selling and speculating on commodities—wheat, gasoline, and gold. Georgian currency was depreciating rapidly and gold was used everywhere—in restaurants, gardens, bookshops. His visa to France had been refused, and he had no means of support, no contacts or relations in Constantinople. He wandered through the city, teeming with refugees and émigrés, a mélange of British and American forces, crammed with White Russians selling their jewels and furs for the price of a meal. He entered the area near Hagia Sophia and was barred from entry to the grounds by guards who took him for an Armenian or a Greek, people prohibited from entering the mosque. At a café he inquired about a place to stay and found lodging with a baker, Hadji-Baba. He worked for Hadji-Baba searching out pigs' teeth, which the Muslims used for cures by grinding the teeth into ink to write on papers they swallowed. As a Muslim, Hadji-Baba could not traffic in the pigs themselves, and for his essential service, Iliazd was given shelter in the shadow of the Hagia Sophia, whose beauty struck a deep chord with him.[10] He slept in a room with four straw mats; the other three mats were taken up by the baker and his two assistants. Iliazd's knowledge of Armenian and Georgian churches, acquired firsthand in the drawings he had done on expeditions with Takaishvili, provided a basis on which to appreciate the full splendor of the building and reflect on its historical transformation from Greek Orthodox cathedral to mosque. Though he could not enter the sacred place, he finally managed to be smuggled onto the grounds in one of his night wanderings:

> From here one could see St. Sophia in her entirety; close enough to see each separate volume, far enough away that I could see her dome.
> I drank in the crystalline fluidity of her forms, light and dense; I rejoiced in the sharpness of her curved and straight lines, delighted in their perfect relations. After so many wanderings, without limit or end, after so many days, so much work, so many hours dissecting and studying other church forms which had never achieved their full realization, I saw at last a perfect and fully realized form.[11]

Unsure of how long he would be staying in Constantinople, he at first spent his time in cafés, playing cards, amusing himself and others with tales of his travels in Asia Minor. He described diversions such as watching cockroach races or a man who hypnotized flies and made them dance with his flute, and even his own efforts to start a journal. A handwritten text, intended to serve as the basis of a poster, showed that he also tried to continue his futurist activities even in this period of transition:

> Proposed lecture at the Black Rose, December 25, 1920
> 146 Grand Rue de Pera, Mullatier, 1er Etage, Constantinople
> The very distinguished director of 41 Degrees, Ilia Zdanevich, is going to offer an evening which will never fade from your memory. He will talk about "The countryside of Mohammedans, the hairy surrogate, Prosper Merriment, a Pushkinist drunkard, the landscape of Crimea, Greek Iscariot solders, Koktabel, the city on the Black Sea which is full of poets, fireman poets, the whore's son, with Adam and without Adam and Eve, 'I am a donkey and the subject of verse.'"
> Ilia Zdanevich is in Constantinople and this professor of poetics will speak at the Black Rose. Ilia Zdanevich has arrived in Constantinople: Prepare to Repent.[12]

This event seems never to have taken place. The displacement from the context of his peers, and the shift in time and mood, were already registering. Constantinople in 1920 was a long way from Moscow in 1916 or Tbilisi in the years after.

The ennui of this existence wore at his spirits. He records a night's wandering filled with despair, overwhelmed by the difficulties of his situation, far from friends and family, when he wept in the darkness. Searching for solutions to his material situation, he wandered into the flea markets where the émigré population bartered goods and traded currency. He encountered two friends from Georgia, whom he identified in his writings as Zhemchuzhin and Serebryakov, both of whom were surviving through speculation. They invited him to come and share their lodgings, but no work was forthcoming. Winter advanced; the city was cold and snowy. He had no winter coat, no money, and he fell into profound depression. His interest in the city receded. He felt only isolation and difficulty. With his two friends, he put together a study of the various currencies that had been printed during the war and by provisional governments. The long article he wrote on the topic seemed to produce little or no financial recompense.[13]

He recorded the dullness of spirit produced by the winter sky and the deep melancholy into which it plunged him. He reconnected with the blond Turk, but when he was invited out for an evening, he worried about the shabbiness of his clothes and his asocial habits, acquired from spending so much time alone. The beginning of an autobiographical novel, *Philosophia,* gives a sense of his mood:[14]

> Beneath the sky of events, among the grandeurs visible to the naked eye, Iliazd is lost. And more, for no reason. Lawyer by his education, he despises legal science. Poet by situation in his culture, he has written nothing but a few rebuses. A convinced atheist, without god, he dreams of Constantinople, and loves Christian antiquities. Rejected by himself, he throws himself from one side to another, giving himself all kinds of different goals. And without having created anything, he disappears from the horizon. After having done everything he could not to be sent to the Front, he went as an observer . . . after working in the press of the State, he went quickly to the provinces and passed whole days writing all kinds of things on his views of the State with his collaborators.[15]

Finally he found work with an office of the same Near East Relief organization he had worked with in Georgia. When he presented his letter of introduction, the administrators were at first unwilling to believe that the shabby individual before them was the one being referred to in the note. He took up work as an accountant, spending his days entering items into a large ledger book with apparent contentment. Graft and corruption surrounded him, and he tried to ignore it. Steady work, steady pay, and no doubt steady nourishment made a difference. Again, from the *Letters*:

> This work didn't bother me in the least. On the contrary, I was quite happy with it. I came to the office around nine o'clock in the morning, to Taxim Street, #25, and I went to the fourth floor where I opened my ledger book, wrote, rewrote, multiplying, dividing, subtracting and adding until the midday bell sounded, at which point I abruptly shut my book and went out down the stairs.
>
> Now the whole city, the whole world, was mine. The animosity and malevolence of the months in which I suffered from isolation and confinement were past. I took pleasure in everything I saw and heard, as if it had been made expressly for my enjoyment, and everything attracted me, distracted me, whether it was the boutiques or the passersby. The variety of it all fascinated me, intrigued me. In the Greek restaurants in the quarter near Taxim Street, or in the fish market nearby, the cuisine no longer seemed disgusting, but appetizing, appealing, no matter what was served to me. I wanted to taste everything, to know everything, and I asked the name of all sorts of Greek and Turkish wares; I greeted everyone with questions, with demands for explanations, details, particularities and tried to eat in a different place every day. I entered into conversation with anyone and everyone and talked, asking questions and exchanging stories. And after lunch I wandered around the quarter of Pera, going into boutique and cafes, into the baths, into any open door, strolling, walking without stop as if I were looking for something, anything content with everything . . .
>
> Then from two o'clock until five I wrote more numbers in the account book, going up and down the columns of figures, turning the handle of the calculator while in my mind I thought about a wonderful Greek meal or other impressions of my day's meanderings, repeating to myself the names of all of the streets I had passed in the course of my walk, recollecting the means of passing from one part of the city to another, thinking about the boutiques or the architecture of the houses in streets I had passed through, etc. I repeated these thoughts aloud to myself and time passed with great rapidity. At five o'clock I did the same as at midday—I shut the large ledger with a bang, ran down the stairs from the fourth floor past Miss Cook, and this time, it was not just Pera which offered itself to my wide eyes, nor Galata, but Istanbul, all of Istanbul.[16]

The *Letters* to Price, detailed though they are, serve as summaries to a period already past for Iliazd personally at the time that he wrote them. The descriptions of life in the year in Constantinople are detailed but succinct.

The duration of living through a period, with its many lulls and shifts of pace, is never the same as the recapitulated account. But the time Iliazd had to compose those letters in the 1920s was rare as well, given other demands. This was not the only nonfiction account he would write of events in his life, but it was the most sustained and, according to Régis Gayraud, by the end of the project he wished he had put the energy into a fictional version instead.[17] The novel *Philosophia* may have provided that alternative account.

The period in Constantinople had been difficult and muted his earlier optimism about continuing his futurist activities outside of Russia or Georgia. But, during the months in Constantinople, he had finished the fifth *dra, Ledentu*, the production of which would occupy him in Paris in October 1921. At last, through the intervention of a relative, he obtained his visa and arrived in Paris.[18]

The Enormity of History

Large-scale historical conditions overwhelm an individual life. Iliazd was raised in Georgia, an independent state that had been annexed to Russia in the nineteenth century. In World War I, Russia was on the side of the French, Italian, and British allied forces, eventually joined by the United States. Georgia is contiguous with Turkey, Armenia, and Azerbaijan, as well as Russia. The Caucasus region was the scene of military and political conflict throughout the war and the Russian Revolution, with bitter fighting and considerable losses and damage and slaughter of Turks and Armenians. Iliazd had witnessed incidents that were part of these conflicts, as his account in the *Letters* and other documents makes clear.[19] These events were connected to much larger conflicts and forces, with the decline of the Ottoman Empire, struggles among ethnic and religious groups, as well as struggles for national identity and independence in the Caucasus region. But the founding of Forty-One Degrees, and its series of lectures and events in Tbilisi in 1918-19, took place as if the region were remote from conflict. Iliazd had worked as a war reporter, and he wrote about the consequences of the war and the consequences of the revolution. The letters he addressed to Price in the 1920s dwell in detail on the period from 1916 to 1920, but they provide little sense of how political events affected his artistic work or creative vision.[20]

Iliazd was not mobilized in World War I, though he was in his early twenties, perhaps because his brother Kirill had already served. Nor did he get drafted in World War II, when he was in France. By then, he had children to look after. His goal during the early 1940s, when Germany occupied France, was understandably to be as inconspicuous as possible. His life in the 1930s, during the Depression, was clearly affected by the economic downturn. He was forced to lay off workers at the textile factory where he was a manager before being terminated himself. Of the Soviet Union and the changes it wrought on the colleagues with whom he had shared his youthful undertakings, he said very little. Return was not an option in the first years he was in Paris (he had no money for a trip), and by the time he was in a more secure economic position, he had a wife, children, and other commitments. News from the Soviet state was not good. The optimism of the avant-garde and conviction that a new vision of social order would in part arise from poetic innovation was crushed in repressive realities.

These are large general statements. They paint historical periods and conditions with very broad strokes. But they suffice to raise the question of how biography is imagined in relation to events of such scale. Though some events had a direct and causal impact on Iliazd's movements or choices (lack of money, closed borders, and family circumstances), the question of how to understand Iliazd—or anyone—as a *historical subject* arises. Iliazd has a sense of his own history, but largely in terms of his projects. The futurists had created sound and visual poetry in the 1910s and this mattered very much to him. He did also occasionally write as a historical subject (*Rahel, The Brigade, Letters*), and he was critically aware of his own historical and historicized accomplishments. And yet, for all of the determining effect on his life and choices about where and how to live, the forces of history were rarely in the foreground. They were atmospheric, not determinative. You pull up your coat collar against the winds of change and set your sights on whatever destination or goal has set your individual path. But this metaphor—of life as a path or route or time as an unfolding ribbon—depends on and fosters a concept of the self as an individual atomistic being moving through, rather than emerging from, such conditions.

Iliazd was far from autonomous, but perhaps because historical conditions were impossible to alter, he seems to have taken them so little into account, except as the constraints and opportunities for his work. And the work? The history of which it partakes is that of the trajectory of twentieth-century art from a disruptive avant-garde into a gradually more classical modern aesthetic. Iliazd was in sync with these periods, radical among the futurists and more conventional from mid-century to his final projects. He participated in modern art in collaboration with its pantheon without any sense in the final decades of his life that modernism was already fading. Though he embraced the notion of "falling into oblivion" as a fate for artists and poets, he was surrounded by giants of the modern period whose prominence seemed established for all time, outside of history—which was precisely the premise on which they would be historicized.

Iliazd was inside the mythologies of modernism. For many collectors, scholars, or critics, the projects he did with Picasso and the relationship that sustained them were the outstanding mark of his success and status. But are those associations with the "great" figures of his period still the only, or even primary, terms on which we assess the value of his work as an artist, writer, and designer? The grounds for evaluation shift over time, as do the perspectives through which work is viewed. He collaborated with various women, beginning with Natalia Goncharova and Sonia Delaunay, then the little-known Roch Grey and Marie Laure de Noailles. But it was mainly the men who mattered, who had credibility and status. His emerging interests in African explorations and Byzantine architecture expanded his view beyond Europe, but that was true of many other modern figures. The terms of modern art—claims to universality, innovation as revolution, and poet as radical individual—were imprinted in everything he did. In that sense, he was a fully historicized subject, and his conception of his identity as an artist was forged from frameworks he adopted, largely unquestioned, from the period of his formation and maturity.

1921-1926
Paris

The New Context

Material evidence for the period following Iliazd's arrival in Paris was considerable. The combination of his own activity in that period, his inclination to maintain documentation about his work, and the continuity of residency in Paris resulted in a much richer collection in the archive than for the earlier periods. The chronology for 1921 lists the following events immediately upon his arrival:

November 27: First lecture in Paris, in French, on "New Schools of Russian Poetry" at the home of the singer Olénine d'Alheime [sic] in Passy (see Raymond Cogniat in Comoedia of December 4, 1921).

December 21: Soirée Poetique at the Café Cameléon in Montparnasse, presided over by Charchoune. Iliazd did performance in his mezzo-soprano voice. (The poster for this evening can be found reproduced on page 297 of Arturo Swarz's Almanaco Dada.)

He soon becomes a regular at the Café Cameleon and, occasionally, The Rotond, in the company of Serge Fotinsky or Lado Gudiashvili.

End of December: Writes to Marinetti to give him a summary of his poetic activities since 1914.

He is somewhat disappointed by Parisian life, as he indicates in a letter in February 1922 to Ali Bey, a friend in Constantinople.[1]

Again, the kind of evidence varies and the scope of the accounts was often limited. But some activities were very well documented by Iliazd and other sources. In contrast to reading the childhood "relics" and the futurist "frameworks" in the earlier periods, or the retrospective accounts of the war and travels, we could find multiple witnesses for corroboration and contradiction within the networks of his activity following his arrival in Paris.

Iliazd gave about a dozen lectures on Russian poetry and his own particular poetic theories between 1921 and 1926. His schedule of public speaking and other activity in the eighteen months between November 1921 and an event known as *The Bearded Heart* (*Coeur à Barbe*), which took place on July 6, 1923, make clear that Iliazd was optimistic that he could transplant the work of Forty-One Degrees, particularly its *zaum* poetics, to fertile soil in Paris. The 1923 *Bearded Heart* event, and all that it indicated about changes in the aesthetics in Paris of the postwar period, put a check on that optimism. The linguistic specificity of his poetics (*zaum* would have been difficult even in a Russian language context) circumscribed their audience in advance—the specialized vocabulary of his theoretical propositions and the typographic radicalism made for a difficult cultural translation.

On his arrival, Iliazd circulated in an émigré community that intersected with French avant-garde poets. Contacts and friends from his earlier activities, as well as new acquaintances, included Viktor Bart and Lado Gudiashvili, Vladimir Pozner, Serge Férat, Marc Chagall, Robert and Sonia Delaunay, and Paul and Gala Éluard. He frequented the Café Chameleon and the Rotond, also frequented by Delaunay and her husband, and went to gatherings at their house in the rue Malherbes. Various *bleus* (those messages delivered around the city by pneumatic tube) in his papers attest to appointments made, rendezvous set, or requests for connection. His signature can be found on a Robert Delaunay drawing of the Eiffel Tower from this period—among those of Man Ray, Robert Desnos, André Breton, Louis Aragon, Marc Chagall, Vincent Huidobro, Blaise Cendrars, Pierre Reverdy, and others.[2]

A note from Francis Picabia, dated January 22, 1922, attempted to fix a meeting, as do notes exchanged with Paul Éluard later that year and one from Jean Cocteau early in 1923. Iliazd made initial contact with Pablo Picasso and also Max Ernst, Roch Grey, and Marie-Laure de Noailles—all connections that would result in collaborations decades later. While his Russian and Georgian friends also appear in archival materials—correspondence about a calligraphic composition for a dress for Vera Soudeikine, invitations to dine with Salomé Andronikov (whom he had known since 1909), and others—he was also cultivating new connections in the milieu of the Café Cyrano and other venues.[3] A brief collaboration on a *zaum* play, "The Teacher of the School for Bread," with Vera Choukaïeff and Erik Satie was never completed.

But evidence of the project shows the vitality of his exchanges and range of efforts. Some of these names no longer resonate with immediate recognition, but others have become canonical within the annals of modern art and literature.

Among his acquaintances of the 1920s, Lucien Scheler was one of those still alive and accessible in 1985. Hélène sent me to see him. I recall an elegant man, white-haired and well-dressed, but not formal. He was welcoming but vague in relation to my mission. He remembered Iliazd, of course— they had done a book together in the late 1950s. But many characters had appeared in Paris in the 1920s. His remarks sketched an ongoing artistic scene. But Scheler and his recollection were rather faded, and my notes of that interview amounted to a moth-eaten miscellany of recollections. If Hélène had imagined I would return with a vivid portrait of the young Iliazd, we were both disappointed. Memory fades in living persons. However, in a special issue of a *Bulletin du Bibliophile*, 1974, dedicated as an "Hommage à Iliazd," Scheler's description had been vividly detailed:

> I frequented Montparnasse doggedly in the 20s, going almost every evening into the company of Russian sculptors and painters for whom the only thing that mattered was the universe of ideas and forms whose rules and principles they were always calling into question. Their discoveries and innovations attracted me, young man that I was, with a kind of sorcery. Imaginative and enthusiastic, these pioneers knew instinctively how to put their work into high relief.
>
> But I was not the only one excited by this atmosphere of contestation, investigation, and research. After the four years of absurd waste of war, this maelstrom of concepts, sounds, and colors, of gestures and rhythms bringing together all the artists of the world was transformed into all manner of spectacles: *Le Sacre du Printemps, La Boutique Fantasque, Le Tricorne, Apollon Musagète, Le Pas d'acier* along with the magic of *La Creation du Monde, Les Maries de la Tour Eiffel*, in a period which saw simultaneously the ballets of Diaghilev and those of Jean Borlin. The prestige of the *livre de peintre* was a sun rising on the horizon, African art had just received recognition, and a kaleidoscope of exhibitions, balls were put on at the Bullier.
>
> In Montparnasse, the privileged sector, every literary and aesthetic theory confronted every other. The Rotonde was the small fortress of the Franco-Slavic contingent where expressionism, cubism, constructivism, futurism, simultaneism and dada served nightly as the pretext for inexhaustible discussions; while at the Dome James Joyce, Foujita, a solid contingent of French and a small but active

colony of Americans held forth on a variety of matters with a variety of opinions which vacillated from one extreme to another; a few independents, such as Fernand Léger and Zadkine, took their café crème alternately in one café and then another.

Sometimes, in the company of either Charcoune, Larionov, Serge Fotinsky or Lado Gudiashvili (formerly promoted to the position of official painter of the Republic of Georgia) one encounters Iliazd, whose real name is Ilia Zdanevich. But it is at the Café Chameleon, at 146 Boulevard Montparnasse, that one is absolutely certain to encounter this Georgian Dadaist at the end of the day. This is the locale in which he prefers to sit, and since his arrival in Paris, Iliazd has installed there his University of 41 Degrees, indicating the temperature of his intellectual fever and his intention to contribute to the elaboration of the extreme wing of the Russian avant-garde.[4]

Scheler's account paints a compressed portrait of Paris life. Extended activity is presented in a single vivid frame. Left out of the quick sketch of Iliazd were the realities of making a living as a handyman in a garage and as an assistant to a hatmaker, the only specific paying work that left a trace in his archives—except when he was employed by the Delaunays to pack and ship artwork and perform other duties in their studio. He briefly painted scarves with Gala Éluard, another activity documented in brief exchanges (one note asked him to visit to bring her one of these objects). The very informality of these communications, a scribbled note, a card, a pneumatic message, spoke of the systems at work before telephones were widespread in the city—but the activities also painted a picture of a living patched together through connections and odd jobs. Habits of stopping by a particular café played a role in this network as well. Chance encounters provided opportunities for connection or event planning.

A photograph of Iliazd in 1922 pictures a vigorous and energetic young man, his face fresh and eager. He is dressed in a good suit, with a handkerchief in the pocket and a bowler hat on his head. A firsthand description by the émigré writer, Vladimir Pozner, published in the Dutch language journal, *Het Overzicht*, in 1924, paints a striking portrait:

> A young, vigorously built man with short, strong legs . . . he is always well shaved, well washed, with a clean head. In the room where he lives there is a bed, a desk, and a wireless. His room looks like a monk's cell. No heat. Since it is freezing there, the inhabitant is obliged to perform all sorts of exercises of physical culture every morning in order to get warm.

Iliazd in dress outfit after arrival in Paris, 1923. Courtesy of François Mairé and the
Fonds Iliazd

After eight o'clock, Zdanevich visits friends. He has a fondness for feminine
companionship. The two most elegant women in Paris receive him, Madame Salomé Halpern, to whom was dedicated the famous fox-trot "Salomé," and Madame Vera Choukaïeff, whom one never sees though her portrait is everywhere.
He tells them all the stories of the day and goes off content. Towards midnight he
often goes to La Rotonde where he encounters his worst enemies. He never talks
about them. Neither do I. No one does.

. . . Although it is not necessarily apparent, Zdanevich is a very serious man. He never talks about anything he doesn't know about, but then, he knows about everything.[5]

How far does one go in detailing these many acquaintances? Salomé Halpern was from Tbilisi, and Vera Choukaïeff worked with Chanel, perhaps serving as connection for Iliazd's work soon after. The fact of these many connections, some with links to common roots and shared experiences, creates a pattern of a life, bit by bit, piece by piece. Day-to-day realities don't appear within the list of who's who, but rather in its interstices.

A list of domiciles attests to the fact that between his arrival in 1921, when he stayed briefly with Larionov, and the summer of 1937, when he moved to the rue Mazarine apartment still occupied by Hélène when I met her in 1985, he moved almost a dozen times, staying sometimes in a hotel, sometimes being evicted, then moving briefly to the suburbs for work and personal reasons, and then back into Paris. The list, and the fact that the final spot was a modest one, gives some indication of his financial circumstances during those many years.

Lectures and Milieu

Initially, Iliazd stayed with Mikhail Larionov, connecting to the international world of artists in Paris, particularly the French and Russian. He makes no mention of Anglophone communities around Sylvia Beach, Gertrude Stein, or Ernest Hemingway, who had arrived at almost the same time. Differences of language, but also aesthetic temperament, no doubt played a part. Iliazd was focused on bringing the work of the Forty-One Degrees to public attention in this new venue. To do this, he launched a series of lectures. In November 1921, he staged his first lecture in Paris, in French, titled "The New Schools of Russian Poetry." He was introduced by poet Sergei Rafalovich:

> Mr. Ilia Zdanevich, whom you have come to hear tonight, is one of the first, if not the first, champion of Russian Futurism. I will not describe to you what the manifestos of the young Russian Futurists have been, nor what procedures they have employed to make themselves known and to spread their propaganda. . . . Mr. Zdanevich took the Futurism of Marinetti as his point of departure. You are already all familiar with the manifestos of Marinetti. These basically battle against all conventional aesthetics and traditionalist attitudes. It is also the affirmation of the visible and modern reality of life, as it exists in its most vital and intense move-

ment, with everything that applied science, industry and technology bring to bear on ancient forms and rhythms."[6]

Rafalovich distinguished the work of his colleague from that of the Italian futurist. As Iliazd would soon find out, Marinetti's standing had fallen, rather than risen, since the 1910s. The strident militarism of his work, clearly instantiated in his 1911 manifesto, "War, the only Hygiene of the World," was out of sync with the battle-fatigued population of Europe in the early 1920s. In his extended comments, Rafalovich characterized Italian futurism as a form of *presentism* and the Russian as the real *futurism*. The Russians were not merely "taking liberties with grammar" but attempting a complete renovation of language. Rafalovich also called attention to the oral qualities of his poetry, saying "it would be difficult to find the same emotions which he invokes in us by his own rendition of his work."[7]

According to Régis Gayraud, Iliazd began his talk with an extended joke. He said he had tried to invite Victor Hugo and Honoré de Balzac—but was defeated in his *poetic* efforts by the *prosaic* quality of the post office (poetic discourse, he implied, transcended death). This rather labored introduction put in place an opposition between poetic and utilitarian functions for language. The work of Forty-One Degrees, he asserted, was to free language from the limitations of meaning (its utilitarian function) through the scientific exploration of the potential of sound (poetics). The concepts were not unique to the Russians. The French poets had their own engagements with sound symbolism, musical analogies, and onomatopoeia. The highly influential Stéphane Mallarmé had published "La Musique et les Lettres" in 1894 and had played with sound symbolism in "The Demon of Analogy" many years earlier. Other instances of investment in the materiality of visual and vocal properties had been part of the avant-garde in the 1910s and 20s, including the *Calligrammes* of Apollinaire and work published in the pages of *SIC* (whose title *Sons, Idees, Couleurs,* reflects a synaesthetic sensibility) under the stewardship of editor Pierre Albert-Birot.

Iliazd's account reflected his own point of view. Some of the references might have been familiar to his audience, but other names and figures would have been new:

In Russia there exist a number of Schools of poetry which, in spite of the Revolution and the War, have not abandoned the study of pure art. Politics has not touched them. During the last few years, they have made such a huge leap forward, such tremendous progress, such a quantity of discoveries and inventions, and so completely changed our attitudes towards poetry, that all the theories of the Symbolists have been completely surpassed; and I am proud to belong to one of these Schools.

In a few lines, here is the history of these schools and the names of the poets: the pioneer is Khlebnikov, whose first works date from 1908. Very quickly, a group of poets and theoreticians formed around him, of whom the principal were the three Burliuk brothers, Elena Guro, Kruchenykh and a little later, Mayakovsky and Kulbin, a critic and a theoretician. Larionov, in spite of being a painter, played an important role in the destiny of these groups. In the beginning of 1912, we already had a large number of editions being illustrated by Larionov and Goncharova, and well-studied system of poetics at the same era when Marinetti was beginning, tentatively, to form his own ideas in Europe. Marinetti had begun to prepare his propaganda for "The Words in Liberty" and "The Wireless Imagination" when, in Russia, we were already talking about *sdvig* and when syntax had already been demolished. In 1912, the school of the poet Igor Severyanin (Ivanov, Olimpov, Shirokov, etc.) and the school of Vadim Shershenevich (who united around him the poets Bolshakov and Ivnev). At the same time, in Moscow, the poet and theoretician, Sergei Bobrov, in collaboration with the poets Pasternak, Aksenov, Bozhidar and Aseev, launched their school of purism, whose principles were borrowed nine years later by Mr. Ozenfant and others who brought them to Paris and claimed them as their own invention. At the same time, I had begun to work in literature. Guillaume Apollinaire had not even visited the Imprimerie Union on the boulevard St. Jacques when, at the end of 1912, the poets Lotov and Sergeyev made their first Rayonnist works in wet cement. The years 1912 and 1913 were exceedingly rich in new editions which have not yet been seen to this day and filled with novel things. In 1913, in the spring, I was the first to talk of the "Shoe more beautiful than the Venus de Milo" and began a series of meetings and reunions with artists which were tumultuous. . . . In Autumn 1913, in collaboration with Larionov, Goncharova, Fabri . . . I invented "Everythingism" in reaction to the strictness and exclusivity of Futurism. When in the spring of 1914 Marinetti came to see us, we teased him for being so late and offered him editions of our new creations.[8]

Self-mythologizing, historical reconstruction, and a fair amount of hubris and exaggeration were evident throughout the talk, but it was deliberately intended as a provocative event. The latent distinction between futurists and *zaum*niks—Mayakovsky versus Khlebnikov, Kruchenykh, Terentiev, and

Zdanevich—would become more pronounced as the lectures went on. By the time of the seventh lecture, November 1922, a year later, this distinction was reified: "The radically modernist school of poetry in Russia is commonly and crudely designated by the general label of Russian Futurism, just as in France all avant-garde art is called Cubism. However, Russian Futurism is actually divided into two independent schools, the 'Futurist' school, headed by Mayakovsky, and the *zaum* school—I will explain later what this bizarre term means—at the head of which are Kruchenykhh and Zdanevich."[9] He elaborated further:

> The revolutionary climate of years 1917 to 1920 defined the order of things. While the *zaumniki* lived on the periphery in those years, constantly pursuing their activities—Khlebnikov at the front and in the Caucases, Kruchenykh and Zdanevich in Georgia—Mayakovsky was in Moscow where he became one of the most active figures of the day. His monopoly and that of his friends and disciples continued until 1921, when Kruchenykh and Khlebnikov appeared on the Moscow scene. Khlebnikov died the same year from starvation, whereas Kruchenykh increasingly gained solid ground, and, if Mayakovsky, and along with him, Futurism had by then become defined and crystallized, the influence of Kruchenykh and the transmental *zaum* school continued to grow, as Mayakovsky himself acknowledged during a recent visit here.[10]

Though the first lecture, in 1921, was given in the private home of a singer, Olénine d'Alheim, it received critical attention in the press. The young art historian and critic Raymond Cogniat published a review on December 4, 1921:

> Last Sunday there was a small gathering which will no doubt cause a stir in the world of letters. In a peaceful studio in Passy a curious company assembled. Among them, Canudo, Raymond Duncan, Larionov, Pierre Albert-Birot who all seemed more or less interested: Mr. Zdanevich gave his first Paris lecture on the 41 Degrees (which is the name of the movement he described to us). He introduced several genuinely interesting documents and a number of ideas, which, if they are not immediately accessible or assimilable to everyone, cannot help but initiate passionate discussion.[11]

Riccioto Canudo was an Italian film theorist, Raymond Duncan, brother of the famed Isadora, was a dancer, and Pierre Albert-Birot, a well-established publisher-editor with a commitment to visual as well as verbal poetics. This was distinguished company. Cogniat went on with a brief exchange between himself and Iliazd:

> RC: This research into sonority also occupied our poets and one finds all sorts of applications of it: Baudelaire, Verlaine, and Stuart Mill found all sorts of interesting sonorous ideas.
>
> IZ: Yes, but in a different domain from ours. We have tended towards a larger interpretation of the word, towards its unknown sense, that which I dare to call its "transmental" sense.
>
> RC: Mallarmé or Rimbaud?
>
> IZ: Not exactly . . .
>
> RC: Do you have followers among the Dadaists?
>
> IZ: I don't think so, our ideas are quite different.
>
> RC: They destroy, you build?
>
> IZ: Exactly. As I said, I depend upon tradition. I left Russia because there we cannot work any longer for pure art and because we were so isolated, the world knew nothing of our work. It seems that in Paris people will quickly become interested in this sonorous and transmental poetry.[12]

Cogniat's review finished with a description of Larionov, "large, blond and jovial" translating for the smaller, darker Iliazd, both of them full of optimism about the future reception of their work in Paris.

The second lecture, also rendered in French, was delivered in February 1922, at the Faculty of Medicine. In English the title can be read as "41 Degrees Synapsed" or "Sina-pissed" and carries medical and scatalogical meanings. This lecture elaborated his theoretical principles, rather than merely situating them within contemporary poetics.[13] The lecture depended upon a single metaphor, the "malady of pearls," the cure for which was to be found in the clinics of Forty-One Degrees. Here I translate from Gayraud's French version:[14] "This illness consisted in the formation of 'hard grains in the living language.' It occurred in two stages, at first benign and then malignant. The malady affected language in more developed animals and humans. The cells of language, healthy in primitive animals, became more and more specialized as one reached the higher orders of the animal kingdom. The 'malady of pearls' in its benign form promoted the regeneration of language, and thus served some purpose."[15]

The "pearl malady" was analogous to the "grain malady" and caused language to "cake-up," but it is possible "to replace the grains of words with those of other structures if the grains are filled with kernels of similar con-

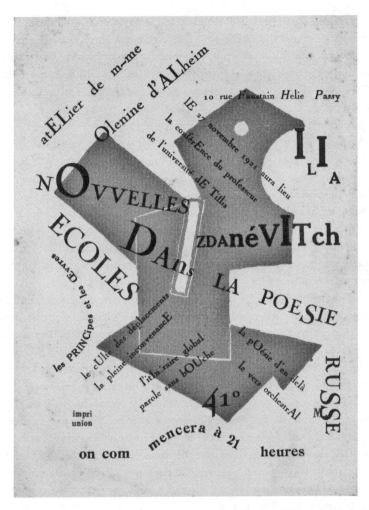

Poster for Iliazd's lecture at the house of singer Marie Olénine d'Alheim, "The New Schools of Russian Poetry," November 27, 1922. Courtesy of François Mairé and the Fonds Iliazd

ception." The text goes on to switch attention to levels of sonorous association in language for which a *sdvig* revelation works to bring to light puns, "phonetic somersaults," and other feats of liberation. He had a three-tiered notion of the ways the *sdvig* coefficient could increase: simple awareness (puns), incomprehensible language (like that of "Gods, apostles and sects," or glossolalia), and his own experiments with *zaum* as direct evocation through pure sonority. Orchestral verse used multiple voices to surpass the limits of the human vocal organ. Whether these principles had been clearly articulated in his lectures in Tbilisi or not, in Paris Iliazd made them explicit. The power of sonority "to act directly on the emotions, and to excite them" was a principle of all *zaum* work, not just his own.

In addition to the *sdvig*, he spoke frequently about *verbal mass* and *global itinerary*. But the verbal mass of words, their sonorous value, had found graphic expression in the volumes and values Iliazd created with letters in combination. The global itinerary was a form of research that could be found just behind someone—not by turning, "but by taking a trip around the world in order to come back to the same place." Another tenet of his early poetics was the creation of a "word without a mouth."[16] Unuttered, unspoken, but sensually available language reflected *zaum* as bodily, a physical, corporeal level of experience, also realized in his typographic handling of poetic expression.

Drawing on Gayraud's work again, it was possible to get a sense of the ways each of the first seven lectures Iliazd delivered within the year of his arrival dealt in some detail with the poetic theories of Forty-One Degrees. His tone was playful, humorous, often stretching elaborate figures of discourse which rendered the details of his argument absurd. He frequently referred to Terentiev's *Seventeen Tools of Nonsense*, and he employed elaborate puns and wordplay. A lecture on April 16, 1922, "A House on the SH(it)ore," subtitled "Intellectuals and Empire," used the image of Siamese twin sisters, Zozefa and Roza, to represent the entangled relation between the intelligentsia and the empire. Iliazd gave the name Pushkin and Tyutchev to the two children they bore. Tyutchev had been preoccupied with anal eroticism, and Pushkin's work, Iliazd suggested, could be read entirely in terms of obscenity. The linguistic and poetic logic of this work extended Iliazd's preoccupations with infantile sexuality in his own work.

Curiously, Iliazd suggested that the use of *zaum* had not only forced the abandonment of ordinary orthography but had compelled the *zaum*niks to abandon writing for the use of wax disk recordings. If Iliazd ever made such recordings, they did not survive.

A 1922 letter to Marinetti (the opening of which was cited in chapter 3) attested to his ongoing project—as well as his desire to continue relations with the Italian, at once aligning himself with futurism and keeping distance, as per the statements above:

In Paris I have already given a preliminary lecture the program of which you will find enclosed and I will reopen a branch of the University at the "Closerie des Lilas." The French school, like the Russian one, will be opened in order to diffuse our works to the French and Russian public.

You are still the most energetic and reliable leader of the struggle of contemporary art, and you are also the master of our movement, and I ask you to take part in the opening of 41 Degrees which will be at the end of January or the beginning of February.

We ask you to reply since we hope that the committed struggle which we talked about in Moscow will continue and even grow, since the last few years have devastated Europe to such a great extent.

Send us a few words and a paper we can proclaim at the opening of the University of 41 Degrees, as a symbol of our friendship and our homage to the founder and leader of Futurism.

Please accept, dear leader, my most respectful and sincere homage.[17]

Within a few months of his arrival in Paris, however, Iliazd began to be discouraged. He reported his disappointment with the Paris scene in a letter to Ali Bey, with whom he had worked at the Near East Relief office in Constantinople. The letter indicates mood as much as detail:

February 9, 1922

The artistic milieu which I had hope to find here, and by which I was so attracted, is faded and powerless. Modernism in art, for which I have struggled all my life, has become transformed into a new academicism, dry and rigid. There is no fresh blood here, no new ideas. Everything has become stuck in an impasse from which I do not know myself how to exit. The principal reason for this must be the war. The end of European culture is inevitable and we Russians have known that for a long time.[18]

Nonetheless, the chronology of Iliazd's activities for 1922 contains more than three dozen entries. In addition to dates and locations for seven lectures, there are notes about contact with Francis Picabia by letter, meetings with Robert and Sonia Delaunay, a proposal for a Swedish ballet, letters from his relative, Jeanne Mojnevsky, an indication that he worked briefly, and other matters. He organized a banquet on the occasion of a visit by Mayakovsky in November 1922 and also became involved in the organization of Russian émigré artists, OUDAR, with which he quickly parted ways to establish another organization, Tcherez (also in 1922). These organizations created a series of "*bals*"—entertainment events that showcased talents in a variety-show format. Posters for the *bals*, notes from various contacts, and other ephemera were the testimonials to these activities.

Iliazd continued to give his public lectures. The bilingual poster announcing his May 12, 1922, lecture, "L'Éloge Iliazde," was the most graphically compelling. The hand-drawn letters spell out the address, the title, and some bits of textual commentary. "The praise of Iliazd for himself, named the angel, cretin, sluggard, traitor, assassin, shithead etc." can be read in French next to a Russian text. It read, in translation:

> A bastard talent, lazy, idiotic cretin, a dirty (Turkish) king. On the day of his birth it was shown that he had been conceived triumphantly with three teeth and with many curs. He crawls like a crab and is full of vices and prophecies. After many other things, he will talk of pants which have already been worn by someone else. He will talk of his language which is "GI." He will talk of his secrets and illnesses, his voyage to Albania, the tender record, the donkey in place of the man and vice versa, the sculptural occupation, the half of Bizke-Bizke, the two and a half idols, the half of which is a noisemaker, and he will explain his last play by means of the Holy Prohibition (Ghost) (Saint Interd'esprit), and Orpheus with the Stiff Cadaver (characters in the play), as well as the unmentionable and unacceptable possibility of a play in the bedroom of some children.[19]

The mock-up for the poster had been sliced diagonally in several places and then reassembled into a collage so that the parts appear to jitter slightly. Black rules separated the several sections, and these, too, were slashed and shifted out of alignment. The poster is disturbing on several levels—the self-denigration of the text, the uneven hand-drawn type with its erratic size and scale change, and the violent ruptures in the graphic field. All register their pathology in various ways, even as they express the transformative effect rendered on language through material intervention.

The lectures continued and attracted critical attention. A long essay by the journalist André Germain, written in response to the lecture given on November 28, 1922, appeared in *Créer* in early 1923. Germain referred to Iliazd using a phrase borrowed from the Russian writer, Dmitri Merezhkovsky, "a pig who flies in the sky," citing Tristan Tzara's descriptive phrase, "a trickster of fleas and dancing master of flies." The long essay tracked Iliazd's development and course through the Russian scene and into Tbilisi during the aftermath of the revolution and then to Paris and his presentations. Germain praised Iliazd:

His greatness lies in his having, in the depths of Georgia, already superseded and conquered Dadaism as well as Futurism, and with all the ardor of dizzying adventures which he understood in the peaks above his native land of Elbrus, topping even the craziest dreams of his more timid European brothers. He has rendered Soupault, Tzara, and Éluard reactionary and totally outmoded; these battered poets have come tonight, however, to show their loyalty and homage to this little brother who, so cavalierly, has surpassed them—an exceptional act of confraternity since in general the demi-extremists hate nothing so much as a super-extremist.[20]

But this November 28 lecture lacked all optimism. A major figure, the *zaum* poet Khlebnikov, had died in June of that year. Mayakovsky had just

Poster for Iliazd's lecture, "The Praise of Iliazd," May 12, 1922. Courtesy of François Mairé and the Fonds Iliazd

been in Paris a week earlier, honored at a banquet Iliazd helped organize. But in this lecture, his comments on Mayakovsky turned negative. He characterized him as "the poet of the revolution, of new ideas, a strong and varied poet," but then went on to condemn the predictability of his verse on formal grounds, "the monotony of his rhythms, the inevitability of his rhyme."[21] Finally, he registered his disappointment at the lack of recognition from Mayakovsky for his own work. The lecture ended with a morbid pronouncement of the end of Russian lyricism from internal defects. Only a handful of lectures followed in the next few years, and the theme of *zaum* dropped away.

In December 1922, he took a trip to Berlin. A safe-transit visa, an invitation letter from Viktor Shklovsky, and Iliazd's notes on the experience—as well as the text of the talk he gave there and soon after his return—give a good sense of the extent to which humor had drained out of his approach. When he returned to Paris in January 1923, he delivered a lecture entitled "Berlin and Its Literary Fraud." He saw careerism and opportunism among the Russian writers in Berlin, including a highly polarized competition between two camps, one led by Andrei Bely, the symbolist, spiritualist poet, and one by Ilya Erhenberg, whose strong Bolshevik and revolutionary beliefs were well known. He saw publishers vying for manuscripts, and a slick, rapid turnover in literary output driven by desires for real or imagined profits. These same publishers recommended to Iliazd that he write boulevard romances if he wished to become successful.[22] He returned to Paris angry and disillusioned, filled with "such disgust that even now it makes me want to vomit just with the memory of what I have seen and heard."[23]

In February 1923, Iliazd distributed an announcement for his forthcoming book, *Ledentu as Beacon* (*Lidantiu Faram*) and, soon after, started regularly using the name Iliazd (a contraction of syllables from his first and last names into a single word).[24] At the time, it felt useful to distinguish himself from his brother, Kirill Zdanevich, who had also arrived to spend time in Paris. Work on this project must have begun to consume considerable time and energy. But before its publication in October, other momentous events occurred.

The Bearded Heart (Coeur à Barbe), July 1923

As should be clear from the multiple sources cited above, the evidence in the archive for this active period was abundant, and between published and manuscript materials, reconstruction of events can be achieved with only minor transitions to provide a coherent narrative. Such coherence is problematic as well as necessary. The smoothing over covers not just gaps but emotional peaks and valleys. Affect is stripped away from evidence, unless it is explicitly described. Iliazd's activities within the émigré community were affected by events in the Soviet Union, and loyalties split along lines of political affiliation.

A letter written in 1924 recorded his disgust with these internal politics.[25] Iliazd noted that he established the artistic entity Tcherez to provide a platform for organizing benefit events. These informal arts organizations had no funding, offices, or bylaws, and were modeled on similar groups that had created exhibits and events in Russia in the 1910s. In the postwar circumstances, many émigrés were in need of assistance, however little they wanted to advertise this fact. The *bals* and other events generated some modest revenue. Among the many activities documented in Iliazd's papers in the period from his arrival in Paris until he moved to the suburbs in 1926 are those in which he participated through planning or presence. For instance, an exhibition of Russian artists, organized by OUDAR, the Union of Russian Artists, opened at the gallery La Licorne on February 2, 1923, with works by Viktor Bart, Kirill Zdanevich, and Chaim Soutine. This and similar events served as the basis of an article published by an L. Volguine describing the "Artistic Life of Russian Artists and Painters in Montparnasse from 1921-24," which prompted the letter of clarification noted above. Addressed to the head of OUDAR, and signed by various persons, the letter stated that the group had been founded by Russian artists "with the goal of providing aid to each other. Not only was the group completely free of links with political emigration, but it was somewhat hostile to such connections." The letter does state the group's leftish sympathies and attempts to establish artistic links through its loyalty and connections with the Soviet Union.[26]

In February 1923, Iliazd was one of the main organizers of the *Bal Transmental* at the Salle Bullier. The poster stated explicitly that "Iliazd, Kruchenykh, and Terentiev are the creators of Transmental poetry without images, without descriptions, without ordinary words."[27] In April, an event organized by Tcherez in honor of the Russian painter Boris Bojnev included participation by a long list of writers and artists, including Antonin Artaud, Georges Auric, Lizica Codreanu, Robert Delaunay, Paul Dermée, Paul Éluard, Vincent Huidobro, Fernand Léger, Jules Pascin, Pierre Reverdy, Georges Ribemont-Dessaignes, Phillippe Soupault, and Tristan Tzara. The presence of so many illustrious figures willing to share the stage and evening appears to be testimony to community cooperation on a shared undertaking.

N. Granovsky.   Construction spartiate

PROGRAMME

SERGE ROMOFF. Éloge de Tchérez.
GERM. TAILLEFERRE. Quatuor : Modéré. Intermède. Final vif,
   exécuté par QUATUOR CAPELLE (Mlle FERNANDE CA-
   PELLE, ALICE PIANTINI, MARGUERITE LUTZ, MA-
   RIKA BERNARD).
CÉLINE ARNAUD. Cavatine de marées. Jeux d'anneaux. Poèmes
   inédits, — dits par ANTONIN ARTAUD, de l' ,, Atelier ''.
VINCENT HUIDOBRO. Océan ou dancing. Globe trotter. Poèmes.
MAX JACOB. Poèmes des cornets à dés, — dits par PIERRE
   BERTIN, de l'Odéon.
Diversités divertissantes. Conférence de TRISTAN TZARA.

TCHÉREZ
Galerie La Licorne (110. Rue La Boëtie - Paris VIII°)

Dimanche 29 Avril 1923
à 21 heures
SOIRÉE DU POÈTE
BORIS BOJNIEFF

Program for Tcherez event organized by Iliazd, April 29, 1923. Courtesy of François Mairé and the Fonds Iliazd

Given these apparent successes, the *Bearded Heart* event organized by Tcherez that took place on July 6, 1923, was expected to follow a smooth course. The event was one in a long series of such activities that had begun with the first Russian *bal*, *"La Fête de Nuit"* ("The Night Festival"), on June 30, 1922. The *bals* contributed vivid color and variety to the Paris scene. For one week in March 1923, the program of Tcherez included eight different events—lectures, an exhibit, readings and discussions of dynamic music, Russian poetry, decoration in Russian theater, and experimental aesthetic activities of various kinds.[28] Iliazd was evidently actively engaged in Parisian artistic life, in spite of setbacks and disappointments.

Iliazd designed the poster for the *Bearded Heart* event, and it is one of the few French-language projects in which he uses typographic techniques that

Poster designed by Iliazd for the *Soirée du Coeur à Barbe* (*The Bearded Heart*), July 6, 1923. Courtesy of François Mairé and the Fonds Iliazd

echo his *zaum* graphic style. He broke the words into letters and played with their arrangement without regard for units of sound. For instance, he did not present the *ée* of *Soirée* as a single unit but treated the letters as two distinct graphic elements. The dynamism of the page is generated by attention to the letters, then the visual form of a curve, block, and line. The playfulness of the poster, however, could not prevent the disaster of the evening's events.

Iliazd's account here is excerpted from a much longer piece about his relations with Paul Éluard, composed between 1965 and 1969, which will be cited further ahead as well:

> Among the Dadaists with whom we were particularly involved was Tristan Tzara, who lived in the Rue Delambre at the time and whom I had known along with Éluard.
>
> In the organization of the *soirées* he had helped by taking care of the posters and pressing people into service of various kinds, and the society (Tcherez) did not exclude him from its program. This is the reason why Tcherez came to have the idea of organizing an evening for the benefit of Tzara, the evening of the *Bearded Heart* in which the key piece was the play of Tzara's, "Le Coeur à Gaz" ["The Gas Heart"], which was to have been performed in the Théâtre Michel. At this time the Dada group was fragmented, but I thought that Tcherez would present a neutral ground. The explosion which ensued showed not only that we were wrong, but also brought about the downfall of Tcherez.
>
> The explosive part of the program was the entrance of Marcel Herrand who was supposed to recite the poems of Tzara, Éluard and Cocteau.[29] Tzara had made this selection since he directed the program for the evening, and after the Bozhnev soirée where Éluard shared the program with Tzara, I had no idea that the choice of Herrand could provoke any protests. But no one had thought to ask Éluard. In addition, of course, there was Cocteau's name on the program, and the two together were totally unacceptable to Éluard. The night before I had received a letter from Éluard taking back his promise to write the preface for *Ledentu* and the next day, arriving at the theater, I met him at the corner of the street. There was no question of his changing his mind about the preface, but he needed to be escorted into the hall. Whoever was in charge had been warned of the possibility of an incident and instructed to deny Éluard—and Breton also—entry to the room.[30]

Lucien Scheler's written account in an homage to Iliazd published in 1974 recalled the first half of the program in particular detail:

> The future surrealists, Aragon, Breton, and Éluard, had proposed to boycott the event owing to their hostility towards Tristan Tzara and also Jean Cocteau, whose names shared the program. On the schedule were a number of musical pieces by Stravinsky, Milhaud, Auric, and Satie, short films and poems of Cocteau, Soupault, and Tzara, and a one-act piece by the latter, "Coeur à Gaz," as well as a number of *zaum* poems in Slavic [sic], an invention of Iliazd, in which the vocabularies were,

by inflection and onomatopoeia, given multiple and simultaneous sense so that abstract and concrete values were revealed at the same time.

As soon as the three clacks sounded, Pierre de Massot read a proclamation and then cried, "Picasso, dead on the field of battle!" Breton, seeing that the painter was present in the room, provoked the first incident of the evening. Followed by Desnos and Peret, the future author of *Nadja* jumped up on the stage and gave de Massot such a strong rap with his cane that he broke the poor man's arm. The spectators, disgusted, began to take Breton to task—and not without reason— and Tzara, anxious above all to restore calm, hastened to call the police to put out those making the disturbance—an act for which even his supporters later condemned him. However, the atmosphere did not exactly quiet down, and when Marcel Herrand began to recite a poem of Soupault's, Aragon, who had a completely striking appearance thanks to a black silk shirt under his smoking jacket in the manner of Judex or Fantomas, called to Éluard and the two began to attack Soupault in the most insulting terms possible and the whole mess began again.

The film projection began and had a momentarily calming effect, and then *zaum* poems were displayed on the screen which revived the uproar—but being supporters of Iliazd, myself and my companions, Lado and Serge, refused to get involved in this combat between troublemakers and rabble-rousers. In any case, we did not want to get thrown out before we had a chance to see the rest of the program featuring our charming friend, Lisica Codreanu, who had already, at the start of the evening, performed a number of dances in costumes designed by Sonia Delaunay and a set of Theo von Doesburg and was still to interpret the work of Iliazd in choreographic terms while he recited it—a poem destined to fill out the last act of the "Coeur à Gaz" which had been determined, during rehearsal, to be a bit thin. Suddenly we spotted Iliazd, followed by Lisica, as they appeared, jumping out furiously from between some props to declaim their piece. Paying careful attention to the quality of his phonemes, Iliazd punctuated his inspired delivery by pounding his cane on the stage—an enormous cane reminiscent of that of the caricatures of Balzac. In spite of the grace and talent of Lisica, the general hilarity overwhelmed everything, and our applause and appreciation were lost in the final hubbub. As the curtain fell, we took off, leaving Iliazd to finish out the evening with his fellow organizers while we went to offer our support and encouragement to the lovely dancer, trying to overcome her slight disappointment by taking her to dine in Montparnasse.[31]

But after their departure, a significant scene occurred: "When the curtain rose on Tzara's 'Coeur à Gaz,' a battle broke out between the two Dada clans.

The police arrived. Who let them into the room? Some people say it was the director, others say it was Serge Romoff. More likely it was a frightened member of the public."[32]

Éluard's distress, caused by being placed on a program with Tzara and Cocteau without his knowledge, was documented in his own account of the evening, given as testimony in front of a lawyer, Maître Boulard, and witnessed by Breton, Desnos, Aragon, and Picasso. Iliazd noted: "In order to answer the charges brought by Tzara, Éluard wrote an account of the incident for a lawyer on the Boulevard Montparnasse, of which I kept the original, while the dossier of the case stayed with the lawyer, who was not retained, and therefore, it was eventually thrown away."[33]

Éluard's detailed account noted that he had written to Zdanevich in advance to be removed. Considerable confusion existed about what precisely occurred, but Éluard, who was present, asked for an invitation to read. Several people in the room protested, and Tzara pointed them out to the police. As Tzara's play was being performed, Éluard rose to explain his attitude. By his account, "the actors, technical crew, and personnel threw themselves on him, turning him back down the ramp, and breaking several lamps in the process."[34]

Éluard's and Iliazd's accounts both agreed that Tzara attempted to tear the large cane out of Iliazd's hands, while Iliazd protested, "No, not with my cane." The prefecture of police prohibited the second night's performance. Éluard further claimed that "all the Dada performances previously organized by Mr. Tzara have been of a scandalous and anti-theatrical character. The public always protested violently. . . ."[35]

Iliazd did not take sides in the argument. Some years later, he wrote to Tzara, saying clearly that in the matter of the Tcherez incident, his attitude had been one of "non-intervention."[36] Éluard was ashamed of the incident, as he said in a note written to Iliazd a few days later. The trial of Tzara v. Éluard did not take place, but the effects of the incident had a considerable effect. The rupture between the Dadaist and the nascent surrealists was made evident, again, from "Approaching Éluard": "The battle of the 'Coeur à Gaz' finished a lot of things. It marked the end of the Dada movement and also of the group Tcherez. A sad and unfitting end, with the participation of the police and the law."[37]

The incident tormented Éluard, who fell on hard times. A year later, Gala Éluard organized a sale of the art collection he had assembled. The sale took place on July 3, 1924: "We were all present at this funeral of an era. Several nasty comments addressed by Serge Ferat about the photomontages of Max Ernst only added to the melancholy of the afternoon. . . . Were we aware of what was happening? For a year we had lived day to day thinking everything would work out. The catastrophe of the *Coeur à Barbe* and the departure of Éluard only took on their real significance after awhile. . . . Dada was dead and Surrealism was born."[38]

Interpretation of the Events

What to make of the events of the evening of *The Bearded Heart*? The multiple accounts all agreed on the specifics of what occurred—Éluard was annoyed, struggles broke out, some physical acts of violence took place, Éluard was to be charged, and all the legal proceedings were dropped. But beyond these basic descriptions, what can be said? What was the cause of the tension between Tzara and Éluard? Why was Herrand controversial and Cocteau's presence a problem? One may read into these accounts all kinds of motivations and crosscurrents of personal and aesthetic conflict. But they are not present in the texts or documents; only the outcomes and actions were described, the external manifestations of these tensions. Causality is specious at best, and guessing at psychological states is mere fiction.

The case provides a perfect example of the differences between reading *between* and reading *across* materials. The correlation of the accounts is produced by reading *across* the accounts written by Lucien Scheler, Iliazd, and Paul Éluard. We can compare their versions and see alignments with some difference of inflection or importance, but the materials reinforce each other. Scheler was writing in the context of an homage, not at the moment of struggles for power or control over the narrative. Reading *between* is impossible here—no amount of speculative projection tells us what else occurred, what the protagonists were thinking or feeling, or how they processed their own behavior. We have a note of regret in Éluard's communication with Iliazd, and an account of his desperate circumstances a year later. A certain dissonance arises from our sense of these figures as established features of an aesthetic history—what would French surrealism be without Éluard?—and the difficulties they were facing in their lives in material and social terms. History flattens the past, of course, into figures whose complexity is reduced to caricature at worst and cartoon at best. Motivation escapes without documentation, and even where it exists, its relation to events has to be questioned. Are explanations self-justifications? Apologies? Every retelling refigures events according to the agenda of whoever gives the account.

Iliazd's life mapped onto, around, and through these events. He was almost thirty years old, and the questions of what the displacement had cost
him and how he was to use his position in Paris as a platform were not easily
answered. Nor were options readily available. His circumstances trapped
him alongside the need to make a living while promoting the contributions
of *zaum* poetics in its final fully realized phase. To say that a work's moment
is past even before it appears is complicated. What is the moment of a work
if not that in which it appears? But the conceptual foundation of *zaum* and
the futurist agendas it served had eroded by the early 1920s, and the documents attested to that realization. Even as *Ledentu* appeared, in the aftermath of *The Bearded Heart,* Iliazd wrote its epitaph. A memorial work, monumental, it was an ending. Nothing in the archive suggests that Iliazd had
any sense of what lay ahead. We cannot extract or project a teleological arc
from that point of termination. The odds that Iliazd would cease his work
as an artist and poet were just as strong as those that he would not. All biographical trajectories are written after events; nothing predicts what will
occur, and reading causality is problematic, at best, and often spurious in its
overdetermination.

Ledentu

The major artistic event of Iliazd's life in 1923 was the publication of
Ledentu as Beacon (*Lidantiu Faram*). Strong graphic and poetic continuity
connected this work with the four *dras* published in Tbilisi. The typography,
book design, and conceptual foundations were more ambitious and more
polished. The cover design, an inlay collage designed and executed in cork
and leather by Naum Granovsky, was an elegantly accomplished work, far
from the paper wrappers and hand-sewn or stapled or pinned pamphlets
produced in the 1910s. The production signaled the importance of the book.
This was not an ephemeral, rapidly produced object, but a work whose very
appearance signaled that it was a publication of substance. But the book
was simultaneously a final and retrospective work, already out of sync by
the time it appeared. It was a culmination, but also a termination for this
period of Iliazd's poetics. It contained the fullest expression of Iliazd's ideas
of orchestral verse and *zaum*, as well as his typographic scoring, but it fell
into a void.

The subscription announcement contained twenty-one brief attestations
of support. Iliazd cited the individuals who had praised his work, among
them Tristan Tzara, Phillippe Soupault, Robert Delaunay, and Filippo Mari-

Cover of *Ledentu as Beacon*, with collage by Naum Granovsky (Paris: Forty-One Degrees, 1923). Courtesy of François Mairé and the Fonds Iliazd

netti, as well as his Russian colleagues. Forty-One Degrees listed offices in
Paris, Moscow, and Peking, a joke on Iliazd's part:

> Subscription notice for Ledentu
> Some new thoughts on Iliazd:
>> Rafalovich: "The final scrutiny"
>> Soudekine: "The millionaire angel"

Terentiev: "The tender record"

Kruchenykh: "The best pastime"

T. Tzara: "The most resolute and decisive master of the alphabet"

Ph. Soupault: "Nothing is finished for him"

R. Delaunay: "You are the true French genius"

F. T. Marinetti: "The only real Russian Futurist poet"

A. Remizov: "The little Turk has arrived"

M. Gorky: "We have had enough talk"

Charchoune: "The professor who signed a contract with the operetta"

Mayakovsky: "The fake crab"

V. Shklovsky: "Pushing and Zda" [Zda is short for Zdanevich]

Bogatyrev: "Ostrovsky and Zda"

V. Bart: "Zda has surpassed Barkov"

G. Ivanov: "The only real man in Paris

Revue La Veille: "The sleight-of-hand tricks of a prestidigitator"

A. Levinson: "If there were a congress of medicine tomorrow in Paris, Zdanevich would find himself in the podium"

O. Zadkine: "Napoleon of the attic"

A. Feder: "An excellent dancer, but . . ."

Iliazd himself: "A talentless cad, traitor, idiot, and dirty bastard"[39]

None of these were comments on the book, or its text and design, just endorsements for the author. Responses would come after its publication, mainly in the form of personal notes and correspondence. After the *Bearded Heart* falling out with Paul Éluard, Georges Ribemont-Dessaignes, a writer well known in the Paris Dada scene, wrote the preface for the book. Iliazd himself described *Ledentu* this way, also in the text from the late 1960s:

> During this time, I worked on my fifth *zaum* play, which can be roughly translated as "the face of the donkey, the accused donkey, or the donkey accuser" which was dedicated to my friend Ledentu who had been killed in an accident in 1917 on returning from the Front. When he had been in Georgia he had been responsible, along with my brother Kirill and myself, for discovering Pirosmani, the Georgian naïve painter. The poem, *Ledentu,* was composed thanks to the help of Dimitri Snegaroff in his Imprimerie Union (Blvd. St. Jacques) where all my later editions were also printed.[40]

Ledentu had a higher degree of sophistication and development than earlier futurist books, including those of Iliazd. André Markowicz remarked that

Interior pages of *Ledentu as Beacon* (Paris: Forty-One Degrees, 1923). Courtesy of François Mairé and the Fonds Iliazd

every time he opened the book he was reminded of the comment about it made by Jean Cocteau, "This book is star-like." For Markowicz, and perhaps Cocteau, the reference was meant to suggest a connection to Stéphane Mallarmé's "constellationary" *Un Coup de Dés* (*A Throw of the Dice*).[41] The timing of its variations and sequences is carefully calibrated from the very first page through the last. The first open pair of pages were punctuated by dense black letters printed in high contrast. The following pair continued this compositional approach on the left while putting the grey, composed, evenly spaced and neatly arranged lines of orchestral verse on the right-hand page as a foil. These modes alternated, so that the imaginative impact of the typographic invention never tired the reader's eye. When Iliazd exceeded the large-scale display fonts and needed a word as tall as the page, he went into the ornament drawers and composed letters from decorative elements. He was intent on creating variable volumes as well as patterns and rhythms. The results were stunning. Unlike the renowned pages composed by Lazar El Lissitzky for the chapter openings of *For the Voice*, published the same year (1923), Iliazd's work remained fully linguistic. This was the typography of *zaum*, of poetry, not type elements put at the service of picture-making. The visual graphic qualities of type as an affective and inflective system had their full dramatic presence on the page in this work, expressive of sound and feeling. Nothing was left to chance.[42] Every typographic design decision was at the service of the text.

Since *zaum* was an invention, there are no fixed relations between the sounds and their graphical representation. No one spoke in *zaum*; it was purely literary. Though intended, at least in principle, for recitation, the plays were difficult to pronounce. As Janecek has noted, "the correspondence between written and oral language would be highlighted were it not for the absence of an *a priori oral* correspondent." He goes on to say that the "*zaum* word is a precise visual representation of itself."

Ledentu contains a pronunciation key, a feature lacking in the earlier plays. According to Janecek, the scoring shows "a fully developed system which included not only stress, but vowel reduction, consonantal elisions and so forth, as well as . . . tempo, pitch, volume."[43]

Iliazd made use of two crucial visual properties of the page—the capacity to form an arrangement of lines in orchestral relations and the use of different typefaces and sizes to establish the relative values of stress and to indicate "character." Iliazd considered orchestral scoring one of his main contributions to contemporary poetics. As he had stated clearly in 1921, "Orchestral verse, invented by me in 1913, pushes the work of the liberation of poetic language in a new direction. We consider 'orchestral verse' poetry written for several voices along a particular theme. The voices speak, all at the same time, sometimes synchronized (the moment of the chorus) sometimes individually. In orchestral verse, poetic language is immediately and definitively liberated."[44]

In some instances, orchestral scoring forced actors to speak in unison, while in other cases, it was used for different texts recited simultaneously. In *Ledentu* five corpses served as a chorus, and the sounds on which they were to coincide were aligned vertically. *Ledentu* was never performed, and it can be argued that it was the performance on the page that Iliazd emphasized in this work, not as a substitute for live production, but as an equivalent.

Again, Djordjadze provided the summaries that I paraphrase: Themes of representation and likeness, the power of images, doubles, murders, and linguistic play wove through this homage to the lost companion, Ledentu. The action began with Iliazd's descent into Hell to bury Lilith, the woman in him, still present from the earlier *dras*. The woman was guarded by five stinking cadavers and a nauseating Holy Spirit who greeted him in the name of "god the donkey" while the cadavers responded by saying, "he belongs to mother."[45] Then a realist painter appeared and did a portrait that all five corpses adored for its conventional realism. Iliazd was having fun and promoting the superiority of futurist experiments. But then the portrait reproached the painter, accusing him of making her in the image of Melnikova, by whom, apparently, Iliazd was still haunted even in his Paris days. Ledentu appeared and made a new portrait, Non-Likeness, and this revived the woman. Then the portrait and the woman made love in spite of the fact that the Holy Spirit was telling them the portrait was his mother and that they must all leave Hell. The revived woman attacked the realist portrait and then a whole series of murders ensued. Non-Likeness destroyed Likeness, the five cadavers assaulted the revived woman who insulted them, the nauseating Spirit attacked the cadavers, the realist painter killed the Spirit, Ledentu killed the realist painter. Finally Ledentu, acting as the beacon of the title, led the revived woman and Non-Likeness out of the abyss.

Iliazd's radical aesthetics were apparent here. The power of nonrepresentational art was so strong that it could even raise the dead, since it was Non-Likeness who revived the woman. The fury of the woman at being painted in the Likeness of Melnikova suggested Iliazd's desire to be free of the actress and her image so that Lilith/Ilia could come into his/her own.

André Markowicz explained to us that the language is carefully and thoroughly organized in this play. The Spirit spoke only in consonants, in a language without breath and virtually unpronounceable. The only vowel he used was an *I* borrowed from Church Slavonic to indicate a degree of solemnity. The five ugly realism-oriented women spoke in grating voices, one in a lisp, one in abrupt tones with clicks and brutal brusque commands and outbursts, one in all vowels, soft and liquid, and two in coarse idiom. All had names suggestive of necrological, scatological, and sexual references. The realist painter was depicted as a lisping phony, impotent and ineffectual. He salivated and used diminutives while the living portrait spoke in a tongue close to Russian. The portrait of Non-Likeness was virile, hard, with lots of "j" and "ch" and "k," "which recalls the 'chacadam' of the sorcerers invented by Khlebnikov."[46] Still, the play ended on a note of greater resolution and hope than the earlier ones.

Iliazd said he finished the manuscript while he was en route to Paris, during the year he spent in Constantinople. Though published in 1923, *Ledentu*, like the other plays in the *Aslaablitchia* cycle, can only be understood as part of the earlier concerns of futurism. *Zaum* was the activity most central to Iliazd's futurist aesthetics, its most unique invention. Iliazd embraced the conviction that the material of language could be transformed to replace the impossibly worn-out poetics of the past. Iliazd did the same with his typography, exploiting the tonal color and weight of type, making it work as visual and emotional impact through a set of radical transformations. No other writer or designer produced such an extended, sustained, and systematic typographic innovation.

Iliazd believed the primary significance of words inhered in their sounds. He was far from the structuralist world of modern linguistics, with its emphasis on arbitrary values and systems of relations. But he was not alone in studying sound symbolism and its impact. The linguist Roman Jakobson made the poetic and communicative functions of language one and the same, with sound reinforcing meaning. But Iliazd remained committed to an opposition that was not shared by Jakobson—between an emotional language and a rational one. He made this clear in his 1921 lecture, "New Schools":

> The word is always dualistic. In the word, the universe is known and understood rationally by logical knowledge, by sense. Sense limits the birth of the word in a practice. At the same time, sense indicates the place of fact, its position. The phonetics of a word indicate the substance of the object in its transordinary sense. The world which is found beyond the frontiers of reason and rationality, the world of instincts, the world of intuition, that is what the sounds talk to us about. Each sound has its quality, its character, its nature. For this reason, ordinarily, the sense of that a word can be different whether the words are made of the same sounds or not, and words of similar sense can be made of different sounds. The world of sound and the world of sense are the two poles of our life, the two roads on which we travel. This is eternal dualism, the sky and the earth, night and day, body and soul, reason and intuition, thought and emotion . . .[47]

In other comments, Markowicz referred to a draft of notes in the archive that appeared to be an intended "postface" to *Ledentu*. Iliazd's text was direct, blunt, and poignant:

> This book is a crown on the tomb of my dead friend, and it is a crown on the tomb of everything we brought to life during ten years. It is ten years since we began to paint our faces, organize our battles, and print manifestos every day or make books by hand.

We threatened to transform the world, reconstruct the earth, and we glori-
fied a new spirit. With a stroke of the pen, we made masterpieces, we wrote
poems in three words and brought out books with blank pages. In all of these
risks, and errors, and broken glass, we discovered laws, and set ourselves to build.
We got lost in the world of abstraction, of games of spirit and sound and words
and ideas.

And now we know that everything has remained the same, everything is as it
was. We know that our youth was useless, and that it is useless to claim we tri-
umphed when all we were was young.

This book finishes the second period of my work, the second period of modernism, which has lasted five years. The idea of *zaum* typography has been taken
to the point of perfection. This is not a decline. This is the peak. Having attained
it, I abandon this book. Farewell youth, *zaum,* the mind set, the long road of an
acrobat of equivocation, and all, all, all.[48]

A handful of responses to *Ledentu* remained among the correspondence
and notes. A note from Jean Cocteau thanked him, as does a letter from an
intermediary writing on behalf of Marinetti, who "very much admired your
book." Additional brief notes of appreciation from colleagues or critics making vague promises of mentions ahead communicated very little. Vladimir
Pozner wrote a notice about the book, calling Iliazd "a babbling poet . . . for
whom I have great esteem."[49] He commented on the dramatic typography—
"the sort of eyechart one finds at the oculist"—and the cover with its "bits
of foil wrappers from candy bars, gilded strips, and cigarette cork." And he
wondered if the leather cover is actually donkey skin, which he hesitates
to touch.[50] André de Massot was more exuberant: "One is dazzled glancing
through this incredible book," but he notes that it is "written in *zaum* which
makes it almost indecipherable."[51] Indeed, this was the problem, the book
was very difficult—unfamiliar in concept, unique in appearance, and linguis-
tically and poetically complex and dense.

A letter from Viktor Shklovsky expressed a more direct and informed
appreciation:

Iliazd has transformed all of his enormous talent into an artistic experience. He is
a writer for writers. He has succeeded in elucidating the pronounceable and sonorous sides of words. But the *zaum* of Zdanevich is not simply the use of words
denuded of sense, it is the deprivation of the sense of the word in order to excite
a whole ocean of senses, which gives birth to many different meanings. The typographic side of Zdanevich's work is one of the most curious successes in con-

temporary art. Zdanevich uses typographic composition not merely as a means of noting words, but as an artistic material. Every writer knows that writing provokes specific and particular responses. On Egyptian papyruses the scribe ends with an incantation, but I think this is read in the form of enormous characters which do not have a happy appearance. Zdanevich gives typographic composition the power of expression and calligraphic beauty of a manuscript of the Koran. The visual side of the page provokes new sensations, and coming into contact with different meanings gives birth to new forms.

If one cannot be a Pushkin, a Racine, or a Goethe, it would be nice at least to be a Zdanevich.

As for me, I would like to consider myself a friend of Zdanevich."[52]

Shklovsky's perception exceeded the frivolities in responses from other people, who simply seemed baffled. Shklovsky was able to address visual-verbal materiality as an integral aspect of language—high praise from the person who was arguably the most important theorist of Russian literature of the period.

In the production of the plays, Iliazd had developed a typographic vocabulary as well as a poetic vision that became the foundation of all of his later work. The obvious continuities are less conspicuous than the differences, since these early plays are so outrageous and virtuosic, but the control is the same in both periods. If his later works are less overtly dramatic, his early theatrics taught him how to maximize the communicative impact of typography and design. He had moved through a sequence of increasingly complex and sophisticated approaches to setting and scoring a text, as well as making use of materials as an integral aspect of the book as an experiential phenomenon. Many experiences would occur before he produced another printed book. When he did, the *zaum* work of this era would be invoked within its historic framework.

Ledentu was published in October 1923 and exhibited in the Gallery Paul Guillaume, accompanied by a portrait of Iliazd by Robert Delaunay. It was also exhibited in 1925 at the Soviet Pavilion in the *International Exhibition of Modern Decorative and Industrial Arts*, an event that gratified Iliazd considerably. Then *Ledentu* fell into its own kind of oblivion until scholars of *zaum*, Iliazd, and typographic design rediscovered it. When Hélène first showed me a copy of the book in 1985, with its exquisite collage cover by Granovsky, the complexities and subtleties of its design were only beginning to garner attention after more than half a century of being ignored.[53]

Anticlimax, 1923-1926

In September 1923, Iliazd drafted a novel, *The Parisians,* that was never published. The advance subscription notice gave some idea of the impression it was trying to create:

> This is an ordinary novel by Iliazd, who forces his readers to speak of a "capitulation" of the creator of *zaum* poetry. The readers can decide if this book represents a surrender on the part of the author of "The Image of the Donkey," who offers us miracles of his virtuosity, juggling with sense, overwhelming us with the elegance and richness of his vocabulary and the diversity of his processes and showing us the Parisian confusion constituted by eight friends caught up in hysteria, revolution, affection, naivete, application, impotence, and homosexual love in which all sorts of nonsense keeps them from being able to sit down to eat together during two and a half hours.[54]

Iliazd combined themes of frustration with artistic ambition to reinvent himself as a writer. But the manuscript remained unpublished. Following the momentous events of 1923, the chronologies for the years 1924, 1925, and 1926 have an anticlimactic feel. They suggest contact with the surrealists at the Café Cyrano, a visit to Éluard and Gala, contact with Max Ernst, and other activities. A handful of *bals*, a plan for a *zaum* performance, some work as a translator, all indicated the ongoing but intermittent commitment to artistic life. He notes that when the Soviet Union was recognized by France in 1925, he began to quarrel with Breton on the subject of Soviet functionarism—by which he may have meant putting aesthetic activity in the service of the state, or merely the overbearing administrative bureaucracy of the Soviet brand of government. He reworked various articles for Russian publications as well as French ones, but by the end of 1925 had withdrawn considerably from the more organized activities, such as the *bals*. A typewritten outline of a lecture planned for Tcherez, dated "9.2.24," was titled "In advance or behind" and its sections included statements like "Invented problems and real problems," under which the subheads include "Dogmatism, lamentable and leading nowhere," and "What the world is at an impasse."[55] The tone continued with the phrase "the end" punctuating the proposal after mentions of Dada, Tzara, and Éluard, along with other indications of disillusion. Not a happy note appeared anywhere in the outline.

As noted above, in 1925 Iliazd was invited to exhibit at the *International Exhibition* as part of the official delegation. On January 4 he presented a lec-

ture in Russian at the Geographical Society in Paris on the poet Sergei Essenine and his suicide, "The Salt of Essenine." The lecture raised objections,
to which he responded in another lecture, "The Poet and Society," on January 28. By December 1926, the Soviet Union had officially outlawed futurism. Iliazd, who had been working at the embassy in various capacities, lost
his job. "I was forced to return to fabric design and ten years were erased
from my literary life." The ten years were the ones to follow.

On September 18, 1926, he married Simone Elise Brocard, known as
Axel. The young woman was an artist's model, and only seventeen. They
would have two children in quick succession. He needed to support his
young family, and this fact, among other changes in context and circumstance, shifted his priorities. The part-time work of painting silk scarves,
making designs, and trying to patch together a living from this freelance
activity proved insufficient.

1927–1946

Family, Fabric, and Fiction

Taboos about the Personal Realm

Where do personal matters belong in a biography when the study is motivated by attention to professional accomplishments? The intimate records of a deceased witness or participant carry their own aura and suggest their own prohibitions. Here the biographer must tread carefully and not overread or interpret the materials which, nonetheless, are not merely witnesses, but partisan documents. In the case of Iliazd, a period begins in 1926 with his marriage, the birth of a child, and family and domestic responsibilities. It is harder to say when this period ends. The events of the global Depression and World War II and his own personal matters merge in ways that have no easily identified boundaries. Much occurs that can be reported and documented, but the segmentation of a life into discrete periods feels ill conceived when its spans of time are crosscut with multiple agendas. I had some hesitation about looking into Iliazd's family matters. Given that the family had very little presence in his work, it felt gratuitous to inquire about the fate of children or his first wife, and yet, some account of these belongs in a biography. But from what evidence?

Marriage, Work, and Novels

If Iliazd had any sustained romantic relationships with women in the Russian period, all trace of them had vanished. His attachment to Sofia Melnikova, the "muse" of his Tbilisi activity, is marked in his writings and publications. In Paris, his circles of acquaintance were considerable, but no mention of romantic involvements remains before his marriage to Axel Brocard. He may merely have been very discreet and private about intimate

Axel Brocard with Iliazd around the time of their marriage, 1926. Courtesy of François Mairé and the Fonds Iliazd

relationships. Do these intimacies matter in telling the story of a life if they do not show up in any way in the artist's work? At certain points in Iliazd's life, relationships brought about structural changes of location and priorities. Iliazd's feelings with regard to Axel are hard to decipher from the scant evidence. She was strikingly pretty, stylish, and young. Was he a mentor figure as well as lover? His motivations may have been very conventional: the desire for female companionship, marriage, emotional connection, domestic stability, and family. By 1926 he must have been wrestling with the realization that he would probably not return to the Soviet Union, and he needed to make a life where he was. Axel was pregnant when they married, so no excess of prudery constrained their relations. In terms of concepts of gender roles in relationships, Iliazd had seen a few remarkable examples—such as that of Natalia Goncharova and Mikhail Larionov, a partnership of equals in an artistic collaboration. But these were rare, and certainly among the Dadaists and surrealists in Paris, women were more likely to serve as muses and models than peers or colleagues. Many strong intellectual women were part of the Parisian scene—Sylvia Beach, Gertrude Stein, and others—but no evidence exists to suggest Iliazd had any contact with them.[1]

We get a tiny glimpse into Iliazd's attitudes in a note written to Axel shortly before their marriage:

> A reputation is a serious thing, for a woman as well as a man. I have often heard you say that you don't care, but it's not that simple, and these things are both difficult and annoying. If you want to stay all your life in Montparnasse, end up like a Kiki or Marcelle, as an infamous girl of Montparnasse, fine, I understand, and in that case you can go right on living the way you were before our engagement. But the moment you decided to get married, to become an established woman, and not a girlfriend, not a model, you have to understand that people are sufficiently wicked to use all kinds of pretexts to gossip and spread rumors which will bother you for the rest of your life everywhere you go. Therefore, it must be obvious that at this point you have to abandon your old ways (and with good spirit, too) which you were used to from September of 1925 until March of 1926. But you have continued your flirting, your coquetterie, and I do not know how many times I have been embarrassed by your behavior at the Rotonde and elsewhere, which I find compromising for both of us.[2]

The tone is understandable. The particulars of the note are clear. A lover may desire fidelity, but a husband will expect it. The marriage went ahead. Iliazd asked Axel to keep a journal, and excerpts from it present a barely fictionalized image of Iliazd: "In a bar near Montparnasse I met a little Russian whom I found both ridiculous and sympathetic. I saw him a few times after that at the Rotonde where I only said hello to him, nothing more. However, as the Russian Ball was approaching, I got the idea that I should ask him for tickets and so about a week later, seeing him at the Rotonde, I went right up to him and asked him if he could get me tickets."[3] A few more excerpts tracked the course of their romance:

> I began to love Serge, but I held back against a sentiment which I knew would cost me my freedom.
> . . . He sat in the armchair, his head in his hands, giving in to his state of mind. I threw myself at him, "Oh, my dear Serge, I don't want—" "You are wicked, Simone, you know that I love you and you make me suffer." "Serge, if I have really made you suffer, it wasn't on purpose, you know how unaware I am sometimes, and I beg you, please, don't be upset with me—"[4]

They were married in September 1926 and the journal concluded. The style of the journal told its own story. Iliazd was in his early thirties. Axel was barely more than half his age. A photograph of her showed a slim, elegant woman. With such minimal evidence, one cannot venture into any analysis of the relationship or even their intermittent cohabitation. Whatever the impact of marriage on Iliazd, he made little mention of it. Lacunae are just that, absences that cannot be assessed.

In January 1927, their daughter Michelle was born. These simple statements punctuate the chronologies, but nothing is fleshed out around them. Iliazd became inscribed in the Register of Professions as a fabric designer and was hired by the company Blacque Belair. The company was in turn acquired by Coco Chanel in March 1928. These tiny scraps of information remain, between which there are large gaps. A letter to an M. Bianchini, artistic director at *Vogue*, recommends Ilia Zdanevich as a "great talent in fabric design," and he created a line of fabrics named for his wife, Axel, which he tried to market.[5] Vivid, geometric, and very *moderne*, they were professional enough to land him work in the industry, though he did not pursue freelance design. His wife was frequently away, and letters addressed to her give some idea that she was often in Cagnes, a bathing resort, on account of claims of delicate health. Their son Daniel was born in February 1928, so the couple must have had at least intermittent contact. Where was the infant daughter when Axel was away? Who looked after her? Iliazd's archive was almost silent on the topic of his children. Hélène's comments about Axel

Design by Iliazd for fabric printing. Courtesy of François Mairé and the Fonds Iliazd

were oblique, and always included the phrase, "a little Kiki," referencing the famous model of Montparnasse. Whether from discretion or ignorance of details, Hélène said little. By the time she met Iliazd, he had been divorced from Axel, had remarried, and had become a widower.

In early March 1928, Iliazd was hired by Tricots Chanel to stay on at a newly acquired factory. He worked on the knitting machines and even filed legal paperwork for an improved loom design.[6] Drawings for a device called "Zdanevich" remain in his archive, demonstrating that he put considerable energy into these new activities. His work with Chanel continued until 1933. During these five years he moved to Sannois, a suburb of Paris near the factory, and finally into a house provided by the firm. Nor was he the only poet who found work in this industry. Pierre Reverdy was also working for Chanel. Iliazd noted, "Instead of signing poems, [he] was signing work orders for me." Indeed, a one-year contract, dated October 3, was signed by Reverdy.

In 1929 Iliazd wrote this description of his existence to Philips Price: "I work in a factory which manufactures wool jersey; in the evenings I sit in a café, I collect paintings, I love my children and my wife, and I am getting hopelessly bald. I read rarely, and only French authors. I never see Russian books or newspapers, and . . . I rarely hear Russian spoken. The past has drifted out of view and questions which used to stir me deeply now leave me in peace. I make love and am becoming the perfect petit-bourgeois."[7]

Here we get a description that seems—what? Does it read as resigned? Reconciled? Is Iliazd disappointed or content? The description misses a few key points. The hazards of self-narration are concealment of evidence, deliberate or incidental omission. For one thing, Iliazd never fully ceased writing during this period. In 1928 he completed a text in Russian titled "Posthumous Works," which critic Elizabeth Klosty Beaujour described as "an ironic view of the world of *haute couture*."[8] He had written *The Parisians* and *The Rapture*, both in Russian, and the latter was published in 1930. The novel is about mountain brigands, with a strong strain of magic realism. The book drew heavily on the scenery of the Caucasus, and a kind of primitivism pervades its themes as well as its style. One scene of violence followed another, beginning with the murder of a monk, followed by images of rape, death, and pursuit. Beaujour summarized the book this way:

> The bandit Lavrentii, the beautiful Ivlita, and the patriarch of the high mountain village all resemble the vividly colored characters portrayed by Pirosmani—with their clearcut outlines stark against the background. These characters inhabit an atmosphere charged with ethnographic detail, and the descriptions of mountain life are among the most striking in the book. The description of the annual hunt, with its rules and ritual, its superstitious pursuit of a buck, "the crucifix," which, although real has become legendary, is not merely a depiction of local color. It creates a sense of intensified reality, surreal, where tiny winged angels sing in the storms, and a goat-man crunches the barrels of the rifles of imprudent hunters in his teeth, and the dead are transformed into trees. . . .[9]

The continuity with the *dras* was evident in the strange but aggressive logic, folktale themes, obscenities, and violence. The book was printed in an edition of 750 copies, and Iliazd sent copies to friends and writers throughout Europe, including Filippo Marinetti, Dmitri Mirsky, one of the Burliuks, Vera Soudeikine, Aleksei Kruchenykh, Viktor Shklovsky, and others.[10] Seven hundred and fifty copies was ambitious, and mailing copies to Russia and Italy suggested that in spite of his multiple changes of domicile, Iliazd must have been keeping good records of his far-flung acquaintances. The addresses of many of his colleagues must have changed many times in that period as well.

Dmitri Mirsky, the distinguished historian of Russian literature, published this favorable review of *The Rapture* in *La Nouvelle Revue Française* in December 1931:[11]

> This is a remarkable book, which deserves to be met with more than silence. The action takes place in a nameless country which resembles Georgia or one of the Balkan states. It unfolds between a mountain hamlet, a village at the edge of the mountains, a small seaport, and the corrupt and abject capital where the Emperor has the name The Masterbator [*sic*]. In this juxtaposition of worlds which are historically so distinct but neighboring upon each other intimately, one sees that Iliazd possesses to an eminent degree a virtue which is rare in a novelist—intelligence. This quality of synthetic observation which could have made him an ethnographer or geographer of the first rank blends with a literary materialism which recalls the great materialist painter Courbet. This combines with a narrative rhythm which is both rapid and ample, and an adventure story which would make an admirable cinema script. But what, for me, contributes the greatest value to the book is its style. The profundity of the literary prose style strikes anyone who is concerned with Soviet literature today, especially if it is compared to the finely chiseled and admirably precise language of a political writer like Stalin. In contrast with most novelists, Iliazd demonstrates a style which is structured without being rhythmic, rich without being spoiled, neutral without being emasculated (quite the contrary!), master of his material without being "artistic" or picturesque. His is a masculine style, heavy with content, a style which, nonetheless, is sufficiently objective not to be inseparable from its original language and which would survive translation.[12]

Mirsky mentioned that the book contained language some Russian booksellers found objectionable, and they boycotted the book on those grounds. In Leningrad, the book met with some enthusiasm, as an old friend, Olga

Lechkova, communicated to Iliazd. But the official mood in the Soviet Union had changed dramatically. Artists and writers still dedicated to the avant-garde were wary of expressing their support. Iliazd's novel was out of sync with the cultural tone. This was an era in which Soviet realist works began to claim center stage. A book that "included among its characters an itinerant monk" was unlikely to find a large following in a Soviet setting.[13] Lechkova, writing to Iliazd from Leningrad in 1930, noted that Iliazd might have need of such a character for aesthetic reasons, but the state had no need of a religious figure in any role whatsoever.[14] Her letter carried other poignant, if coded, remarks about conditions there. The cultural distance was marked. The passing of time registered differently in Paris than in the Soviet Union, and Iliazd was further than he realized from the Russia he had left in 1920.

While Iliazd worked at the textile factory and composed his novels, he did not give up recreational activities. A trip to Spain in September 1933 provided an opportunity to reflect on the similarities between his native Georgia and the Catalan landscape.[15] The pleasure he took in the mountains had been evident in this note to Axel from a journey in 1929: "I left the pass of Auberne at 5:30 this morning. After a wonderful hike, I was glad to finally arrive at an old chalet. A shepherd, goats-milk, all fresh (drawn before me), flowers, glaciers, a conversation about the mountains—what beauty. I was completely happy, except that there were so many fleas attacking me that I was lucky to get any sleep before my body was completely chewed up."[16]

Family duties demanded attention. In early 1933, Iliazd records that he paid for piano lessons for the two children. A note from a nurse in Spain on November 2, 1933, indicated that the children were still with her, suggesting Iliazd had deposited them there earlier in the autumn. Another note in 1934 indicated they were with a different nurse in St. Quentin. In July 1934, he wrote to Axel asking her to be sure to correspond with the children. Where were they and where was she? The children were about six and seven years old. No judgment can be passed on this situation without evidence, but questions arise in its absence. In March 1935, Iliazd returned to Spain on foot, without a visa, by way of Andorra and the mountains, and reconnected with his children in Cartagena.

As a biographer, one does not have the right to read between these lines, merely to read the lines themselves. But the gaps are enormous. The children seem barely present and family life seems nonexistent. How can this be? No access to his feelings or thoughts remains.

But a passage from a lecture on the topic of Spain given to the Cercle de

Cervantes in 1935, following another hiking trip in March, reinforced his enthusiasm for the mountains: "Allow me to tell you why I think a Georgian feels so much at ease among the Spanish whose society substitutes so readily for his own, which is far away, and why, instead of having to go all that distance, it is sufficient for me, whose stay in France has extended itself a bit longer than I had expected, simply to cross the Pyrenees to recover some of the ambiance of my youth."[17]

His appreciation of this landscape never ceased. Within a few years he bought a small house in the Var district of France, in the village of Trigance, the only property he owned in his life. The house was basic, and years later it exercised the magic of its rustic authenticity on Hélène as well. Iliazd was well known in the region, but only when he died and the local paper published an obituary were the local people aware of his profile and accomplishments as an artist and publisher.

Changes of Circumstances and New Books

Iliazd's work with Chanel continued until December 1933, but increasingly the Depression made the factory economically unfeasible. During Iliazd's last year in the position, the letters exchanged between him and the director of Chanel's operations, Paul Iribe, showed Iliazd's repeated attempts to prevent layoffs for the workers he supervised. Nevertheless, cutbacks continued, and Iliazd wrote the final report on the plant as he himself was being terminated. He returned to Paris from the suburbs, and life was difficult. He found work intermittently and relied on the hospitality of friends for shelter. He pawned a few items—a vacuum cleaner, a brooch, and other things. The receipts remained among his papers, showing he had not redeemed the pawned items. In June 1934, he wrote to Axel saying with relief, "At last, a bed!" His circumstances were never easy, and often difficult, as in this period. Work was hard to find, and skilled though he was, he struggled. Again, there is the question of the children's whereabouts.

In spite of these limitations, he pursued projects and plans. A Russian theater director, Nikolai Evreinov, contacted him a few times to discuss a possible production of *Yanko,* or perhaps *The Rapture.* A new exhibition of work done for the expedition led by Professor Takaishvili years earlier contained drawings by Iliazd, and he was able to see them appreciated. He had elaborate exchanges with booksellers dealing in the architecture and archaeology of Asia Minor and Greece as he developed his studies of Byzantine churches. He corresponded with the director of the Museum of Fine

Arts in Istanbul, M. Halil Edhem Eldem, on points concerning an ancient palace that had once existed near the site of Hagia Sophia. In 1934-35 he obtained a library card for the Bibliothèque St. Geneviève and occasionally earned money doing commissioned research. He collaborated with a Mr. H. Kazandjian on an article on the "Star Shaped Edifices of Armenia." These succinct statements each indicate work and labor as well as social networks of communication and correspondence, but what they felt like on a day-to-day basis is hard to imagine. How was he paying bills and managing to keep his household afloat?

In 1935 he wrote an article titled "Paris Fashion for the Year 1935," stressing the strong blow struck to the world of fashion by the Depression. He was finally reduced to going on unemployment. A card dated 1936 entitled him to "a meal for 3 francs at the Famille Nouvelle, resoling of his shoes for 13 francs, a haircut at reduced rates, entry to the Worker's Fair at reduced rates, and free legal advice."[18] Iliazd, like many others, was at the mercy of much larger forces than those of his personal circumstances.

In 1936, he occupied an apartment in rue Seguier with his wife and children, but the arrangement did not last. Axel filed for divorce. In 1937 he moved alone into the apartment in the rue Mazarine—which he occupied until the end of his life—and continued to concern himself with care for his children and a number of cats. A flirtation, crush, or love affair with an English painter, Joan Spencer, occupied him briefly in 1937. Notebooks from this period describe their relationship and a portrait she was painting. The accounts are full of missed appointments and other details of Iliazd's attempts to meet:

> Day after day, Iliazd passes his evenings in the streets, searching the cafés in hopes of seeing Joan. But Joan doesn't appear. Iliazd goes home late, and often a little drunk. Waking up the next morning, he calms himself saying, "Tonight I have a date with her." In anticipation of the evening, Iliazd sits on his bed or at his table and works on a book. If Joan would fall in love with Ilizad it would make him crazy with joy, maybe they would even have children. And there wouldn't be a book. But, so it goes, passing the days in vain hopes, languishing from despair, and being unhappy. One must write a book.[19]

Iliazd was now in his early forties. He was vital and ambitious. Never in these years, or at any other time, did Iliazd in any way imagine a return to the Soviet Union. Occasional correspondence from his father appears in the archives, along with correspondence from friends in Moscow or St. Petersburg. Nothing about the circumstances seemed positive, particularly for those figures who, like Iliazd, had been part of the avant-garde. He sent money to his family when possible. He also pawned his camera and his phonograph, and these tickets also remained unredeemed. He got work contracts for a few months here and there in the fabric industry. Following his own interest, he continued work on Byzantine church architecture. A list of works for which he requested research permission from the Conservator at the Bibliothèque Nationale attested to the scholarly specificity of his work, which he pursued by contacting the librarian of Barton Guy de Rothschild's collection.

From time to time, the historical changes through which he had passed registered with immediacy. In 1938, at an event honoring the anniversary of Guillaume Apollinaire's death (November 9, 1918), Iliazd encountered Marinetti. Iliazd's unpublished account contains these details:

> The wife of Apollinaire covers the tomb with roses brought by Picasso and Paul Dermée. Then Marinetti arrives. Iliazd has not seen Marinetti for over a year. He is glad to see him, taps him on the shoulder. He is radiant. Marinetti holds out a hand to Picasso. But Picasso says no, we are at war, wait for the peace. Marinetti attempts to change his mind, but we are here, in front of this tomb, it seems to me. Picasso turns his back. He has become crazy, says Marinetti, speaking to Iliazd.
>
> Bellini and Salmon arrive. Seeing Salmon, Picasso says, "Shit," and takes off through the tombs. Iliazd stays. He hears all kinds of stories explaining the situation, long explanations from Salmon, then justifications, and Salmon defends his pro-Franco position.[20]

The full depth and complexity of emotions escape from this account, even as it registers the stresses of the situation. Allegiances and betrayals, deep and long histories of political alliances and scars of recent events—are all compressed into a telegraphic rendering. As a scene, this must have been crosscut with glances, looks, body language, tones, asides, and exchanges that broke through the surface. The amount of history that was being accessed in the process was also enormous and filled with emotionally charged memories. None of this is recoverable in the archive; only the bare bones remain.

In November 1939, his divorce from Axel was finalized. She stated she had left the conjugal domicile of her own free will, abandoning her husband and children.[21] The children were about eleven and twelve at the time.

The book Iliazd had mentioned working on contained sonnets in Russian that would be published in 1940 under the title *Afat*.[22] This book launched his production of the deluxe editions that would occupy him for the rest of his working life. The work followed the protocols of the *livres d'artistes* standards in its use of a large format, fine paper, and the inclusion of two aquatints and four engravings by Picasso of nude figures in elegant line drawings. The book was produced in the shop of Chalit and Snegaroff, the Imprimerie Union, whose cases of Cyrillic type provided the means by which Iliazd's Russian poem could be put into print. The sonnets portray a painter as the chief counterpoint to the first-person voice of the writer. The contrast between writing and image making, between "I" and "Pablo," allowed Iliazd to contrast the working tools and identity of the different arts. The typewriter, under its dust cover, "plagued the imagination" of the writer, while in an attic the artist made engravings "with a sure and golden hand." Iliazd knew the contrast with his earlier work would be noted and in anticipation wrote: "Who could have foreseen that in 1938, Iliazd, the eternal clown, would demonstrate his complete control over Russian meter and become the most severe and rigorous practitioner of classical poetry?"[23]

Afat was the first book on which Iliazd collaborated with Picasso, and it contained features that would become signature elements of his work. The book was structured as a whole, not just a series of text-image juxtapositions. The sequencing and number of pages were ordered by a mathematical scheme. The image was not linked directly to the text, thematically or physically, and the interaction produced a dialogue rather than subordinating one to the other as illustration and/or caption. The sequence of blank sheets, title, half title, and justification of the edition were laid out symmetrically so that the closing of the book echoed the opening. The supersaturated, dense pages of the futurist period were gone. The typographic style was restrained, and the pages produce subtle equilibrium instead of dynamic activity—no confusion, no clamor, no crowding, no elaborate display faces. The sole decoration on the cover was the stamped title, *Afat* (a term that invokes unhappiness and/or beauty that causes it) rendered in *kufic* (an ancient Arabic script).[24] The paper in the book was thick, almost as heavy as cover stock. The use of the blank pages as a delay, a physical halt that is both a pause and a mechanism of deferral, intensified the anticipation of the reader. With this work, Iliazd's architectural approach to book structure, with strong emphasis on symmetry and balance, made its appearance.

The engravings were printed between December 4 and 8, 1939, and the text between March 2 and 30, 1940, all dates he noted precisely. Each of the author's copies, numbered I through VI, had a special dedication: Joan Spencer, Dora Maar, Picasso, Chanel, Dmitri Snegaroff, and Volf Chalit (these last two were owners of the Imprimerie Union where the book was printed). Chanel's copy contained an extra, seventy-seventh sonnet. Clearly these were the figures most closely connected to Iliazd. Maar and Picasso lived a few blocks from Iliazd at the time, and the other figures were closely tied to his daily life, livelihood, and the book's production. The limit of the intimate circle was defined by the numerals I through VI of this part of the edition.

This publishing activity could not save him from difficult financial circumstances. The book appeared just as the war with Germany was intensifying. The timing was bad, and the book had little success. Classical sonnets in Russian had few readers, and buyers for deluxe editions were scarce. Iliazd had no track record or established subscription list: "I walked the streets with my copies of *Afat*, illustrated by Picasso, but these treasures only met with blind stares—in the cafes of St. Germain des Prés faces one was used to meeting with every day would suddenly disappear, responding to alarm, and then reappear a week later. Gas masks left little space on the café tables for glasses. . . ."[25]

The Stalin-Hitler pact had been signed in August 1939. Less than a year later, in early June 1940, Paris was occupied. Chanel sent a messenger to Iliazd, telling him it was not safe to visit her (she was reputed to have a lover who was a Nazi officer). Iliazd said he wanted to remain as inconspicuous as possible. Though he was summoned by the draft board, he was excused from military service after a review on account of his children. Iliazd was in his mid-forties. He worked at a secondhand bookstore run by Guy le Prat and did research for clients with special requests.

Though the war interrupted his renewed interest in literary projects and book production to a large degree, Iliazd wrote two sonnets on the theme of the war. In 1941 he published them under the title *Rahel*. Paul Éluard, with whom Iliazd had struggled to maintain relations, and whose work he would publish in the future, translated the sonnets into French. Two wood engravings by Léopold Survage accompanied the text. Survage's iconography is reminiscent of Picasso's *Guernica*. A raised arm, a crying woman with her head thrown back, and layered intersecting planes of action cut in the bold lines of the woodblock. The graphic impact was strong, and the Rus-

Rahel, with images by Léopold Survage (Paris: Forty-One Degrees, 1941). Courtesy of François Mairé and the Fonds Iliazd

sian text was rendered calligraphically by Marcel Mée. The edition of this set of prints was only about twenty copies, and the printing was completed in November 1941. The poignancy of this effort was brought home by recognizing the austerity of the conditions in which it was produced, and the classical form of the sonnets. The title *Rahel* derived from the Russian radical *RHL*; it meant "sheep," and the evident connection with war victims destined to be butchered was clear.[26] The text describes a war "that devastates the last village" while "a fresh moon perseveres, illuminates elms dressed in tatters." It goes on: "The ravaged countryside is afraid, harsh words roam everywhere."

Iliazd's personal life changed dramatically in 1943. Through a woman named Luna Michonze, the wife of a former friend of Axel's who frequently looked after Iliazd's children, he had become acquainted with a Nigerian princess named Ibironke Akinsemoyin.[27] A British citizen, she had been interned in a German camp for foreigners, and on her release came to Paris with Luna. Details are lacking. But the connection was made, and a new romantic relationship began.

Meanwhile, Iliazd went on with his work with the book dealer Le Prat and also continued writing. In 1944, he put into the hands of his friend Prince Gleb Eristoff a manuscript of verses written in response to the Spanish Civil War. The poems were in Russian, titled "One of the Brigade," and Iliazd described them as "the writing of a condemned poet." As he gave the work to Eristoff, he said, "You are my only reader . . . I will let you know when the time is right to publish this work."[28] In a set of reminiscences sent to Hélène at her request, Eristoff wrote:

> Here is one of the situations which you have asked me to write about, among the many diverse events which have surprised us. It was, if my memory serves me correctly, in 1944. Paris has just been liberated. Iliazd and I went frequently to the bistro at the Reine Blanche, a little bistro located above the Brasserie Lipp, on the Boulevard St. Germain, near the hotel Taranne. It was a little café, frequented by the people in the quarter, and which was recommended by Roger Blin to those of his friends who preferred small spots to sitting in the Flore, as was true in our case. From this café, we often went to eat at the Petit Saint-Benoît and came back pacified to the Reine Blanche where we stayed until it closed, which it did fairly late in that happy era. I had been good friends with Zdanevich, my compatriot, for a long time. I was very respectful of his tremendous learning, and for me he was a great Russian poet.
>
> I remember this night very well. Zdanevich was in a great mood. He had begun to rework his great poem, *Brigadni*. He was feeling very confident and recited several changes he had made. He was very concerned with finishing it. I had never tired of hearing him read his poetry, and occasionally, that of others. That evening, or rather, that night, after the café closed, we walked toward the church on the Boulevard St. Germain, then turned and retraced our steps, completely

absorbed in our conversation. Finding ourselves at a standstill with our backs to the church, we were suddenly surprised by the sight of a staggering silhouette coming out of the Rue du Dragon, and weaving across the Boulevard St. German; he turned his steps in our direction, increasing his pace, and ended by falling into our arms. He died instantly. He had just been stabbed, probably in the Rue du Dragon, or in one of the nearby streets. Thank heavens, two police agents on duty ran up to us so that we avoided any complications in the matter. A bit dazed and shocked, Zdanevich said, "It happened that a man, whom I did not know, just died in my arms, assassinated, without my knowing the reasons for the murder; on the other hand, at that moment, I realized that my long poem on the Spanish War, 'Brigadni,' is finished. The poem is done." He embraced me and we said goodnight.[29]

Eristoff was one of the many individuals Hélène encouraged me to visit. Through the usual exchange of letters, I set a rendezvous and went to meet him at his "studio," a classic early twentieth-century atelier space with glass skylight, kitchen alcove, mezzanine, and bedroom somewhere out of sight. The room had the air of a time capsule, unchanged throughout the decades of his long residence there. He received me in this light but cold environment. It felt more like a stage set than a domicile. He was seated in a large chair and held a cane with a carved handle. He gave the impression of a man from an earlier era, with starched white shirt cuffs and collar, and stickpin and foulard. His hair was swept back, his thinning mane and regal profile still dramatic. He never looked directly at me during the interview but kept himself in profile the entire time. He was a White Russian émigré, aristocratic by birth. What were the terms of his connection with Iliazd? The erosion of so much that had separated them, perhaps, and the attachment to shared language and frames of reference? No notes of mine remain from that visit, only the impression of the man, diminished and elderly, but maintaining a posture of grandeur in an empty space.

Such a visit yielded little of substance but much affective force to my sense of Iliazd. Eristoff was a living reminder of a lost era, still able, in his own recollections, to touch that world of Tsarist Russia. We did not talk politics or history, and we barely spoke of art or literature. I might as well have visited a monument or a portrait for the information I received. But I was there to pay homage, to give him the recognition of his identity and his connection to history. That was my role, and if I received no information, I had a sense of the long duration of a life lived after its frameworks and contexts were gone, one in which a man continued to preserve within himself all that had vanished externally. I had had an encounter with a living connection to the past.

Second Marriage

In May 1943 Iliazd married the Nigerian princess, Ibironke Akinsemoyin. Two almost identical cards, one with and one without a black edge, bracketed the short extent of this second marriage. Printed with engraver fonts, elegant and conventional, they announced a wedding and a death. Their similarity reinforced the proximity in time. The font, the printer, and the conventions in layout and appearance remained unchanged between the card announcing the marriage on May 22, 1943, and the one with its announcement of Akinsemoyin's death, June 18, 1945. Just a little more than two years separated the events. You cannot read those dates without sadness. But what right do you have to these emotions as a biographer? The tragedy is not yours. The vicarious grief is voyeuristic. You are not inside the life you describe. But you feel the human consequences.

The wedding license listed Akinsemoyin as the daughter of Prince Mobolaji and Princesse Remilekun, and listed Iliazd's mother's maiden name as Gamreklidze. Their son Chalva was born on October 7, 1943. Akinsemoyin had become ill in the detention camp before she met Iliazd, and she died of tuberculosis in a sanitorium at Bligny. Another acquaintance of Iliazd's, Cecil Michaelis, recalled the circumstances of her death, and Iliazd's attempts to buy penicillin on the black market, and being cheated. Penicillin had only recently been discovered, and supplies were scarce. Hélène communicated the pain—and horror—of this experience in her expressions, shaking her head.

Iliazd's two older children were in their teens, but Chalva was an infant. Iliazd struggled to make contact with his late wife's family in Nigeria, in order to secure the legal inheritance for his son within the family line. He also worked to get him British citizenship. A note in October 1945 states that he had not baptized Chalva and intended to raise him in the Georgian Orthodox Church. This note was the only mention of religion anywhere in the archive. A 1945 note from Daniel, Iliazd's older son, on the day that his sister, eighteen-year-old Michelle, was to be married, says that he will take care of Chalva for the day. We get a glimpse into the connections among the family members. Nothing more.

I probably never would have heard of Chalva Zdanevich if I had not arrived one afternoon for our usual work and found Hélène in a terrible state. Everything was amiss, even her capacity to explain. Her usual demeanor was deeply disturbed, her gaze was unfocused, her energies rambling. Chalva, Iliazd's son by his second wife, lived in the apartment just above (or below) the one occupied by Hélène. I had known nothing of this fact despite our months of regular contact, though clearly Chalva had occupied the domicile for a long time. How long, under what circumstances, or how this had come to be—during Iliazd's life or sometime after—was never clear. But some crisis was immediate, and fell on Hélène, whose shrugging and incomplete statements indicated that this was not a topic to be gone into in detail but that it was a responsibility she felt she had to shoulder. Chalva, she barely continued, could not, would not, for whatever reason, manage on his own. He was a prince, after all, Hélène said, but one without the resources for his position. That was all she said. We did not speak of this again. For that day, we suspended our work while she dealt with the emergency.

One picture of Iliazd showed him on the beach with the young Chalva held high and proud in his arms, the only visual record in the archive. Along with his curly brown-black hair and tawny skin, he had a clear imprint of his father's features combined with his mother's beauty. Hélène was always respectful in speaking of Akinsemoyin, the deep connection she had had with Iliazd, and the tragedy for them both in the brevity of the marriage.

In 1954, a short message from Iliazd told Chalva that he had not purchased a certain diving mask they had looked at together on the Quai du Louvre, because it appeared to be dangerous in the water. Instead, he promised to buy him one the moment he arrived in Cannes. These were missives from well inside familiar reference frames, undertakings together, business ongoing, a chain of events interlocked across one moment and a next that showed the family connection was active.

Another note to Chalva in August 1955 informed him that his brother, Daniel, was getting married in September and that Chalva would probably not be able to lodge with him (Daniel) after that. His father assured him, however, that he would not lose his trip to the beach, and that he would see him soon. Another note soon after to a caretaker of some property belonging to Iliazd detailed his interest in saving a batch of kittens, and he offered one hundred francs for their care until he could arrive to see after them himself. The cats were part of his life in Trigance, his other residence, and a constant part of his domestic life in the rue Mazarine. Hélène said he would

Iliazd and his cats, 1960. Courtesy of François Mairé and the Fonds Iliazd

arrive in the country, open the shutters to the house, and call out through the valley. The cats would come running.

A note written in 1965, when Chalva was about twenty, suggested the young man had money troubles. Iliazd could not bail him out, and he characterized himself as "a poor man who earns money irregularly," adding that Chalva's recent trip to England had imposed a heavy burden that he could not sustain.[30] Frustration was evident. But Iliazd continued, into the 1960s, to attempt to establish Chalva's legitimacy with his Nigerian family. Lives lived and not described, but intimate to Iliazd, included those of the children. The intimate connections were there but remained out of sight, undocumented and undescribed. Michelle, his firstborn child, committed suicide. Hélène communicated this fact succinctly. The topic was not to be explored. Daniel died in due course of natural causes. Chalva struggled on.

Notes from the Dead and Boundary Lines

Because the dead are gone, we read their private notes. But what of the living?

I never met Chalva, and in the play of presences and absences that define a biography, he was close by and impossibly distant. Hélène was protective of him—and about him—and these limits were to be respected.

In the task of moving from statements in the chronologies to understanding, some lines could not be crossed. Many statements were left just as they were. A note from Iliazd to the wife of Robert Desnos in October 1945 consoled her on his death with the recollection that he had run into the poet daily at 1 pm on the bridge as he was leaving for work. What bridge? Which work? F. Victor Hugo, an acquaintance who had sent Iliazd a message of congratulations on his marriage, moved to Golfe-Juan sometime in 1945 to set up pottery works there with a woman named Hélène Douard (later Iliazd's third wife and the Hélène of my acquaintance). Iliazd met her a year later, on a visit to the Midi to see Picasso. Iliazd worked with Hugo on a project related to fabrics while Hugo's ceramics factory, named Elektra, was being directed by Hélène.

Iliazd's children were never present in the circle around Hélène, but I met a few members of her own family, including the vibrant niece, Hélène, who worked in the perfume industry, and a brother, Henri, warm and engaged, with a lively, intelligent wife, who lived in an apartment with comfortable reading chairs and many books, and was an active force in establishing the Iliazd Club. Hélène's sister lived in the sixteenth arrondissement and had us to an intimate family tea one spring day in her elegant apartment after I had worked with Hélène for months. I took it as a sign of my having gained trust and status in her eyes that she would introduce me to her family circle even in this minimal way. The formality that governed our relationship simply seemed part of French bourgeois society, a way to keep boundaries intact, not a way to shut me out.

Hélène was circumspect but not silent on the topic of the women who had been in Iliazd's life in the early decades. For Melnikova, the Georgian woman who had served as Iliazd's muse, she had only admiration. She was of another era, and another order of being, as if the change in political circumstances and times had erased any connection to her except as an icon of the past. Toward Axel she was sharply critical, though she said little and did not dwell on the subject. About Joan Spencer she said less, sighing and shaking her head. And on the subject of Ibironke Akinsemoyin she was grave and serious, saying that this had been the true love of Iliazd's life, the great romance and tragedy. None of these women still existed, and so they posed no threat and no possibility of contact. Herta Hausmann, a friend from mountain hikes and rambles, was alive and in Paris. Hélène, with her characteristic dignity and reserve, suggested that I talk with Herta and learn what I could from her, but that this I must do on my own. Herta was lean, athletic, a hiking partner and friend of Iliazd's who wanted me to know that she had had a special friendship with him, though she stopped short of details or improprieties. I did not ask, as this felt unnecessary. Something undisclosed was hinted, but only enough to make clear it would not be revealed. I felt that Hélène's desire to have before her a living portrait of the man, of Iliazd, was strong enough to overcome most hesitations, but not to attend to many details. What facets of experience were being turned forward, and which turned away, in Hélène's presentation of Iliazd's life to me? She wanted me to glean as many details for that portrayal as possible from the living memories of any who retained them.

The only one of Iliazd's relations I met was his granddaughter. In the summer of 1985, I went to stay with Hélène very briefly at her house on the southern coast in Golfe-Juan. Iliazd's granddaughter visited, a thin young woman, nervous and narrow, whose father, Daniel, was the child of the first marriage, with Axel. She told me they had had very little to eat in her early years and during World War II. Just "pâtes," she said, almost spitting out the word. Noodles, nothing but. The implication was obvious. She had benefited very little from her grandfather's work and had been undernourished in that relationship as well—and her resentment transferred onto the persons she felt might profit from engagement with his legacy. I could not blame her, but still, none of that history was of my doing. As a biographer, one is also the object of projection for unfinished business.

1947-1950

Lettrist Provocations and *Poetry of Unknown Words* (*Poésie de Mots Inconnus*)

Letters from the Past

With the few exceptions already noted (Gleb Eristoff and Lucien Scheler), the companions of the earlier decades of Iliazd's life were mainly gone by the mid-1980s. But beginning with our chronicling of the events of the late 1940s, we entered the period of many living witnesses. New challenges were added to the biographical task as a consequence. The living memory of Iliazd was held by many different individuals, each with their own agenda and each with their version of the man, his work, his role. The work became partisan, a matter of assessment and advocacy within disputes whose impact was still present. Research, documents, and other materials had to be balanced with impressions and opinions about Iliazd's character and actions.

Still, as usual, Hélène and I began with the chronologies and the documents to which they led. For 1946 and the years immediately following, these show Iliazd actively involved in plans and projects. His work in the fabric industry led to new business endeavors. He continued planning various theatrical productions, such as one with Yvette Chauviré (at the time a star of the opera company in Paris and a much-celebrated prima ballerina) on the theme of an underwater ballet. His financial difficulties persisted. At one point in January 1948, books were seized from the apartment in the rue Mazarine to recover some money on outstanding debts. But Iliazd also began making books again in earnest.

The first of these was *The Letter* (*Pismo*), published in 1948. One of Iliazd's last Russian-language books, it was written in part at the urging of Olga Djordjadze, with whom he had rendezvoused in Cannes in 1946. Their mutual enthusiasm at their common languages prompted a hiking trip in Provence during which Iliazd asked, half-rhetorically and half seriously, for whom he should write in Russian at this point. She had replied, "For me."[1] According to André Markowicz, the text of *The Letter* was full of longing, unrequited and unrequitable love, and the theme "What good does this passion do me?"[2] Details of Iliazd's relationship with Djordjadze surfaced in a series of letters that give evidence of a strong connection and emotional bond, and the "Letter" of the title details an impossible romantic love.[3]

My access to *The Letter* was mediated through summaries and descriptions until André Markowicz's translation appeared in 1990, so as I was working with Hélène five years earlier, I found the poem opaque and remote. Djordjadze was alive, but she was not in Paris, and Hélène did not seem to be in contact with her. By contrast, access to the entire dossier of materials for *Poetry of Unknown Words* made it feel present and vividly alive, even though the two books were published in the same year.

Even as *The Letter* was gestating, a second project emerged from a very different set of conditions and promptings. These were initiated by a lecture Iliazd gave on his return from Provence to Paris in the fall of 1946. Titled "Twenty Years of Futurism," it was a reflection on the activities of many decades earlier (though which twenty years he was factoring into his title is unclear, since by 1926 the futurist era had passed, though the span may have referred to the 1910s and 1920s).

The lecture provoked the ire of Isidore Isou, a megalomaniac Romanian poet and theorist who had arrived in Paris at the end of World War II, very young and very ambitious to make an impact on the literary scene. The exchange between Isou and Iliazd inaugurated the battles that would lead to the landmark publication of Iliazd's anthology, *Poetry of Unknown Words* (*Poésie de Mots Inconnus*), in 1948. Published in an edition of sixty copies, it is, as far as I know, the first anthology of experimental visual and sound poetry from the twentieth-century avant-garde to appear in print. The circumstances of its conception and the details of its production warrant detailed discussion.

The development and publication of *The Letter* and *Poetry of Unknown Words* overlapped chronologically. Work on the first was ongoing as the events that prompted the second were unfolding. *The Letter,* the Russian work of melancholy, and *Poetry of Unknown Words,* the elaborately coordinated anthology of "unknown words," could not have been more different in their aesthetic profiles. The first was interior and personal, the second a public claim to aesthetic invention within a historical frame. This was a crucial and pivotal moment in Iliazd's personal development as an artist and his professional transformation as a publisher. One senses, from the retrospection in the lecture and the inwardly reflective tone of *The Letter,* that Iliazd was thinking about how his past and future work and identity were to be related. How far was he from that past? How distant aesthetically and culturally? In the few years that followed, as he put the *Poetry of Unknown Words* anthology together, Iliazd would promote the accomplishments of futurism, Dada, and early modern experimental work—his own and that of others. At the same time, he shifted his own creative focus into the production of *livres d'artistes* that had begun in 1940 with *Afat*, and continued with *Rahel* (1941), and then *The Letter*. Significantly, after *The Letter*, the only Russian text he published was a virtuosic "crown of sonnets" that formed the text for *Sentence without Words* (1961), and the only other writings of his own that he published were highly self-conscious bookends to the arc of his career as a whole.

When *The Letter*, known as *Livre sans titre* (*Book without a title*), was published in 1948, it met with critical success. The book was reviewed in the company of two other publications, both issued by very established and renowned editors: Matisse's *Jazz* (produced with pochoir from stencils) and Georges Braque's *Notebook* (*Cahier*). *Jazz* was published by Tériade (Paris), and *Notebook* by Curt Valentin and Maeght (New York and Paris). The review by Raymond Cogniat grouped the three, thereby putting Iliazd in highly esteemed company: "Here are three remarkable publications, which are also exceptional works on account of their technical quality. The perfection of their execution marks this year as an exceptional one for bibliophiles, giving them three productions, three rare works, which, no matter what reservations one might express, will remain absolutely typical of this era and its art."[4]

To this day, *Jazz* is considered a classic in the *livre d'artiste* tradition. The highest level of artistic engagement with the book format was being demonstrated by these works, and for Iliazd's Russian-language text to find itself in such company was due to his production standards, design, and vision, as well as the Picasso engravings. The *livre d'artiste* format, established in the early decades of the twentieth century by editors Daniel Kahnweiler and Ambroise Vollard, was the product of atelier printmaking and fine printing in limited-edition formats. What distinguished Iliazd's work in this genre was his choice of texts, his role as editor, and a design sensibility already formulated in the earlier avant-garde work and mid-century productions.

The Letter was published in an edition of fifty copies with six engravings by Picasso. Many of the formal features of the production anticipated the

Pismo (*The Letter*), cover image by Picasso (Paris: Forty-One Degrees, 1948). © 2020 Estate of Pablo Picasso/Artists Rights Society (ARS), New York

luxurious designs of Iliazd's books in the decades to come. The pages were folded to create a stair-stepped sequence of sizes, and heavy printing paper formed "guard" pages at the start and end of the work.[5] No glue or sewing held the signatures in place; they were folded tightly and then placed in an envelope of parchment (buffalo skin, very stiff and resistant) which he worked himself.[6] He bought his Japon and Chine sheets from warehouses and storerooms where he sought the palettes on which the paper dealer's markings had left red streaks or other uneven variations in the margins, preferring these to the unblemished sheets, perhaps for their variety. (They may also have been discounted in price on account of these markings, thus making another virtue of an aesthetic decision.) The plates were printed in the Atelier Lacourière, where Iliazd produced the images for his subsequent editions. The reception of the book could not have been better. Cogniat's comments were high praise indeed. Iliazd's credentials as a publisher had reached a new level.

But a completely different set of events put in motion the struggles that placed Iliazd in the headlines in the Paris literary scene and motivated the publication of *Poetry of Unknown Words*.

The list of documents and events related to the *Poetry of Unknown Words* is long and provided much material for research as well as a dramatic demonstration of the social networks from which it arose and in turn embodied.[7] Among the four dozen or so entries, many refer to articles in the press, as well as various correspondences, lectures, public debates, and of course the dossier for production with its multiple maquettes and design materials.[8] In addition, I developed a connection to Maurice Lemaître, one of the original members of Isou's group.

In January 1946, almost immediately after his arrival in Paris, Isidore Isou (then just barely in his twenties) organized a public event to proclaim the importance of the movement he had founded, Lettrism. He attracted attention. He was a fresh voice, he had already written a considerable monograph on his theories—which he was in the process of pressuring Gallimard to publish—and he saw himself as the spokesperson for a new literary generation. The historical conditions of a post–World War II culture seeking rejuvenation combined with his individual ambition made a perfect combination for success. Warranted or not (Lettrism was more claim and provocation than substance in 1946), the movement and Isou achieved high visibility in short order. In August 1946, the journal *Arts* published a succinct account of the claims of the Lettrists. The movement, it noted, was not very old but had already established itself by such statements as "You don't imagine that modern poetry is really represented by the stupidities signed Aragon, Audiberti, Emmanuel, La tour du Pin etc."[9] The author cited excerpts from several of the Lettrist works that were meant to outstrip the regressive verses of the authors just named. One excerpt, from M. Brasil, that cannot be translated (not because it is obscene or offensive, but because it is a nonsense poem) is an example:

> Li sis li sis
> Cradoul isolvo tuss
> Na
> Na
> Sisna[10]

The author of the piece (whose name was not indicated) went on to talk about other writers insulted by Isou in public and lineages within which he wished to be considered—notably James Joyce, Henri Michaux, and Raymond Queneau. The distance from early avant-gardes is conspicuous, and the mid-century sensibility of these writers is far from Dada or surrealism. But the author went on to say that the one "prophet of lettrism" conspicuously absent from Isou's discussion was—Zdanevich. This acknowledgment was accompanied by citation of one of his untranslatable works: "Baoutca zefir cafoufou penataloun." This was at least a recognition of Iliazd's place within the history of sound and visual works that experimented with the atomization and play of language for the voice and on the page. But the author commented that in a single blow, Isou had interned all of his predecessors, calling them "old carrion." Isou, he said, "had his youth working for him" and was "full of talent." His major claim? That poetry was "not made of words, but of letters," and that soon "all the poets will write as we do."[11]

Isou's outrageous behavior was designed to be provocative—precisely as that of the futurists had been decades earlier. Over the course of 1947, the conflicts escalated. On June 21, 1947, Iliazd staked his territory clearly in a lecture titled "After Us, Lettrism," given at the Salle de la Société de Géographie. The lecture had been prompted by the public performances by the Lettrists, led by Isou, in which their claim to innovative originality included complete denial of any prior experimental work along similar lines. On the eve of Iliazd's lecture at the Société de Géographie, a notice in *Combat* laid out the arguments: "Isidore Isou did not invent Lettrism. Certain Dada poems of Tzara, of the Berlin Dadas, and of the Russian Futurists were committed to the letter."[12] This notice at least put Isou's claims into context.

But Iliazd could not bear to be erased from a history that was not yet written and in which he had so actively participated. His longtime friend, Ribemont-Dessaignes, explained to the *Combat* reporter that Iliazd's *zaum*

Salle de la Société de Géographie

184, BOULEVARD SAINT-GERMAIN

SAMEDI LE 21 JUIN 1947 A 21 H

une conférence par

ILIAZD

APRÈS NOUS LE LETTRISME

LES CARTES EN VENTE A LA SALLE
ET CHEZ DURAND 4, PLACE DE LA MADELEINE

"After Us—Lettrisme," poster for lecture given in Paris at the Société de Géographie, June 21, 1947. Courtesy of François Mairé and the Fonds Iliazd

work, *Ledentu,* had used consonants without vowels as the speech form for one of its characters. A similar notice in *Arts* did the same, and its author stated at the outset that from the very first Lettrist manifestos they had reservations on the originality of the movement. Isou's major publication, *Introduction to a New Poetry and a New Music (Introduction à une Nouvelle Poésie)* (1947), had been brought out by then under the Gallimard imprint. But the claims in that text were also refuted by the *Arts* author, citing Iliazd's statement that "the Lettrists are today making use of techniques we discovered more than twenty years ago." He used work by Christian Morgenstern, Kurt Schwitters, and Hugo Ball to demonstrate the earlier engagements with elemental components of sound and letter as poetic materials.[13]

The lecture ended in a minor melee. The painter Camille Bryen, a friend of Iliazd's who was serving as the chair of the session, was wounded in the head by a blow from a chair in echoes of the unfortunate events at *The Bearded Heart* from more than twenty years earlier. But this incident became the instigation for *Poetry of Unknown Words.* The June 21, 1947, lecture received multiple press notices in *Combat, Arts,* and *La Gazette des Lettres.* The simple issue at stake for Iliazd was that the innovative work of the early avant-garde, in which he had personally participated, was being erased. His sense of historical accuracy and his sense of personal pride were both affronted.

The reports that followed these events described dramatic struggles. The reporter for *Combat,* identified by the initials P. L., began by describing an audience composed of professional literary people, riffraff of the Latin Quarter, and amateur hecklers. He described the program and a long lecture by Iliazd on Russian poetry and futurism, accompanied by slides of *Words in Liberty (Mots en Liberté),* which, he claimed, were identified as "lettrist" only in order to justify claims of historical priority. The young Lettrist group around Isou, described as between eighteen and twenty-one years of age, created an uproar. Chaos ensued. *La Gazette des Lettres* published a similar account on June 28, describing the bandaged head of Camille Bryen as the culmination of hostilities.

Lectures, readings, and public proclamations occurred through the rest of 1947. One review in *Arts* published on December 12, 1947, described Iliazd at a lecture given by Isou.[14] He stood in the back of the room waving his arms frenetically, attempting to read his *zaum* work while Isou jumped on a table among the glasses and proclaimed that the time had come for an aesthetic revolution in France. Isou and the Lettrists, through their connection with Guy Debord, Asger Jorn, and others, were in fact part of an early youth movement in France that would lead to development of the situationists and their role in the activities of 1968.

None of that could be anticipated in 1947 or 1948, and the struggle between Isou and Iliazd played out in the press, in letters, and charges back and forth of plagiarism and imitation. One very droll note from Iliazd to the editors of *Libération* described his presence at a conference where Isou denounced his existence, and then, having denied that he existed, proceeded to describe in detail the various things Iliazd did not do. Insults abounded.[15] Isou called Iliazd a fake, an imitator, and Iliazd called Isou a false prophet. Isou's arrogant claims to be a messiah did not help matters, nor did his exaggerated ego, bolstered by his good looks (later, when Elvis Presley shot to stardom, Isou played up his resemblance to the star in his grooming and haircuts). At that time in his early fifties, Iliazd resented being called an old man, or worse, being described as a dead man, by the brash young poets. Isou's language of attack became more and more strident over the months ahead, filled with crude slang and constant accusations that Iliazd was an "impostor" and a "scoundrel" who was a plagiarist in reverse. Iliazd and the futurists and Dadaists, Isou insisted, had copied Lettrism in the past, stealing their ideas from Isou and the future movement. This perverse logic has a wit to it, but not much historical sense, and it only served to further provoke Iliazd.

In Iliazd's view Isou was not the only offender in misrepresenting the history of avant-garde poetry. In 1947, a work titled *Panorama of New French Literature*, edited by Gaeton Picon, was published by Gallimard. A study of the twentieth-century French writers Picon considered of significance, the book did not contain a single profile from among the avant-garde poets. During the opening at La Hune, a bookstore in St. Germain celebrating the book's appearance, Iliazd pointed this out to the organizers of the event. The idea that the mainstream literary establishment *and* the emerging avant-garde were equally determined to forget the history of earlier twentieth-century experimental work irked Iliazd. He began to formulate his project. At first, he imagined the title might echo that of his 1947 lecture, "After Us, Lettrism." But he soon dropped all references to the group, not wishing to define his poetics through any relation to them.

Isou's megalomania did not subside. In an open letter to the publisher Gallimard, who had already published the enormous 1947 *Introduction to a New Poetry*, he described another work in progress, *Youth Uprisings (Les*

Soulèvements de la Jeunesse), a twelve-hundred-page manuscript he demanded be brought out immediately. The first volume of this work was published by Aux Escaliers de Lausanne, with the title *Treatise on Nuclear Economy* (*Traité d'Économie Nucléaire*), in 1949.[16] The theoretical text had nothing to do with poetry, though its theories of economics, meant to find an approach that was neither based in the concept of an autonomous individual nor a Marxist collectivity, had some influence on revolutionary social thought. Isou continued his campaign of accusing Iliazd, the Dadaists, futurists, and surrealists, of being copyists and imitators, in spite of their historical priority. At other times he focused his criticisms simply on Iliazd as a derivative artist working in the mode of Tzara.

The outcome of these public battles was Iliazd's decision to edit and publish the *Poetry of Unknown Words*.[17] While journal publications among the avant-garde had included visual poems in their pages, no anthology of this kind had yet been assembled. Iliazd began thinking about the project during 1947. He was still working on the production of *The Letter,* and the correspondence, editing, production, and final publication of *Poetry of Unknown Words* lasted into 1949, as is evident in an exchange with Raoul Hausmann dated January 16, 1949, asking when the book would be finished.

The book was a major undertaking. The sheer scope of the correspondence necessary to enlist his collaborators, get their texts, manage the image designs and production (by sending blocks or plates back and forth), and keep the project on a production schedule was daunting. Add to this that he was dealing with figures with whom he had, in many cases, relations of long standing, but who had become famous artists and writers and had to be persuaded to contribute.[18] A few he may have contacted for the first time to engage them, such as Hugo Ball or Georges Braque. A handful of the correspondence was available when I was working with Hélène, but not enough to get the full picture of the social relations involved.

Not every work in the anthology had previously been published, but all that were newly written for the work were noted in the colophon. Twenty-one poets and twenty-three artists were involved, and each page was a collaboration orchestrated by Iliazd. Velimir Khlebnikov, Aleksei Kruchenykh, and Igor Terentiev were among the poets with whom his earliest connections had been made; then there were the figures from the time of his arrival in Paris—Pierre Albert-Birot, Serge Férat, Oscar Dominguez, Camille Bryen, Léopold Survage, Georges Ribemont-Dessaignes. Names that recalled the programs of the Russian *bals*—Fernand Léger, Henri Laurens, Boris Poplavsky,

Paul Dermée and others—took their place alongside the farther-flung networks of modern experiment in visual and verbal arts: Hans Arp, Antonin Artaud, Jacques Audiberti, Hugo Ball, Nicolas Beauduin, Raoul Hausmann, Vincent Huidobro, Eugène Jolas, Pablo Picasso, Kurt Schwitters, Michel Seuphor, Georges Braque, Marc Chagall, Alberto Giacometti, Albert Gleizes, Alberto Magnelli, André Masson, Henri Matisse, Jean Metzinger, Joan Miró, Sophie Taeuber-Arp, Edgard Tytgat, Jacques Villon, and Wols (Alfred Schulze). Some were of very recent acquaintance (he'd met Matisse in the summer of 1947). He also included Akinsemoyin. His deceased wife's "Lullaby for Chalva" appeared with all its rhythmic and syllabic structure carefully arranged on the page. This and the woodcut done after a drawing by Sophie Taeuber-Arp, who had died in 1943, are the sole contributions by women.

The project, begun as a response to immediate events, dragged on over two years. Each page contained a unique typographic design as well as a printed image. Matching the artists with the typographic elements was a part of the challenge.[19] Once the actual print production was begun, the work itself was considerable. An unpublished note from 1949 reads:

> I pass my time pulling the sheets of my book; the work goes very slowly since I have only candlelight and still not electricity and the days are very short. Here it is autumn already. And summer? I did not see it this year. A year has passed, the pages of the book have returned, printed—it has taken a year for this?
>
> No one helps me and I have no aid at all. I make no progress at all in my writing, which is natural in such misery . . .[20]

And another: "At last my book begins to take shape. Only now have I begun to get hold of the paper, begun the composition of the text at the printer's, and the image and the text are both far from being complete—how long this all takes!"

The *Poetry of Unknown Words* was composed of single unbound sheets folded into quarters. On the outside of the sheet, the names of the paired artist and poet appeared. On the inside, the sheet opened to a full-page work. The typeface Iliazd chose was Baton, a strong sans serif face, unfussy and bold—a harbinger of the Gill Sans he would soon adopt for his subsequent editions. The texts ranged from pure sound poems, their elemental components meant for reading aloud, to works that had slightly more recognizable lyric structures. For texts originally in Cyrillic, transcriptions had to be made and substitutions determined as much by sound as by literal match.

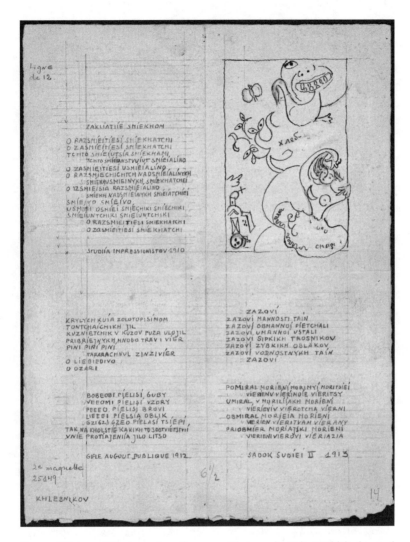

Poetry of Unknown Words, mock-up for page with poem by Velimir Khlebnikov and image by Marc Chagall (Paris: Forty-One Degrees, 1949). © 2020 Artists Rights Society (ARS), New York / ADAGP, Paris

The images were created using woodcut, linoleum, etching, drypoint, aquatint, lithography, and engraving.[21] The maquettes produced by Iliazd are highly detailed, exploring the layout of the type for each different poem, and placement of the images. Nothing was left to chance, and every detail

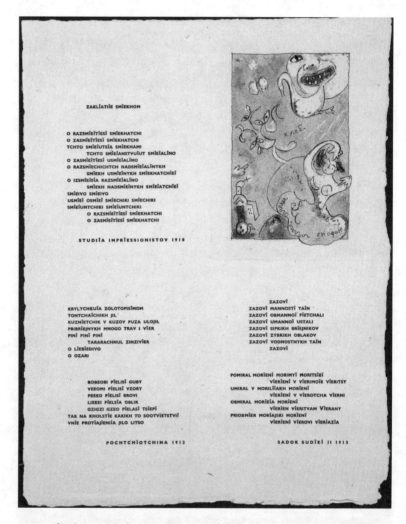

Poetry of Unknown Words, printed version of the same page. © 2020 Artists Rights Society (ARS), New York/ADAGP, Paris

was carefully calculated. The pages were printed by letterpress by Alexandre Zasypkine at the Imprimerie Union, where he had produced his other editions. The extent of Iliazd's involvement in the composition of the type is not clear, though he frequently did this part of the work himself. The dates April 25 through June 22, 1949, were given as the period for compos-

Poetry of Unknown Words, pleated vellum cover, motif by Georges Ribemont-Dessaignes, with warning "not to cut my pages" (Paris: Forty-One Degrees, 1949). Courtesy of François Mairé and the Fonds Iliazd

ing the work, an adequate time for the twenty-one poems, title, and colophon even if each took two days (the poems are not long, and the actual work of composition was mainly a matter of spacing, not the more complex typesetting of *Ledentu*).

The folded sheets, thick and highly tactile, were enclosed in pleated parchment that flapped over their edges to make a protective cover. The result is a compact and object-like book, with a solid presence and sculptural spine. An etching done by Ribemont-Dessaignes showed a winged harp and the statement, "Do not cut my pages" (*"Ne coupez pas mes pages"*). The warning was necessary since the sheets inside, with their folded edges, could easily be mistaken for the uncut pages of a bound book in the style still prevalent in French production. At one point, Iliazd quarreled with the supplier of skins for the covers, angry that he was trying to swap sheepskin for the goatskin that had been promised.

Iliazd wrote to an unidentified friend: "I have finally finished the printing of *Poésie*. I had begun to lose hope. . . . Now begins the same work which you did a year ago—remember? Folding the pages? But I am so tired that I am not sure when I will begin."[22]

The project as a whole was dedicated "in recognition of our companions," particularly those already vanished from the scene. But the correspondence Iliazd had with his collaborators also demonstrated how much credibility he had among them, and how skilled he was at getting these many people to cooperate for the purpose of putting into place a historical record. The notes he exchanged were pragmatic, asking about plates or a text, or about the delivery of a woodcut so it could be printed, and so on.[23] Indications of any discussion about the aesthetic and poetic scope of *Poetry of Unknown Words*, its goals and aims, are harder to locate. A letter to Georges Rouault written sometime in 1949 simply asked for a contribution to the "new collection" which he was in the midst of publishing. Obviously, the format made the project flexible in terms of inclusion and extension, but Rouault did not seem to have responded. Iliazd said nothing in that invitation about the project beyond the fact that he already had images from Matisse, Braque, and others.

Iliazd chose the collaborations, or pairings, of the texts and images, and each page had a distinct layout and format for its typographic setting.[24] The image-text relations were innovative, and the surprise of opening the folded sheets works as part of the experience of the book, providing a new scene for each work. The planning for each page was specific and elaborate, since none of the layouts were repeated. Errors came up in the proofing, and sometimes artists did not like the arrangement. But if any major negotiations took place, or if any substantive aesthetic discussions arose, they left no trace. The one exception was the correspondence generated with Raoul Hausmann, which was continued intermittently (and infrequently) for a decade. Iliazd and Hausmann shared an interest in the historical dimensions of their work and experience and in creating a record of the generation of which they had been a part.

The opening for *Poetry of Unknown Words* was held on June 30, 1949, at the Galerie Graphique Thesée, in Paris, but correspondence with Hausmann and others indicated it was 1950 before they received copies of the book. In total, 158 copies of the book were printed, and of these, forty-one were printed with customized inscriptions to the "Compagnons." Among these collaborators were the professional artisans who had done the presswork, several friends, and two copies for *dépôt légal* (the French copyright office) lettered "A" and "B."[25] The earliest texts in the anthology were by

Khlebnikov, from 1910-13, and the most recent were by Antonin Artaud, dated 1947-48. All were unconventional in their use of language and form. Again, the absence of any Anglophone artists was notable. All lent themselves to Iliazd's typographic presentation, which stressed the possibilities of phonetic and graphic aspects of language as material. Rhyming, timing, and punctuation of breath were all given graphical scorings, while the printing and occasional overprinting were used to make a simulation of vibration, repetition, cancellation of one voice by another, or overlapping tonalities. He was not so much working at a mimetic redundancy of verbal and graphic qualities as he was demonstrating the theatrical potential of the page.

This book of "forgotten phonetic poetry," as Iliazd called it, celebrated a generation of artistic experiment. But it also provided closure on that period of past work. The next phase of his work was not retrospective. *Poetry of Unknown Words* had brought Iliazd out of obscurity. Though the elements of his identity as a *zaum* poet, a futurist, and a founding member of the Forty-One Degrees were all important to him, the persona of editor/publisher/artist displaced that earlier image in public perception, particularly among the literati and bibliophiles.

Into the Present: The Lettrists

Maurice Lemaître was the Lettrist figure with whom I had the most communication. The first time I met Lemaître was in a well-known bookstore haunted by Isou and somewhere on the Left Bank. Its name has slipped from memory, though an impression remains of a corner store with a heavy black doorframe—a small space with tables piled with books, and the space between the aisles constricted by readers standing with books open.

As in all connections in that spring of 1985, the initial contact was made through letters. I wrote to an address, waited for a reply, and if it came, I sent an answer to work out a rendezvous. In this case, the bookstore was the surveillance site for Isou, who would decide whether a visitor warranted his attention and engagement. If not, he let Lemaître, still his faithful lieutenant after forty years, proceed. My appointment was with Lemaître, as Isou did not respond directly to inquiries. Gabriel Pomerand, the third founding member of the Lettrist movement, had died in 1972, and though other followers and latter-day practitioners still lingered, the two key figures were Isou and Lemaître. They were fused by their early allegiance to the Lettrist agenda, and now their energies bonded in the campaign of securing its historical importance.

So I went to the bookstore, entered, looked confused, and hung around. Lemaître approached me. To my young eye, he was an older Frenchman with worn features, and he was wearing a somber suit. In his late fifties, he was going deaf, a condition he described to me with some poignancy later in our relationship by saying the isolation was horrible as it cut you out of human communication. The sadness was evident in his walk and posture, but he came forward and we talked. Where? How? In a park? A café? He needed environments that had less noise and confusion in them, so our next meeting took place in the Jardins du Palais Royal, where the Daniel Buren sculptures populated the gravel courtyard in striking contrast to the original seventeenth-century architecture.

I never met Isou face-to-face. He either deemed me too insignificant to be worthy or too committed to the Iliazd project to be of service to his cause. Isou's position in the mid-1980s was not strong.[26] The Lettrist movement had peaked in the 1950s and early 1960s. The experiments in cinema, as well as the bold graphic canvases and performances, had been eclipsed in many ways by the very youth movement Isou had predicted in the late 1940s. The Situationist International, which had had a high profile in 1968, and whose influence through the writings of Guy Debord, among other prominent theorists, had eclipsed the Lettrists and largely erased any substantive connection to the aesthetic movement. The role of aesthetics in situationism was a topic far from my work on Iliazd, but the insight I gained into Lettrism through my connection with Lemaître gave me a genuine sympathy with its ideas and practices. Later, when I studied the Situationist International and CoBrA (a postwar international art movement whose name was composed of the initial letters of Copenhagen, Brussels, and Amsterdam), I was surprised at the extent to which Lettrism had been erased and disregarded. A perverse justice, perhaps, given the early tactics Isou had used to erase his own predecessors.

To take any interest in Lettrism, however, was heretical within the Iliazd community. Isou was the devil and Lettrism was anathema. Some family incident also attached to this animosity through Iliazd's daughter's activities with the group (perhaps simply rebellious behavior toward her father). These were topics not spoken of, and so the specifics were never made clear. The tone of allusion, brief and quickly passed over, made it evident that the subject was closed. I kept to myself my interest in Lettrism, my friendship with Lemaître, and my sense that an undone project on that movement also had some appeal. Hélène would, I felt, have experienced a sense of betrayal had

I indicated any interest in that direction. These are delicate matters for the biographer, trying to keep the record straight while maintaining good relations with principal players.

Lettrism had a conviction and force to it. The "hypergraphic" work of each of the three original principals mustered visual features of cartoons, glyphs, calligraphy, and typography in experimental works like the *Saint Ghetto of the Loans* (*Saint Ghetto des Prêts*), produced by Pomerand in 1950, or Isou's *The Journals of the Gods* (*Les Journaux des Dieux*), a glyphic novel from the same period, 1950-51. Lemaître's own hypergraphic work was beautifully designed and executed, particularly in the earliest works, like the *Canailles*, also from 1950. At the moment when Iliazd was opting for a deluxe edition protocol through which to express his aesthetic engagement with books and texts, the Lettrists were making innovative works within their own investigation of crossovers between popular culture forms, languages, and those of poetic tradition. None of this had any appeal for Iiazd.

Lemaître waged a brief but pointed campaign to get me to switch projects. Once, he met me on the platform of a Metro station, walked down the stairs and barely paused, handing me a bag full of materials as he passed. Other times we met in a park or garden to talk. The production value of the works told an interesting tale of the slow decline in perceived importance of the Lettrists and their work. The first books were published in editions from established literary houses. Then the work began to be self-published in smaller editions. After this came mimeographed texts, stapled between plastic report covers and other cheap materials. This approach tended to encourage rather than discourage me, as an authenticity attached to these formats and their material qualities.

I did not meet Lemaître's expectations, professional or personal. His kindness was tempered by reserve, and his drives as well, but they were announced and evident. Had I crossed over to his position and accepted all, any, of the many opportunities proffered, a different historical narrative would have emerged. In spite of some recent attention, Lettrism is a still undervalued movement; their aesthetic qualities offered an alternative to the narrative of high art resistance to the popular. A seepage of kitsch and commercial sensibilities occurred in the product lines of Lettrism (they designed bedsheets and other home textiles from their designs). This work had a wit and irony to it decades in advance of postmodern commercial appropriation. Their systematic engagement with graphics and visuality as an integral aspect of poetics was more eclectic and wide-ranging than that of Iliazd. They had no right to ignore the precedents of Dada and futurism, but their atomistic approach to the letter and the glyph came from a different theoretical framework than that of *zaum* or sound poetry of the 1910s, which was affective in force and motivation. The Lettrist work was always an investigation of cultural production and thought in opposition to the romanticization of essence (in sound, form, or affective force). These were significant distinctions, and the very sullied, contaminated pollution of Lettrism's aesthetic looked forward rather than backward, hence its deliberate distancing from movements of the early twentieth century.

We did not talk of these things, Lemaître and I, and we did not talk much of Iliazd either. We met several times, and we also corresponded. I wrote a piece on his work, focused on the hypergraphic novels, and I accepted his gifts of books and works, gratefully. I did not turn from my project on Iliazd, which disappointed him only slightly more (or less) than other refusals of engagement. But this encounter, more than others, was with a living history, not a past one, even if Lettrism was already really only historical by this time. Lemaître asked me to translate something for him, a script or text, and when I did so he brought me, again, a large sack of Lettrist materials, saying something to the effect that it was the privilege of an older man to be extravagant in his thanks.

Hélène and I went on with our work, the indisputable accomplishment of *Poetry of Unknown Words* fully acknowledged, and its scope also deserving, we knew, of much more scholarship and study than we could afford at the time. Keeping the balance between writing the life and analyzing the work—or situating the two in a dynamic relation—was always present. The book remains one of my favorite among Iliazd's works for its unique role in historicizing the work of the avant-garde innovations of verbal and visual work in a moment on the cusp of conceptualism, pop art, and their interests in the art and theory of visible language. *Poetry of Unknown Words* had a handmade quality to it by virtue of the small size and originality of its pages that remains appealing, each sheet opening to its four-part surprise. Compact and articulate, the book performs its aesthetic vision in material form.

8 **1951–1975**

The Editions: Collaborations
and Projects

Deluxe Publications

My original interest in Iliazd was prompted by his books, and, indeed, without them I would have had no reason to engage with his work or profile. When addressing the "editions," those works of exquisite and luxurious design that came to maturity in the last decades of his life, I faced the challenge of giving each work its due while also weaving them into the double narrative of the life and the process of getting to know the books within the research. To write about each book in turn, in the order of their publication date, is inevitable. The chronology presents an unavoidable logic. But the production of the books overlapped, was undertaken through fits and starts, communications initiated with collaborators such as Ernst or Éluard, then broken off. Even the steady friendship of Picasso and his contributions had momentary bumps when plates sat unfinished or timelines slipped or a proposed project failed to catch hold.

Across the whole oeuvre, certain themes echo and repeat: dance, possible antique precedents for *zaum,* language games, and the recovery of works or authors who had not had their due. These were all topics Iliazd returned to repeatedly. At the level of production, the works are faultless. Every book Iliazd had done throughout his life had been executed with precision. But by the 1950s, he was working with a full understanding of what it means to "orchestrate" a work in the book format—to play with the reader's engagement through a series of unveilings, turning sheets of paper that are a prelude to the title page, the text-image relations, and the structure of the whole.[1] He demonstrated what it meant to understand books as works, as art, as full objects, not conventional vehicles for content. Iliazd used materials and design as his creative means, with an understanding of signatures (the physical division of the sections of the book into gathered groups of folded sheets), of openings (the dialogue of one page to another across the gutter), of intertextual play (image and text, text and text, image and space, blank space and margins). But within this creativity, it is his typographic sensibility that is his signature. The texts he chose to publish were the outcome of research and deliberate choice, and the artists with whom he worked were figures to whom he was linked by professional and personal connections and convictions. All of these elements could have been in place and the books' designs could have been exquisite within conventional terms— but his approach to typographic articulation was distinctive.

In *Skinnybones* (1952) the text is balanced through a perfect bilateral symmetry: almost to the letter, the work builds from the beginning to the center and back to the end so that the size of the text blocks and the placement of images are completely matched from the central point. In *Horses at Midnight* (1956) the type dances across the page, imitating the movement of the horses in Picasso's economical drawings. In *The Wandering Friar* (1959) blocks of type imitate the shape of the banners in the images, again by Picasso. In the *Poems and Blocks* (1961) with Raoul Hausmann, the designs of the type are made in such a way that the features of the woodblock prints they accompany are called to full attention. The typesetting "reads" the image and makes us aware of its features. This is rare work—exquisite, technically challenging, but also original in its conception.

True, by the 1960s, visual poetry and concrete poetry in particular were finding fuller expression within an international community, but if Iliazd was aware of that work, he made no mention of it in his notes or commentary. *Maximiliana* (1964), to my mind the peak of his typographic and book design powers, is a work of complexity and subtlety, with two artists (Max Ernst and Iliazd) working together in full control of their abilities. But the "book" is Iliazd's, not Ernst's: the orchestration, to invoke that notion again, is fully realized in the organization of the whole and use of each of its parts. *A Hint* (1965), the long overdue collaboration with the deceased Éluard, monumentalizes a whisper of a poem through its design, using the heavy, almost sculptural prints made by Michel Guino in combination with the typographic distribution of the letters in free fall, to conjure a solid work from a hint. *Boustrophedon* (1971) and *The Grotesque Courtesan* (1974) are consummately skillful works of typographic composition, the first economical in its settings and reversals of text, the second virtuosic in its use of type turned sideward within the lines. To fully appreciate some of these features requires firsthand knowledge of the type case, composing stick, forms for the press, and challenges in printing. Even without knowledge of the physical work and design constraints imposed by letterpress technology, one can appreciate the look of the pages and their design features for their balance, dynamism, and relationship to the images with which they are in dialogue.

These editions benefit from systematic attention. They deserve to be treated one after another. Each is complex. Each was the result, in most cases, of years of cajoling, persuading, seducing a collaborator. Many overlapped in their production and execution. Publication dates are one of the great deceits. No book is produced in the year of its publication date but is always the result of many years of planning, working, executing, and finishing a project. Books are notoriously easy to consume and hard to produce. The experience of production changes one's appreciation. Every detail of page size, paper, ink, placement of text, and size/scale of image, margins, and organization in sequence requires decisions and implementation. A bad run, a misspelled word, a typo, a fading image on a plate, an over-inked block—these are the daily hazards of production. Any of them can ruin the consistency of an edition.

Iliazd, I firmly believe, had absorbed so profound an understanding of what a book is—how it is organized, how it works, how its physical, material, conceptual, and experiential dimensions intersect—that he thought in these terms. The art and design of books, editorial perspectives, and production skills are not the singular provenance of Iliazd. But he did not have projects and make them into books. His conception of a project was always fully within the book format. *How* would it be a book? What paper, what size, what elements of layout and design would bring the idea into form? This capacity is what makes Iliazd a modern artist of the book.

Each of these works could sustain a full study—for its texts, design, and images, as well as physical form. But the task here is to show how these works are embedded in his life, and in the process, make a case for understanding works of art—not as autonomous entities, but as outcomes embedded in complex conditions of conception and production.

Books and Biography

No other early-to-mid-twentieth-century figure I had encountered, no matter how interesting their writing, visual art, or even design, had taken *the book*—its format, possibilities of drama, formal and conceptual dimensions—and worked with it as their primary form in quite the same way as Iliazd. In the last half of the twentieth century, the field of artists' books, book arts, and related activities blossomed in ways that are more innovative and engaged in contemporary culture than those of Iliazd. But Iliazd, we should not forget, was a modernist. He was part of a generation that came of age with the early decades of the century, exploring new formal and theoretical languages in visual and verbal arts. By mid-century, this generation shifted to work that was more classical. The concept of the "democratic multiple" and industrially produced editions that eschewed any affiliation with the crafts of the book or its arts was coming into prominence beginning in the 1960s. None of this touched Iliazd. Once he established the mode of his editions, he never wavered.

Iliazd not only worked out each book project in great detail, but he created the arc of his entire career within a single trajectory shaped by his books. His first works were echoed in the last in a repetition of theme and persons that brought his life *in* work and *as* work to a carefully orchestrated close. This deliberateness combined with a variation in his conceptions of book design so that each project was distinct as well as part of a larger whole. Iliazd had begun his work in the 1910s and sustained his engagement with the book as an object of aesthetic experimentation until his death in 1975. He started with radical futurist poetics and ended with monumental works in the *livre d'artiste* format with its conspicuous innovations and disregard for conventional protocols, and the highly codified protocol required for deluxe editions. This passage from avant-garde innovation to mature individual vision had trade-offs. Experimentation diminished while an identifiable signature brand of work emerged. He shifted cultural location from edge to mainstream as he got older.

Each book arose from attention to the way a particular text should be treated typographically and visually. His approach to shaping language on the page is recognizable, but he never repeated himself. Nor did he imitate others or produce derivative work. If his books belong to the same rank of *livres d'artistes* as the volumes produced by Albert Skira, Daniel Kahnweiler, and Tériade (Stratis Eleftheriades), his approach was still unique. His casings were vellum, often with raw edges, pleated spines, and no sewn bindings. His text blocks were preceded by many layers of folded sheets—blank, but as essential to the sequence of events that structure the book as the title and half title that follow.

Iliazd had spent many hours in the print shop, standing at the case with the composing stick in his hand, separating letters with brass and copper

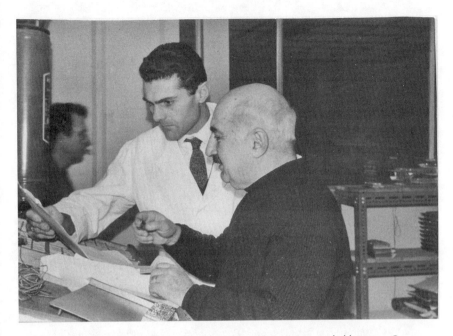

Iliazd with Louis Barnier at the print shop, Imprimerie Union, probably 1950s. Courtesy of François Mairé and the Fonds Iliazd

spacers to get the layout perfect. He had even arranged to stay in a hotel in the quarter near the shop so he could be present when the first workmen arrived for the morning shifts, earning their respect by his persistence. He supervised every aspect of production. But he was not a pressman, and did not print his books, wisely leaving that work to experts whose skills he understood. He was more directly involved in production than other publishers of his day, if perhaps less directly than many book artists who began working in the later decades of the twentieth century. He carried with him that early experience of apprenticeship in a print shop in Tbilisi, and the hands-on knowledge of making is apparent in his approach to design. He had played the part of publisher *and* artist, taking on the roles of designer and compositor, poet, editor, and writer.

These were insights gained as my research had progressed. They provided a foundation for understanding why, in his final projects in the 1970s, Iliazd had returned to some of the first writings he had done. He created two self-reflexive works. In one, he put his early essay on Pirosmani into an edition accompanied by a Picasso drypoint of the artist. In the other, he wrote very short verses that were set both forward and backward, in boustrophedon style, to create a *zaum* inversion of the texts. He was recapitulating, recovering his beginnings in a gesture of completion and closure. He outlived completion of those books, long enough to be working on other projects. But in a very substantive way, with *Boustrophedon* (1971) and *Pirosmanachvili 1914* (1972) he had completed the cycle of his work. To appreciate the poignant resonance of that late gesture we have to begin much earlier and put in place the many points of reference against which he created his life's work.

The related question also persists: What aspect of Iliazd's life warrants *biographical* attention? If only the futurist phase of Iliazd's work remained, his contributions would still merit attention, though his ideas of poetics and *zaum* could be examined without a biographical study. The work of mid-century, entangled as it is with the historical recognition of past accomplishments and the canonization of artists and writers of the avant-garde, benefits from biographical details and circumstances. The editions that occupied Iliazd from the 1940s until the end of his life reward critical engagement, but as biographical artifacts only *Boustrophedon* and *Pirosmanachvili* have direct personal connection to his life. So why a biography? As the details of Iliazd's life became familiar, the narration of the life-work relationship became a continual issue. Were life events a way to get from one book to the next, a kind of interlude of connective tissue bridging one major project and the next? Or did the books just take over and the stories of their production become the main focus? Even the *zaum* dramas, with their themes of gender and language, can be studied directly as texts. Biography does not explain them, and their interpretation does not depend upon the limited details of family life and individual experience available to us at this distance.

If it had not been for Hélène Zdanevich, no biographical study of Iliazd might have been undertaken. Her role in his life, and his importance in hers, were aligned to provide her the motivation and opportunity to support this work.

Hélène (then, Douard) had met Iliazd around 1946-48. She was the director of a ceramics factory and he had come to the Midi region in the South of France with an idea of producing works of his own design, much as he had created fabric designs several decades earlier. Precisely what Iliazd had in mind is unclear. A commercial business plan? Or work that paralleled the ceramics of Picasso, whose output was well known? Iliazd's economic conditions were unclear, and some kind of work and revenue-generating activity might have been a motivation. The ceramic project, however, never took off.

The connection with Hélène, whom he married in 1968, developed over the same period as his work as a publisher of elaborate editions. Iliazd's status rose, even if his income was always modest, through the associations on which he built and the growing reception for the works. The man Hélène knew was of this period. Iliazd was in his fifties, vital and vigorous, and intellectually as well as physically energetic. Her reading of everything Iliazd had done prior to this period was through the lens of this success—which increased over the decades of their relationship. Iliazd became a canonical figure in his own right, established, well respected, and esteemed, and also associated with the major artistic figures of modern art.

His reputation was mainly among bibliophiles and collectors. His editions generally consisted of fewer than a hundred copies. The costs of production were mainly paper, printing costs, and binding materials. The labor-intensive work of typesetting he took on himself. If any money passed hands between Iliazd and his artist-collaborators, no record remains in his notes or correspondence. With the exception of one or two small commissions, Iliazd had no other obvious paid employment in these decades, so he had to have made a living from the editions. He acquired a house in Trigance, in the mountains of the Var district, which brought him close to scenes of his youthful mountaineering. He lived for almost forty years in the small studio apartment in the rue Mazarine, where his design and production activity took place.

From the biographical point of view, starting in 1948, Hélène became a part of the story as well as a witness to its particulars. She was twenty years younger than Iliazd, with her own children, career, and competencies—and she was also a vigorous, energetic person. She played shifting roles in his life as friend, lover, wife, and helpmate-companion. After his death, she was the guardian of the legacy. The profile she passed to me was suffused with her belief in the value of the man and his work. She had no reservations or judgment, no qualifying phrases or reflections. Iliazd was an absolute, a term of replete reference, uttered each time with reverence and resonance, as if no statement could contain the many dimensions of his identity. For her, each book represented a triumph, a culmination of years of research and thought, which it was. Each work stood out as the manifestation of an aspect of character, talent, gifts. For instance, Iliazd produced two texts by a seventeenth-century writer named Adrian de Monluc, who had essentially vanished from public view (and, indeed, traces of his work are difficult to find, even with current digital search tools). Iliazd's recovery of Monluc's work was honored by the town of Toulouse, a point of which Hélène was justly proud. She characterized the book *Treatise on Ballet* (1953) as proof that his interest in dance and understanding of the form was exceptional, and his own skill as a dancer could be painted in extraordinary terms. She saw the elaborate study of the astronomer Guillaume Tempel and its outcome in a small biographical study as well as *Maximiliana* (1964), the elegant collaboration with Max Ernst that stretched over many years, as evidence of a unique intellectual range. The work on Armenian and Georgian churches that resulted in several papers at academic conferences was occasion for awe, deep respect.

The point is not whether these perceptions were warranted, which they surely were, but that the scale of this accomplishment was measured from within a limited perspective. Other artists, writers, and publishers produced equally admirable work, and the issue is not whether Iliazd's accomplishments were important, but whether they were exceptional. Initially, the measure of Iliazd's achievement came to me through the metric of Hélène's judgment. The auratic resonance of the pantheon of modern art, and its celebrity figures, understandably exercised its own power. The Iliazd of the editions, however, was without question Hélène's Iliazd. This was the "person" I came to know, and through whom the rest of the life and work were initially filtered.

In the late 1980s, the canonization of modern artists was still largely uninflected by critical modification. To say "Picasso" or "Miró" was to name figures whose authority conferred immediate status through association. To justify Iliazd by naming the list of his collaborators was to raise him to the level of their pantheon. Again, the issue is not whether these assessments hold over time, but that in that moment of producing the biographical portrait of Iliazd, these were the terms in play. The approaches to which he was attached were formal rather than conceptual or procedural. The figurative imagery, like the texts, was often a matter of historical quotation. Iliazd's collaborators often created visuals that echoed moments of an imagined past, conjured out of scraps of evidence. But Iliazd did not entirely avoid the present, and contemporary approaches to imagery and new editions of poetry by his peers also figured in his works. The study of modernism offered formative frameworks within which Iliazd's oeuvre should and could be read critically, intellectually, aesthetically. Minimalism, pop art, process-oriented work—all of this was irrelevant, just as situationism, art brut, and many other successive stages of visual activity did not factor into Iliazd's work. Nor did radical literary realism or conceptualism of any kind.

Each of Iliazd's books had an origin myth. Sometimes Hélène had an idea of these from conversations with Iliazd; in other instances the stories were in his notes. His research was often elaborate. Iliazd explored his own vision and followed his interests within a combination of scholarly, personal, and artistic affiliations. In the two and a half decades of the editions, he showed the many facets of which his aesthetic consisted. To conflate the aesthetics with the man, however, is problematic, as they are non-equivalent in spite of their link. The books, in all their particulars, are Iliazd's work. They are immediately recognizable by their physical features, typography, and general design. But Iliazd is not the books, and so the relationship does not flow reciprocally. Hints of his character, his respect for artisans and craftspeople, his desire to claim peer status with his collaborators, his persistence, ambition, and dedication—all of these can be gleaned from notes, demonstrated by evidence. But how he lived, what his values were, where his ethical and political principles lay, what he was like as a being in the world—all of that escapes the record. The books do not show the man, even though they are the expression of his individual aesthetic.

A biography is a study of non-equivalences—between evidence and narrative, between documents and character, between projection and impression, between construction and evaluation. A longer list of these points of distinction could be drawn, and in each opposition, the gap between what is present and what is absent is covered by the work of narrating and describing, creating something that passes for the person, stands in as an always inadequate surrogate, radically incomplete. My work involved the process of moving from Hélène's Iliazd into another view of the man, his work, his importance, and the project of attempting to communicate something about his identity created conflicts, not with Hélène—I had too much respect for her for that—but within my own writing. Every sentence, term, word choice became fraught with value judgments that were either too much or too little. The struggle to write without judgment was impossible to resolve; even staying close to evidence was not as simple as it appeared.

Though this discussion of Iliazd's books appears toward the end of this book, it was the beginning, the start point, for the biographical project. We had worked chronologically through the archive and evidence, but the project had been shaped by the arc of the career. Futurism was significant, the Paris arrival and activities crucial, the Lettrist struggle definitive, but it was the editions that defined the Iliazd whose identity initially framed the biographical project.

Editions

The books that Iliazd produced in the context of futurism were poetic texts scored typographically in the service of rendering *zaum*. By contrast, the editions of *Afat* (1940), *Rahel* (1941), and *The Letter* (1948) shared features of the *livres d'artistes*, works whose printed images were artworks in their own right even though they were integrated into book formats. The concept of the *livre d'artiste* had become established in the early decades of the twentieth century. Such works were aimed at a luxury market and meant to create a niche for such products. Illustrated books and folios had been produced for centuries, of course. But *livres d'artistes* included commissions of original art to be combined with a literary text—often a canonical or classical text, and sometimes (more rarely), a contemporary one.[2] In the standard *livre d'artiste* format, the separation of texts and images or the formula of large type, large paper, large margins, was almost never varied. Typography was not innovative or experimental but instead conformed to the decorum of "good" taste and "fine" printing in the tradition of the inconspicuous elegance famously espoused by Beatrice Warde in her advocacy for "transparency" in her well-known "crystal goblet" metaphor for the best kind of typographic presentation.[3]

When Iliazd had turned his attention to *Afat* (1940), *Rahel* (1941), and *The Letter* (1948), he invited Picasso to provide plates for *Afat* and *The Letter*, and Léopold Survage to provide the woodcut for *Rahel*, which has the largest dimensions of the three. With its two sheets of printed work and silky tissues overlaid with the French translation of the Russian text, *Rahel* is more like a slim portfolio than a book. The early *zaum* plays had been bound, their pages sewn or glued into fixed bindings. But *Poetry of Unknown Words* and the books that came after all followed the pattern of loose sheets, folded in sequences of different paper stock, from heavy printing papers, thick as card stock, to papers that rippled in the air and slid through the fingers in light, silky sheets. This orchestration of the "scene" of the book as a series of curtains drawn slowly back in a sequence of physical and tactile events is one of the signatures of Iliazd's mature work. This technique had already been anticipated in *As Though Zga*, published in 1920, which contained variably colored tissues—turquoise, purple, and vivid pink—between its typographic sheets.

For Iliazd, the book was a form with which and in which to think. It was a fully expressive aesthetic object. A book was a site of performance, not a vehicle for presentation of content. The concept of the "artist's book" changed with its appearance in the context of conceptual art and photo-based publications in the 1960s.[4] These independently produced works had certain things in common with the early Russian avant-garde books—a commitment to using mechanical means, an anti-craft sensibility, and goals of achieving a broad readership because they were inexpensive multiples. Artists working in the book format in the latter part of the twentieth century had a wide variety of aesthetic positions open to them under the broad rubric of artists' books. After the 1950s, Iliazd worked in a unique intersection of experimental typography, editorial creativity, and book design. The work does not need to be judged against that of others but succeeds on its own merits. Still, it is useful to consider where it sits in the larger context.

By calling attention to the materiality of formal features, Iliazd's approach feels completely integral to the aesthetic agenda of modernism. Commitment to formal language, innovation within its terms, the self-conscious attention to material features of production as an aspect of the conceptual identity of a work, and a long-standing engagement with typographically experimental approaches as a part of poetic meaning were central to modernist aesthetics. Iliazd had wit and humor in his productions, but no irony, no self-conscious historicization or postmodern critique. He took no stand in relation to popular culture, globalism, racism, or colonial practices, and no political agenda can be assigned to these productions. He was intimately involved in each project from the initial impulse to the final collation of pages. He folded sheets, pleated parchment, and assembled the work for presentation. He was an artisan book artist, hands-on, but also an intellectual one. A defining feature of Iliazd's production was that books are works of art in the fullest sense. The editions he made did not—could not—exist in any other format.

Skinnybones (La Maigre) (1951-1952)

After the critical success of *The Letter* (1948), Iliazd began to produce his editions regularly. Many features of their formats—the fine paper, heavy guard sheets, worked parchment, and unbound sheets—were established elements of his approach and so they won't be described in each instance.[5]

Every book, however, has its origin myths, and Iliazd gave this account of how he came to make *Skinnybones*:

> The year 1941 was remarkable for the fact that I discovered *The Games of an Unknown* while walking through the Passage Jouffroy; I pulled out from a bin a complete edition of *The Games of an Unknown* and, struck by the perfection of the text from the very first line which I read and finding absolutely no indication of the name of the author, asked the proprietor of the establishment, "What is this?" To which he replied, "Thirty francs." I am not in the least ashamed to say that I found my treasure for thirty francs . . . because from this volume I took the text of *Skinnybones*.[6]

The author turned out to be the seventeenth-century writer Adrian de Monluc, and Iliazd spent considerable effort researching the biographical details of his life.[7] This research occasioned various trips to Toulouse to track records in the province and assemble the profile of the author. The original text of *Skinnybones* had appeared in print under a pseudonym, Guillaume de Vaux. The fundamental facts of Monluc's biography were succinctly outlined in Iliazd's notes:

> Adrian de Monluc, an orphan, was raised at the home of Père de Faure, the president of the Parliament of Toulouse and a man of letters. He was surrounded by the shelves of books of one of the richest libraries of the period. But he chose a military career like his father Fabius and his grandfather Blaise, the Marechal, and in forty-two years of active service he took part in twenty major campaigns beginning with that of Le Leion in 1594 and continuing through that of the Mandre les Quatres Tours in 1636, the eve of his imprisonment in the Bastille. But he left us only one account of a siege, that of the bordello of Toulouse . . .[8]

Skinnybones was vivid, funny, and slightly risqué, but also blatantly misogynist in ways that read very differently now, when the idea of men body shaming a woman as an excuse for humor has issues impossible to ignore. The relentlessly satiric text mocked the supposed virtue of a woman so thin her viability as a sexual object was constantly ridiculed: "Don't heap such great praise on yourself for your chastity since no one could ever succeed in working on your flesh. Those who see you will believe it easily enough; since you don't have any flesh or muscles it would be impossible to commit anything but a sin of the bones with you. I would even defy the Casuists to give a name to such a sin—is it fornication, brutality, sodomy, or simply pollution? As for me, I doubt it even *is* a sin to couple with a skeleton . . ."[9]

Though not evident in translation, the work was riddled with puns and wordplay, which Iliazd characterized as "words in liberty," making an obvious connection to Marinetti's phrase.[10] Iliazd said that it was the verbal richness of the work that appealed to him, but he also cherished the idea of Monluc as an anti-academic writer, one persecuted by Cardinal Richelieu. Iliazd commented:

> It is not to admonish the historians of literature that we have become so attached to this book. The best fate for a poet is to fall into oblivion, and Adrian de Monluc certainly merited his oblivion. . . . his garden has become a no-man's land, known as the site of an assassination, his chateau vandalized by people who have never even heard of him, his works attributed to a queen, a magistrate, or a painter, or else locked up in libraries by ignorant folk who nonetheless serve him better than would the ugliness of human recognition . . .[11]

Iliazd had caught Picasso's interest with the project, and by April 1951 his drypoint plates for the images had been completed. They were proofed in May and printed in December. Iliazd described the various stages of the process:

> On his return to Paris, Picasso decided to help print the plates at his nephew's, M. Villato, on his press; but after a few attempts on Chinese tissue we changed our minds and took the plates to the studio of Roger Lacourière. We began with the traditional pulling of three series of proofs (two for Picasso); then the plates were put into acid and we went on to the printing on fine Chinese paper. However, the paper was unsatisfactory, and after some looking around, I managed to find an excellent ancient Chinese on which the edition was printed. Before that, however, we were obliged to try proofs on a number of different papers before we were satisfied.[12]

These details, only mildly interesting in their own right, make Iliazd's direct engagement in the production quite clear. The work he did on design is evident in the outcome, but production histories and labors are generally lost. The book's layout is organized with perfect bilateral symmetry—practically down to the letter—beginning and ending with the same number of lines on the first and last page. He sketched the entire text on graph paper before beginning, a technique he stuck to throughout his works.

The plates were printed in the studio of Roger Lacourière, with whom Iliazd continued to work from that point on. Lacourière worked with other publishers, among them Ambroise Vollard, and a considerable number of major modern artists. The typesetting was done at the Imprimerie Union, a shop inherited by Louis Barnier from Chalit and Snegaroff (one of whom was his father-in-law).[13] Barnier, interestingly, became a member of the Collège de 'Pataphysique, though in his crisp white shirts, ties, sweaters, and vests he gave no hint of his more radical aesthetic leanings. (Pataphysics was the creation of French poet Alfred Jarry, as the "science of exceptions and imaginary solutions."[14]) Barnier was always very correct and formal in his manner, polite and professional in the few instances when we met and exchanged cordialities. He did share an anecdote about the printing of Apollinaire's famous visual poem, "Il Pleut," whose letters drip down the page in imitation of raindrops. The text had been set on a galley, with stabilizing metal spacers and furniture (spacing material), and then, he said, had been held in place with fast-setting dental plaster. This revelation had the aura of occult knowledge offered for view, and though it had been before his time at the Imprimerie, Barnier was clearly proud of the connection with this canonical work, and of the novel solution that had facilitated its production.

Barnier's recollections of Iliazd's working method suggest that Iliazd first set the type without refinement, then went back and justified it with excruciating attention to detail. (Justification is the term for filling out each line of metal type to the same length.) Technically, this makes good sense. The workflow sequence would have had Iliazd pulling the letters from the case, assembling them on a galley between leads (the thin strips of metal that hold lines in place), and then putting together the carefully spaced form for the press. This process would have allowed Iliazd to see the relations among all of the words and letters as a whole, rather than trying to space them as he pulled the individual sorts (letters) from the case and placed them into a composing stick. The physicality of this process can be compared with acts of fitting wooden blocks into a solid shape—it is nothing like using a typewriter (to which it bears no resemblance). Barnier wrote an appreciation of the design of *Skinnybones*, referring to its symmetry as a "counterpoint" within the "structure of a closed system."[15] Iliazd gives this account: "In this book I introduced for the first time the use of variable spacing placed in-between the letters before the lines were justified. This invention showed the error committed by artists of the Renaissance in their search for the correct proportion of letters, which was that they had studied each letter separately, rather than seeing them in their ensemble."[16] The comment reinforces the recognition that Iliazd thought of the whole design, not just its parts. The spacing material to which he refers here consists of very thin slivers of brass and copper, each less than a point wide (the point system is the standard measure for type—seventy-two points to an inch): "My comrades at the printing shop took me for a madman watching me put all the little spacers in-between the letters."[17]

This spacing technique is generally reserved for titling type, large display sizes, where the fit of one letter to another requires subtle optical adjustment. It is almost never used for text type. Iliazd had chosen a typeface called Gill sans serif (or Gill Sans), a delicately cut font that has subtle weight changes in its lines and curves. Unlike the mechanical sans serif types based on strict geometrical models, Gill has some of the qualities of letterforms made from brush and pen strokes in a humanistic tradition. Iliazd used only the majuscules, and this is part of the need for the elaborate spacing. A contemporary font, designed by the British artist Eric Gill in about 1928, Gill was a more elegant version of the Baton font he had used in *Poetry of Unknown Words*. It became his signature font, and he never used any other typeface again.

Other signature features were also present. Iliazd left the sheets unbound, folded between layers of "guard" sheets, the whole encased in a stiff parchment cover. The Picasso drawings depicted the limbs of Skinnybones with such scratchy lines that they resembled umbrella ribs stripped of silk, and he compressed her gawky arms and spindly legs into the spaces of the prints to exaggerate their length and thinness.

Iliazd recorded the date of signing the finished pages as May 18, 1952, and he noted the final printing date as May 21. He signed his books alongside the artists he worked with, giving himself equal billing. These were *his* books.

The book was not an immediate financial success. It sold poorly; although fifty-two copies of the book had been printed and numbered, destined for subscribers, nowhere near that many buyers appeared. Iliazd still had a young child (Chalva) to support, and survival was an issue. The costs of making the edition had been considerable. A private showing was held at the Galerie Bignou on May 27, 1952, and the book was featured in an exhibition at the Bibliothèque de la Ville de Toulouse. Though the Bibliothèque's conservator/librarian heaped scorn on Monluc's text, he praised the work of the "Georgian poet and Spanish painter"—without mentioning them by name—"whose work had rendered the book worthy of being displayed among the treasures of the library."[18]

In an important sense, this book, more than *The Letter*, launched Iliazd's career as the editor of *livres d'artistes*. It contained all of the necessary elements, and was in French, designed to appeal to collectors and bibliophiles. The work was completely legible to its intended audience and sufficiently esoteric to signal erudition. Perhaps only Iliazd would have understood its connection to his earlier *zaum* works and themes of eroticism, but the book was part of a very different publishing and art context, an expression of a mature aesthetic.

Treatise on Ballet (*Traité de Balet*) (1953)

Certain themes repeat across the corpus of Iliazd's work. The challenge is to read the relation among these repetitions without overdetermination. The topic of ballet is one that appeared early in his plans. The initial staging of *Yanko, King of the Albanians*, was in the manner of a puppet show—not a ballet, exactly, but an orchestrated set of movements in which poetic language played an important part as a score. In the 1920s, as part of a program for Tcherez, Iliazd had taken excerpts from his texts and used them as the basis of a performance by the dancer Lizica Codreanu. In 1922 another prospective project involved a Swedish ballet company, though it never materialized. In 1947-48 he had gotten as far as rehearsals with dancer Yvette Chauviré in a project titled "The Ballet of the Underwater Hunt." He described his vision this way: ". . . a ballet in words. Unknown words replace the music and according to their tone determine the characters on one hand while on the other their cadence determines the movements of the dancers' bodies. The key to the rhythm lies in the stops. There are only unknown words, free from the necessity to follow the rules of discourse, which can truly be danced."[19]

The plot of this ballet recalled that of the early *zaum* plays and his novel *The Rapture*. Violence, sexuality, and transformation wove throughout the story of a hunter and a woman fishing and swimming. A fish tail attaches itself to the woman, transforming her into a siren. The tail detaches itself, the hunter shoots it, and realizes he has killed the woman. The tail goes off to dance among the crustaceans. The text of the ballet was completely phonetic:

roco oroco
oroco roco
coroco ocoroco[20]

The 1947-48 ballet was never realized. Pierre Minet interviewed Iliazd for an article in *Combat* designed to produce some advance publicity. Serge

Lifar was named as choreographer in Minet's piece.[21] A storm of attack descended on Iliazd from artists and writers (including Tzara) who claimed Lifar's relations with the Germans during the Occupation rendered him suspect. In fact, Iliazd had never intended to collaborate with Lifar, but pressure to discontinue the project mounted: "This deplorable campaign robbed me of the chance to realize an important work. From this moment it became clear there was a conspiracy against me . . . and that all my work would pass in silence, unreviewed, unnoticed . . ."[22]

The tone in Iliazd's note is bitter. These personal slights and misunderstandings always touched a nerve with him. His own position was never so secure that he could rest comfortably, and the ongoing effort of trying to move projects forward with relatively little support beyond his connections and perseverance clearly taxed him.

For other evidence of his interest in dance we have the records of the lessons he took at a studio in St. Sulpice in 1955, including his enthusiasm for the dances and fancy balls he attended at the home of Marie-Laure de Noailles, an aristocratic artist and patroness of the arts. In an extension of this connection, Iliazd invited her to collaborate on a book, *Treatise on Ballet*, written by Jean-François Boissière, a seventeenth-century courtier and lawyer who had served as secretary to Monluc in Toulouse. A chain of connections helped to propel the project: dance, Monluc, and a patroness of dance who had included Iliazd among her guests at fancy balls. When Iliazd engaged Noailles in creating images, his invitation generated strong reactions, including criticism of Noailles's skills as an artist. But Iliazd defended her: "Victim of an old prejudice about art and the formation of the artist . . . As if everyone doesn't have the right to hold a crayon, as if a precious cult of the 'fine arts' had not been definitively defeated. As if the artist had not always been an autodidact, as if didactic art had not always been false! She, to whom so many owe so much, owes nothing to anyone."[23]

Iliazd remained scrupulously aloof from any financial dealings with Noailles, even when the project faltered for lack of funds. His pride and his sense of propriety were strong.

The text of the *Treatise* was one of the works Iliazd discovered while researching ballets at the seventeenth-century court. Iliazd excerpted sections from the lengthy piece on ballet, and said of Boissière:

Historians of the ballet never mention Jehan-François de Boissière, nor the ballets at Toulouse under Louis XIII. And yet, after the death of Henri IV, the Comte de

Cramail [Adrian de Monluc] who had been the instigator of these ballets at the court of the king, returned to Toulouse. There, in the company of poets like Boissière, Goudelin, Baro, painters like Chalette, and surrounded by friends who were members of noble families or of the Parliament, took place a twenty year program to revive Toulouse. It was at Toulouse that the ballet of the era of Henri IV achieved perfection and became the model for imitation through the rest of the 17th century.[24]

Research on Monluc had led Iliazd to Boissière, including documentation that linked the two noblemen in a sequence of choreographed entrances that formed part of the court ritual.[25] Iliazd pursued this research with skill, ferreting out obscure references. Writing of his own process of editing and publishing, Iliazd reflected: "Should we be less discreet than Boissière? He wrote when the courtiers who danced these ballets were already dead. He neither wished to strip them of their masks nor to reveal their real names. Since the Ballets live forever, we will respect this sentiment. Among the vain attempts of today, one of the worst is that of pretending that poetry is a didactic art. So read this immortal book, dear reader, as proof of a happy time in which Ballets were written and danced by poets."[26]

Art was what mattered, not the individuals. And dance should be danced, not studied and taught. Poetry was not to be turned into lessons. These residual sentiments from his avant-garde period remained with him as guiding principles.

Production on the book was completed in 1953, a year after publication of *Skinnybones*. The book contained twenty-two full-page images and forty vignettes inserted into the text, again set in Gill sans serif. The suggestive drawings imply the splendor of the court rather than depicting it, while providing some openness for the reader to imagine the events of the text. Iliazd had made design decisions similar to those that had governed *Skinnybones*—the parchment wrappers, varied paper stock, and carefully spaced type (though the presentation of the text was more conventional than in the earlier book). In addition, he added thick textured endpapers from a paper stock generally used for wrapping candies so that it was known popularly as *dragée* paper. The sturdiness and tactile-visual character of this paper allowed it to substitute for parchment or be used as guard sheets inside the wrappers. The book consolidated a friendship with Noailles and extended a research agenda. Iliazd attended the Bal des Écrivains given by Noailles in 1956. He came in the role of Afanasy Fet, a nineteenth-century Russian lyric poet renowned in his century but obscure in the mid-twentieth. In this costume Iliazd appeared in the pages of *Paris Match*. In his archive is a list of books on the topic of seventeenth-century ballets, "fêtes et *bals*" at Toulouse under Louis XIII that indicates he was searching for other publications on this topic and period. As will be clear ahead, he eventually succeeded.

Horses at Midnight (*Chevaux de Minuit*) (1956)

Roch Grey was a poet Iliazd had known since the 1920s. Reputed to be the half sister (or cousin) of painter Serge Férat, she was known as the Baronne Hélène d'Oettingen but used several pseudonyms for her publications. Under the name Jean Cerusse, for example, she had published a poem in 1913 in Guillaume Apollinaire's *Parisian Nights* (*Les Soirées de Paris*), and she also published under the name Léonard Pieu. Details of her birth are unclear; what is known is that she came to Paris in the 1900s, divorced (her husband had been an officer with the tsar), and had considerable wealth. With Férat she ran a salon where émigré artists, poets, and musicians were welcome to come for food and warmth. Major figures of the Parisian art scene were among her circle, and Pierre Albert-Birot, publisher and poet, made this assessment of her work: "Never has so authentic a genius been so totally passed over in silence. A genius, yes, a cerebral construction completely unrelated to anyone else, a mind which had been formed in a single and unique example. Read any two lines written by Roch Grey on any of a dozen subjects, and you will immediately recognize a voice full of power."[27]

Grey had died in 1950, and in 1955 Iliazd made notes for a memorial tribute borrowing from the comments of a friend identified in his notes only as Rocherand: "It is thirty years since I first met the Baronne d'Oettingen, alias Roch Grey, and I can testify that the first time I climbed the stairway to her studio . . . I was not at all self-confident. I had been warned that she could be very welcoming to artists, but that she had very little use for those she termed 'merchants.' As fate would have it, she placed me among those 'worthy to enter' and I can be proud, because the lofty domains which belong to her were far above my humble path."

Horses at Midnight was initiated by Serge Férat, and Iliazd agreed to work on the project on the condition that the edition be for private circulation and sale by subscription only. The book by Monluc, then the *Ballet* of Boissière, had put him on course for a next project, a text by another seventeenth-century poet. So *Horses at Midnight* had not been a part of Iliazd's plans, as

he makes clear in the following note. But the combination of personal connections and a disposition toward a project of recuperation prompted him
to take this on: "For many years Serge [Férat] has asked me to include *Chevaux de Minuit* on my list of projects to do with Pablo Picasso. If I finally did
accept, causing upheaval in my schedule, it was only because of the memory of poor Roch Grey, who had fallen into oblivion."[28]

The phrase "fallen into oblivion" resonates across Iliazd's oeuvre and his
personal notes. He repeatedly stated that such a fate was the ideal one for a
poet, and yet his actions in resuscitating lost or obscure works, and even his
continual interventions in public discourse to "rectify" the historical record,
contradict this stance. Iliazd's connections to émigré communities brought
him into contact with individuals from all sectors of Russian society, but
always within an artistic milieu. Whatever differences of class status, wealth,
or politics existed, the common ground of aesthetic activity supplied a justification for exchange.[29]

The thirteen plates engraved by Picasso complemented the dynamic
movement of the setting of the poems. The rendering of the text was dramatic, and here we see Iliazd's graphic imagination at work. The lines of
poetry broke into a frenetic gallop, as if inspired by the capriciousness of a
wildly moving horse. Not strictly mimetic, the layout moved in the spirit of
an animal's erratic spatial dance, "the feverish/thrownback/eyelid of the
midnight horse/breaking into a gallop."[30] Without a manuscript reference,
the decisions about line breaks, word spacing, and organization on the page
cannot be checked against the poet's own design. Aside from the works in
Poetry of Unknown Words, few of the texts in Iliazd's editions were by living
writers (Hausmann and Éluard were the exceptions). Thus, the graphic treatment of the poems was largely based on decisions made by Iliazd, and often
in dialogue with the graphical features of the images in the editions. In this
case, Picasso's capacity to hold a page with an outlined form of horses gave
the right balance to the poem. The text was permeated with dreamlike longing, with its cries of "Carry me, carry me there, only where, my lover, knows,
to wait . . ."[31]

The book's structure alternated between folded text sheets and triptych
arrangements featuring an image in the center panel with the layout of type
mimicking the dynamic motions of the horses depicted. This pattern was
repeated, again in bilateral symmetry from front to back/back to front, so
that the book's shape was spatial and sculptural. The result was that the book
appeared as a volume, in the three-dimensional sense, rather than merely a

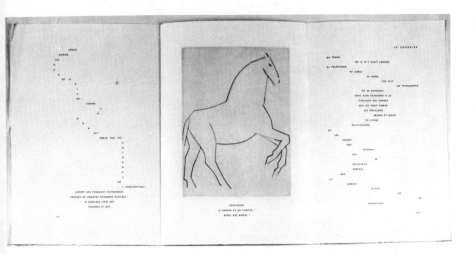

Horses at Midnight, poem by Roch Grey, page showing typography echoing the movement in the image by Picasso (Paris: Forty-One Degrees, 1956). © 2020 Estate of Pablo Picasso/Artists Rights Society (ARS), New York

sequence of pages. The whole effect was dreamlike. The horses cavort, the text gallops on the page, and the book is enclosed in its own set of referential frameworks, as if set apart from the rest of the world, which it is. This quality of insular enclosure is another feature of books that Iliazd fully understood and explored. He created spaces and worlds apart within their covers, exploiting the capacity of books to act in this way.

Tale of the North (Récit du Nord) (1956)

Another continuing interest for Iliazd was in finding historical precedents for his *zaum* work. The discovery of *Tale of the North,* by René Bordier, provided a rare example while also contributing to the work of dance and *bals.* First published in 1626, the text had been performed in recitation as part of an entry procession to one of the more elaborate balls that took place in the court of Louis XIII.[32] The full title of the piece was *Story of the North and Cold Regions for the Entry of the Bailiffs of Groenland and Friesland at the Grand Ball of the Dowager of Billebahaut.* The roles of the bailiffs were in fact played, in that actual ball, by the Duc de Nemours and Adrian de Monluc, Comte de Cramail. The poem was purportedly written in the Topinambou language of Indians from the Brazilian island of Maragnon who had been brought to the

French court by François de Razilly.[33] However, Iliazd gave credit to Monluc
for creating the text, noting that the poem had been recited at the moment
of Monluc's entrance in the procession.

At the remove of several centuries, the syllabic rhythm of the poem and
its nonsense characters justified Iliazd's description of it as a *zaum* work that
"echoed the researches of the most eminent of modern poets."[34] Even if a
connection to an Indian language can be proved, to the European ears hearing these syllables only their musical assonance and sound patterns would
have been evident:

> Toupan mepicho doulon
> Tartanilla noruegen laton
> El bino fortan nil gonfongo
> Gan tourpin noubla rabon torbongo
>
> Pinfa zapaly noucan
> Britanu gogita mouescan
> Vallaguine normdamidon
> Golgon midarman ninbolbodidon.[35]

The short work was accompanied by a colored etching by the painter
Camille Bryen, who had been a stalwart companion in struggles against the
Lettrists a few years earlier. The size of the Gill Sans typeface was larger
than in Iliazd's previous books, and the text was counterposed to the abstract illustration. The colors of the etching—dark red organic lines against
a green field—suggested frozen tundra. The cover of stiff parchment and
thick chocolate-colored guard papers front and back add heft to the volume. As was usual in his publications, Iliazd issued part of the edition, forty-
five copies, on one kind of paper, Chine satine, and several others (four in
this case) on an antique Japon.[36] The edition was finished in 1956, the same
year as the publication of *Horses at Midnight*. Iliazd had hit his stride with the
multiple complexities of its production, but each work still required the
same level of committed attention to detail and persevering spirit.

Intangible Wake (*Sillage Intangible*) (1958) and A Hint (*Un Soupçon*) (1965)

Multiple projects were underway at the same time during these years,
each progressing at its own rate. Neither conception nor execution followed
a mechanistic path. For example, these two works appeared in 1958 and

1965 respectively; although other editions appeared between these dates, the two works were linked by Iliazd's connection to Paul Éluard (who had died in 1952).

Iliazd met Éluard soon after he arrived in Paris in the early 1920s. Iliazd's early connections, like this one, lasted throughout his life, providing collaborators and *compagnons* with whom he shared an aesthetic formation as well as life experiences. Among these were Picasso, Joan Miró, Max Ernst, Roch Grey, and others involved in *Poetry of Unknown Words,* the *bals,* and other activities.

Perhaps none of these relationships was more complex or fraught than that which Iliazd had with Paul Éluard. A leading figure among the surrealists, Éluard had played a crucial, and unpleasant, role in the *Bearded Heart* affair in 1923. He had withdrawn his offer to write a preface for *Ledentu,* feeling compromised by the circumstances surrounding the Tcherez event. At the same time, he had made an extra effort to let Iliazd know that no personal break had occurred between them. As a consolatory gesture, Éluard had offered Iliazd an unpublished poem to use as a basis of a later work. Various misunderstandings and difficulties delayed this publication, but both *Intangible Wake* and *A Hint* arose from the long-standing connection between the two men.

In notes titled "Approaching Éluard," Iliazd describes the relationship as "a failure, a vain blossoming."[37] In 1978, Annick Lionel-Marie summarized this text as follows: "It recounts the declined invitations, the lost preface to *Ledentu,* the battle of Coeur à Barbe, and its paradoxical result: that it permitted Iliazd to see Éluard frequently, but resulted in Éluard's departure. Of the ten years erased from his [Iliazd's] literary life, he retained a special sadness in considering them ten years in which he lost sight of Éluard."[38]

When Éluard died, Iliazd, desirous of paying homage, returned to the unpublished poem Éluard had consigned to him thirty years earlier. But the estate of Éluard refused to allow rights for the publication without exorbitant payment. Iliazd was offended by this on two counts. First, he felt it was a betrayal of Éluard's own wishes. Second, this attitude demonstrated profound misunderstanding of Iliazd's approach to his editions. He was not interested in *publishing* in a commercial sense, but in making work that could celebrate Éluard in a unique presentation, an Iliazd production.

Iliazd decided on an alternative project, taking a poem written in memoriam by another close friend of Éluard's, Lucien Scheler, and combining it with an engraving by Picasso showing the poet's head wreathed in laurels.

Iliazd recounted the chain of events as follows: "Scheler knew I was very upset by the refusal of Éluard's estate to grant me publication rights of the poem, so at the end of 1957 he offered me one of his own poems, one dedicated to the memory of Éluard, as a gift, without any expectation of recompense. And so I took the greatest possible care in its composition . . ."[39]

Of this production, François Chapon said, "Iliazd, consistent with his manner of creating any volume, even the thinnest brochure, struggled to create a unity from which no part could be separated: a visual poem."[40] A single page of text and one engraved image made up the entire contents of this edition, and the role of paper, parchment, and guard sheets became essential. The cover of *Intangible Wake* was made of heavy parchment on which the title was printed in brick color, anticipating the guard sheets with pale brown fibers. According to the bibliographical scholar François Chapon the interior was printed on "the most beautiful Japanese paper to be found in all of Paris, that which the publisher Pelletan had acquired in 1906 from Bing, the exporter of Chinese and Japanese goods."[41] These sheets of paper had survived a flood in the storage cellar of Bing's illustrious shop, and thus had a history as well as pedigree of their own. These details gave extra value to the production, lending it material substance and symbolic dimensions.

But the care Iliazd lavished on this production did not protect him from other offenses of the sort to which he was particularly sensitive. The book appeared in July 1958, and in November of that year Iliazd was confronted with the sight of both image and poem reproduced without permission on the cover sheet of *French Letters* (*Lettres Françaises*), edited by Louis Aragon. Iliazd described his shock this way:

> On Monday, coming out of the Rue Monsieur le Prince into the Carrefour Odéon, I stopped in front of the *crémerie*, which, being closed on Monday, served as a support on which the neighboring news stand propped its journals. I stopped dead before a familiar face. The journal was *Les Lettres Françaises*—which I did not read regularly—and my portrait of Éluard by Picasso was printed above the poem by Scheler. For a few moments, innocent that I am, I could simply not believe my eyes! To have printed the text and illustration of which I possessed the rights without having asked my permission and then without even mentioning my name![42]

The plate was printed in reverse, adding insult to injury, and the work was represented in the publication as a collaboration between Scheler and

Picasso, with no mention of Iliazd or the Forty-One Degrees imprint under which it had appeared. Somewhat unusually, Iliazd had not signed the book, which does not excuse the incident, though it casts it as ignorance rather than malevolence. The subscribers to the book protested to Iliazd, angry that he had let the plate and text be reproduced in so banal and ugly a manner. On November 27, Iliazd wrote a letter of rectification to Louis Aragon, demanding it be published. The affront was painful, and on December 13 he wrote Aragon again, asking why the first letter had not been published.

In 1965, this blow was softened somewhat when Iliazd was finally able to publish the text of *A Hint*. He had located the four-line note in which Éluard consigned the poem into his care for future publication. Iliazd took the small poem and rendered it into a monumental book. For the project he approached a young sculptor, Michel Guino, who had never before done engravings. Guino recalled that one day Iliazd came into the École des Beaux Arts, full of energy for the project, and literally put the burin and plates into his hands, telling him he needed something very strong to counter the delicacy of the poem.

The poem was not only brief and delicate, it was *about* delicacy—hints, suspicions, traces—all subtly nuanced through a series of phrases in which the word *légère* (lightly) was coupled with a series of words such as *tombait* (fall), *dormait* (sleep), and so on. These phrases formed the entirety of the text, and Iliazd worked exhaustively on the arrangement of the letters in what were literally dozens of studies for the pages. Design notes show he experimented with no less than 117 different ways to set the word *légère*. The challenge was to make a few letters, sprinkled on the page, into a successful design that communicated a sense of form, movement, and lightness without disintegrating into chaos or mere scattering. The very sleight of hand by which he achieved such an effortless effect is the strongest testimonial to its success. The pages have the look of having happened, rather than having been made, the look of being permanently in a state of suspended activity, the stop-motion image of particles of breath, falling leaves, a yawn, a stretch, a laugh.

The contrast with Guino's engravings was striking. The images seem like hewn slices, plates of metal, suspended in free fall. Iliazd linked text and images with colored ink tones, the only time he ever used colored ink for type (except for cover titles). Guino recalled that Iliazd brought him small samples of wool to show him the colors he intended to use.[43] The guard

A Hint by Paul Éluard, with image by Michel Guino (Paris: Forty-One Degrees, 1965).
Courtesy of François Mairé and the Fonds Iliazd

papers, or folded endsheets, were thick and gray, enclosing the pale cream
Japanese paper within:

> *Un Soupçon* [was] the book I had dreamed of since the death of Éluard . . . I ap-
> proached the sculptor Michel Guino because I thought his style would suit a
> book in which the word "lightly" was repeated so many times. There are fifteen
> dry-point engravings on copper, unetched, three printed in black, twelve in color,
> all coppery tones showing off the nuances of color. . . . The deep cutting of the

plates posed a difficult problem for the choice of paper; in order to avoid tearing I was forced to give up the idea of printing on the wonderful antique Japon which I had put in the Lucien Scheler book.[44]

Marking the completion, Iliazd noted the publication date as the winter solstice, 1965. No record of an opening party exists for the book, printed in an edition of sixty-four copies. Iliazd's records indicated more than half the edition was promised to subscribers at the time of publication. Guino claimed the book did not sell well, though it was exhibited at the Galerie Darial in June 1976, and he blamed his own poor status in the art world for the unpopularity of the edition.[45]

Intangible Wake and *A Hint* were intensely personal books motivated by slights that Iliazd wanted to rectify. In the latter, the small fragment of Éluard's poetry, fragile as the bond between them had been, had become transformed into a work of monumentality through Iliazd's efforts. His aesthetic vision was more encompassing than the concept of publication could accommodate. The substance of the book seemed to answer the long-standing ambivalence and frustration he had experienced in his relationship with Éluard. In coming to terms with this situation, he spent hours composing and recomposing the shape of those brief phrases—*tombait légère, mangeait légère, dormait légère*—until they occupied the exact configuration that could reconcile him to their place on the page, their permanent inscription, their impression as memory.

Of the many friends and colleagues who formed an integral part of Iliazd's life in Paris, Éluard was only one of several for whom he created such a memorial tribute. He had produced Roch Grey's *Horses at Midnight*, the anthology of *Unknown Words, Ledentu,* and later would commemorate the work of the printer in the work bearing his name, *Roger Lacourière*, the memory of Pirosmani, and the self-reflexive testimonial to his own life, *Boustrophedon.* The themes of memorialization and recapitulation brought the books into being from the events of the life. Any understanding of them is incomplete without this recognition.

Modernism Vanishing: A Day in the Country with Michel Guino

The editions continued to appear. But as Hélène and I worked on the materials related to *A Hint,* the question arose, as it always did, of who was still alive with whom we might speak. On many visits to persons known to

Iliazd, I was sent by myself. Hélène felt no particular personal connection, or had never met the person involved, but felt these conversations were important for my research.

One of these was Michel Seuphor, the famous art historian and critic. The visit took me to a very upscale apartment in a fancy *quartier*, where, with flowers and pastry in hand, I was received by a domestic, shown into a large study, and had half an hour's conversation with the elderly figure whose domed head and shrunken body were a testimonial to his age and endurance. We both wondered why I was there, and I was soon allowed to leave with little gain and no recognition that my visit had had any more value than that of the paper cone in which the pastries had been tied.

A very different event had been a meeting with Antoine Coron, curator at the Bibliothèque Nationale, who spent the entire meeting lecturing me as if I were an undergraduate on a year abroad about why I was not going to see any of the archival materials the library had acquired and why, in any case, I was unsuited to any of the intellectual tasks I had undertaken with regard to Iliazd. Again, the biographer becomes an object of projections.

But with Michel Guino, Hélène had, I sense, a feeling of affection. He had been a young artist in the mid-1960s when he worked on *A Hint*, and Hélène had had some social connections with him during the time as well since she was, by this time, involved with Iliazd and had firsthand knowledge of the ongoing production.

"We will go to see Guino," said Hélène, "now, there is a man who gets it." The statement meant many things, but chief among them was that Guino believed in Hélène's Iliazd. He could be counted on to subscribe whole-heartedly and unreservedly to the image of the man as a great artist and editor, visionary and poet.

Guino was the young sculptor Iliazd had tracked down at his studio one afternoon with the request to make plates for *A Hint*. His father, Richard Guino, had been a famous and commercially successful sculptor, making figurative work, mainly female nudes, with a semi-moderne stylized finish. Guino *pére* had had an unusual history, having been hired by Ambroise Vollard to work with Pierre-Auguste Renoir as his "hands" after rheumatoid arthritis had crippled the painter. The work had required translating images painted by Renoir into sculptures to be cast. These duties went far beyond simple technical assistance and blurred lines between original creation and collaboration in an unusual way. Michel Guino had fought a legal battle on behalf of his father's contribution to the sculptures, and these Renoir editions had given him an income. All of this history had occurred long before our encounter, in an extended process that stretched from the 1960s through the early 1970s.

Guino *pére* had been a figure of recognized reputation and renown. The son had secured credit for his father's work, reclaiming the identity of artistic authorship of the sculptures. But the younger Guino saw himself as a failure, as Hélène had indicated to me before we went to visit. He had become affluent by restoring his father's fame, and he lived without doing anything of substance himself. Hélène, wanting him for a credible witness to Iliazd's talents, needed him to live up to her expectations.

We went in a car that Hélène kept stored in a garage near the apartment, though she rarely used it. The whole event was unusual from start to finish, since we rarely ventured out together. Our work was focused on the table in the atelier, and our exchanges across its expanse circumscribed almost the entire horizon of our relationship. The idea of an adventure into the countryside had many fascinations and was a rare treat in all regards. Régis accompanied us and drove. The route was a tangle of small roads. Where signs were posted, I could not make sense of them. They seemed to point to obscure spots on a map that only listed larger towns. Many of the crossroads had no signage, and Hélène navigated by impulse. The trip did not take long, but we were well out of Paris and into the rural surroundings when we pulled into a long gravel drive, through a lightly forested zone, and onto an open area in front of a house. It was late morning and raining slightly. A handsome man, with a gently aging face and body, was dancing under an umbrella. He wore a dark blue silk dressing gown, over a white toga-like garment, and he held a glass of champagne in his hand.

He greeted Hélène with great warmth, though I could tell from her body language that she did not approve entirely of his demeanor. Not yet close to lunchtime, the hour suggested that champagne was definitely decadent. And he was clearly somewhat inebriated. Continuing his dance, he welcomed us all and we crossed the patio that flanked the house and went into the spacious interior. There we were greeted by his wife, a pretty woman beautifully dressed in fawn-colored slacks, and a couple of children whose identities became less clear when we met his mistress a few minutes later. A skinny woman with big eyes and blond, slightly frizzy hair in ringlet curls, she was wearing some kind of gossamer garment that gave her the appearance of a dragonfly. The children were introduced in connection with their respective mothers, and the group was clearly the assembled outcome of these multiple connections.

Welcomed in, we were offered champagne, under Hélène's somewhat disapproving eye. She accepted the hospitality with the necessary politeness, but only barely sipped at her glass. We sat together while the children and women moved around, the wife remaining and the mistress disappearing.

Hélène was keen to have Guino tell the tale of Iliazd's invitation to him to collaborate on the book, and also to demonstrate the pedigree by which Guino claimed his own status. Guino obliged on the first count and refused on the second, constantly undercutting his own identity and credentials. He was so clearly not his father, nor of the stature of Iliazd, and insisted on this point almost to an extreme. This behavior troubled Hélène in some way as the day unfolded. But in the initial exchange in the salon, Guino, holding off on more drink, gave Hélène the account she had come to hear. He told the story of Iliazd, and in each uttering of his name, made clear that *that* was a man, an artist, one of the truly authentic human beings. Hélène glowed, satisfied. Guino was charming, virile, and charismatic, and his interest flattered Hélène as he paid her all due deference, giving her his full and serious attention.

After about half an hour, the first conversation flagged. We moved from the salon to the dining room, arranging ourselves around the big table in a bright, open room that had doors on to the garden. The light rain had stopped. A general air of affluence prevailed, not quite luxury, but ample sufficiency. The wife presided at one end and Guino at the other end of the broad country table (after he had slipped away to put on slacks, a white open-necked shirt, and sports jacket). The bread was fresh and crusty, the food beautifully prepared and traditional, and the wine was ample. The rivalry between the wife and the mistress was constant, part familiar banter but also edged with rancor. Hélène was not comfortable. A discussion of town and country domiciles went by quickly. The suggestion was that some separation of roles between wife and mistress had been violated. The presence of the mistress in the country house, where they had all been in residence now for some time, was somehow not quite in keeping with the rules. The wife in her deer-colored clothing had big brown eyes, long lashes, ruddy chestnut hair. She kept putting one of the children, her daughter, in immediate proximity to her father. The children were very pretty, and this daughter, about seven or eight, was clearly the darling. But Guino said something cynical about the child's capacity to charm and the wiles of women that also alienated Hélène. Her sense of propriety ran deep, and this was a flagrant violation of bourgeois norms and discretion.

Lunch dissipated rather than concluded, and the suggestion of a walk prevailed. We trudged about in the woods, now steaming, and Guino told more tales. The party broke into clusters, each moving at different rates. I stayed with Hélène and Guino. Régis disappeared and so did the mistress. Hélène was a skilled conversationalist, well bred, sophisticated, and capable of keeping an afternoon's exchange pitched at the right level and pace. But the conversation about Iliazd was over; that had been the first exchange of the day, and homage had been duly paid, respect acknowledged. The rest of the day moved from other reminiscences, Guino's recollections of his father's contacts and circles, the legal process, the many connections that provided common points of reference between him and Hélène. Little substance, but much exchange of familiar names, formed their dialogue. Guino resolutely refused to step into the role of the artist or claim credibility. He was a failure, he said. Hélène chided, but with no effect. Guino knew where he sat in the historical lineage and hierarchy. More, he knew the paradigm had collapsed. The era of giants was over. For better and worse, he had neither aspirations to its terms nor faith in their continuity. He was not a modern artist, but a child of the moderns. He was dissolute, indulgent, living off the accomplishments of the generations that had preceded him.

Régis and the young mistress now reappeared, their composure disarranged. Hélène opened her eyes wide, then narrowed her gaze and compressed her lips. Régis. Really. He was flushed and clearly somewhat at a loss. But the energy of the group took over, normalizing, as we returned to the house and got ready to depart. Some final exchange passed between Hélène and the pretty brown-eyed wife, who held a child close as we parted. Arrangements for some other event and connection ahead were mentioned. All necessary civilities were observed. Régis resumed his place at the wheel, Hélène next to him, and we drove back to the city. Some asides acknowledged Régis's adventure, though no details emerged. His embarrassment could have been the result of innocence, not experience. Hélène seemed amused, even pleased, by his success.

But the deep import of the day was clear. The age of those great figures was over. The children of those modern masters were not going to stand on the shoulders of their fathers. And Guino, at least, understood that Hélène was disappointed—in him, in the defeatism, and in the way the attitude both celebrated and undercut Iliazd's generation. The celebration was easy to understand; Guino paid clear homage. But the undercutting came from a refusal to engage with the world on his father's terms, a sense that they did not fit the current world. In making that admission, he signaled that the father's generation could not determine his work or life. This attitude felt disrespectful to Hélène. Filial duty obliged a son to live up to the expectations of the father, not put him aside as irrelevant. For Hélène this was painful and registered as a major loss. Iliazd had believed in Guino more than Guino believed in himself, and such disregard seemed to squander talent and refuse responsibility. The terms of the present had suddenly reframed the past. The ground on which the biography was founded had shifted. This was not tectonic, not catastrophic, but the reorientation brought the frameworks of what was, at that point in the mid-1980s, the current conversation about the historicity of modernism into focus in the embodied history of participants. Impressions of that day sank in deeply. Historical distance was registered in the living present.

Editions, Continued
The Wandering Friar (Le Frère Mendiant) (1959)

The Wandering Friar, Iliazd's next project, arose from his interest in language and geography. But it must also be read as another of the memorial books, a tribute to his second wife, the Nigerian princess Ibironke Akinsemoyin. By 1946, Iliazd had established contact with his late wife's relatives, the Yoruban family, to assure that his young son, Chalva, would have a connection with his mother's family and heritage. By 1949, Iliazd had become actively interested in research on the European voyages of "discovery" of Africa. He had collected maps, manuscripts, and books that charted these explorations. In 1969, he traveled to Lisbon in pursuit of a scrap of information for one of these accounts. But the 1959 publication *The Wandering Friar* was the most substantial expression of this interest.

The text of the book had been written by an anonymous fourteenth-century Franciscan friar, and Iliazd approached the study by making elaborate lists of all the place names in the work, comparing them with earlier and later versions on maps and writings. Both linguistic study and geography figured in this project as Iliazd compared dates of landings on sites on the African coast with the transformation of place names. A body of correspondence in the Iliazd archive attests to his African studies: he wrote to the Huntington Library in California, to book dealers in France and England,

and to various scholars. From an M. R. Bastide, for instance, he received a reprint of "Afro-Brazilian Social and Religious Structures," and from a musicologist, Dr. G. Rouget, he gleaned references on Yoruban history. The Africanist Pierre Verger wrote a tribute to Iliazd's erudition, praising his passionate pursuit of books, information, and ideas. Iliazd was described as "haunting" bookshops with dogged constancy, a "familiar" in many special library collections, who knew every corner and secret shelf related to topics that inflamed his curiosity.[46]

When it was published, *The Wandering Friar* received considerable praise from scholars in the field. The Secretary of the Société Africaine de Culture wrote in 1959: "The presentation you have made of this ancient manuscript is of great interest to Africanists and anyone with an interest in African studies. If you could send us some proofs, we would be certain to make them known. Your work and efforts deserve to be recognized and continued and we would like to help you in the distribution of your work. We also very much appreciated the work of Picasso, which has a simplicity and rigor in keeping with the spirit of clarity in the narration."[47] Iliazd had relied on a version of the manuscript established by Marcos Jimenez de la Espada in 1877. François Chapon has commented that the text described Africa before it had felt the impact of European culture. Preceded by fragments of accounts of the discovery of the Canary Islands by M. Jehan de Bethancourt in 1402, the text of the anonymous friar had struck Iliazd as having no agenda for either conversion to Christianity or conquest.

Picasso supplied the images, using what Chapon termed great "economy of means" to suggest the vegetable, architectural, and other elements of the African landscape. Here, as in other images by Picasso, the apparent sparseness created powerful suggestions. The thin lines gave an impression of a sun-drenched world of blinding light, balanced against the regular spacing in the usual Gill Sans font.

The type was set in shaped blocks that echoed forms of banners and other features in the images. The relation between the images and the arrangement of the type into blocks, which had first appeared in *Horses at Midnight,* here assumed a solid geometric character within the overall composition of the book. The visual and verbal domains became solidly integrated. The book had a medieval character with its images of knights, castles, banners, and so forth evoking an era of pageantry, but also an African flavor through the full-page images of the landscape. Once again, the parchment wrappings and heavy gray guard sheets performed their work, adding heft

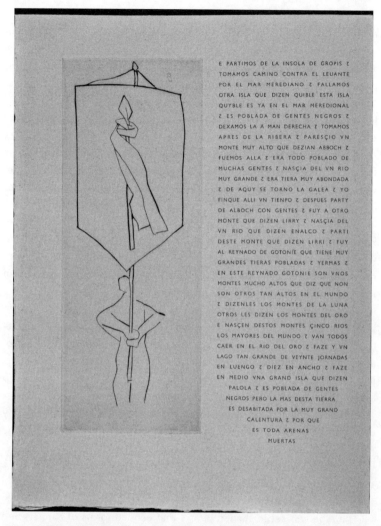

E PARTIMOS DE LA INSOLA DE GROPIS ჳ
TOMAMOS CAMINO CONTRA EL LEUANTE
POR EL MAR MEREDIANO ჳ FALLAMOS
OTRA ISLA QUE DIZEN QUIBLE ESTA ISLA
QUYBLE ES YA EN EL MAR MEREDIONAL
ჳ ES POBLADA DE GENTES NEGROS ჳ
DEXAMOS LA A MAN DERECHA ჳ TOMAMOS
APRES DE LA RIBERA ჳ PARESÇIO VN
MONTE MUY ALTO QUE DEZIAN ABBOCH ჳ
FUEMOS ALLA ჳ ERA TODO POBLADO DE
MUCHAS GENTES ჳ NASÇIA DEL VN RIO
MUY GRANDE ჳ ERA TIERA MUY ABONDADA
ჳ DE AQUY SE TORNO LA GALEA ჳ YO
FINQUE ALLI VN TIENPO ჳ DESPUES PARTY
DE ALBOCH CON GENTES ჳ FUY A OTRO
MONTE QUE DIZEN LIRRY ჳ NASÇIA DEL
VN RIO QUE DIZEN ENALCO ჳ PARTI
DESTE MONTE QUE DIZEN LIRRI ჳ FUY
AL REYNADO DE GOTONIE QUE TIENE MUY
GRANDES TIERAS POBLADAS ჳ YERMAS ჳ
EN ESTE REYNADO GOTONIE SON VNOS
MONTES MUCHO ALTOS QUE DIZ QUE NON
SON OTROS TAN ALTOS EN EL MUNDO
ჳ DIZENLES LOS MONTES DE LA LUNA
OTROS LES DIZEN LOS MONTES DEL ORO
E NASÇEN DESTOS MONTES ÇINCO RIOS
LOS MAYORES DEL MUNDO ჳ VAN TODOS
CAER EN EL RIO DEL ORO ჳ FAZE Y VN
LAGO TAN GRANDE DE VEYNTE JORNADAS
EN LUENGO ჳ DIEZ EN ANCHO ჳ FAZE
EN MEDIO VNA GRAND ISLA QUE DIZEN
PALOLA ჳ ES POBLADA DE GENTES
NEGROS PERO LA MAS DESTA TIERRA
ES DESABITADA POR LA MUY GRAND
CALENTURA ჳ POR QUE
ES TODA ARENAS
MUERTAS

The Wandering Friar, text by an anonymous fourteenth-century friar, with image by Picasso (Paris: Forty-One Degrees, 1959). © 2020 Estate of Pablo Picasso / Artists Rights Society (ARS), New York

and material substance to the edition. The fifty-four copies were each signed by Iliazd and Picasso.

The production activity on the editions had a certain regularity to it. Though projects often took a long time to develop, beginning with the kernel of an idea that might come quickly or very slowly to fruition, the actual work of getting paper, plates, setting type, cutting vellum, collating and binding is production work. It has a certain physical rhythm and demand to it, but it was also work Iliazd was doing to keep a pipeline going, supply his subscribers, and make a living. Nothing about these aspects denigrates or devalues the work; quite the contrary—it makes clear what kind of work the books' production involved. The conceptual and intellectual dimensions drove the projects, but Iliazd had skills in the craft and art of book production that informed his designs. This was work he chose, work that made sense, and work at which he excelled—but it was also essential to bring the editions to an audience of appreciative bibliophiles and dealers, and that necessity of production provided its own drive.

Poems and Woodcuts (Poèmes et Bois) (1961)

Iliazd and Raoul Hausmann had had an extensive correspondence spurred by the initial exchanges around the *Poetry of Unknown Words* in the late 1940s. In them, Hausmann mentioned his plans for a history of sound poetry and discussions of its origin within the early seventeenth-century work of the Spanish poet Góngora. In 1948-49, the letters contained much detail from Hausmann about his activity in the Dada period, where he had been central to the Berlin group's activities. He noted that he had written his phonetic works independent of influence from Hugo Ball, and only learned about Ball's Zurich works from Richard Huelsenbeck in 1920.

The bond between the two poets, Iliazd and Hausmann, sprung from their mutual engagement with experimental verse in the late 1910s. Hausmann asked Iliazd to confirm various points of information about the evolution of Russian avant-garde poetry. Both were keenly committed to documentation of their work and its larger context. But once the *Poetry of Unknown Words* was completed, their correspondence became more sporadic. In 1954, the prospect of a collaboration was broached. The appearance of *Poems and Woodcuts* in 1961 was the result of a slow and careful exchange.

The initial idea was for the work to include some pieces by Kurt Schwitters, some by Hans Arp, as well as Hausmann's own. Hausmann sent a copy of the Dada publication *PIN* to Iliazd, since a number of the works had appeared in print in its pages. But the proposal was vague, and it was unclear exactly what Hausmann had in mind or how it would differ from *Poetry of Unknown Words,* the anthology Iliazd had already completed.

After 1954 the correspondence lagged. In 1957 a letter from Hausmann mentioned that they had not communicated in the intervening years. The new exchange came about when a Swiss publisher approached Hausmann with the possibility of publishing some of the work he had sent to Iliazd three years earlier. Iliazd's interest quickly revived. Hausmann responded with enthusiasm, saying he much preferred the idea of a project with Iliazd, since it would be "a million times more artistically produced" than any commercial work.[48]

By spring 1957, the project was underway (quite likely, *Intangible Wake* and *The Wandering Friar*, which appeared in 1958 and 1959 respectively, were also in process). Hausmann had begun making woodcuts and pulling proofs, sending them to Iliazd. By this time, the book was envisioned as consisting solely of Hausmann's poems and prints. Hausmann's enthusiasm increased as the project continued, and he was more sympathetic than most collaborators to the actual production tasks and labor involved. He wrote to Iliazd in October 1957:

> Well, vacation is over, and I see you have returned home and are now faced with all of the difficulties involved in producing a book. Have you found the Chinese paper? Do you already have the parchment? Have you made a contract with the printer?
>
> I am very happy, now, that my poems and wood cuts will soon be produced by you. It is certainly time that something of mine appeared . . . because I have, after all, often been the precursor . . . But I know that you are aware of this, and also, understand the urgency and importance of my appearing in your production, with your *mise en page*. There is absolutely no one at all who is capable of better typographic design.[49]

The long process of production caused another of the snags that irritated Iliazd profoundly. Three of the poems that were part of the manuscript appeared in print in another collection, apparently printed without Hausmann's knowledge or permission. Their appearance prompted a series of letters from Iliazd to Theodore Koenig, joint editor of *Phantomas,* where the poems had appeared, asking him to print over them with black ink to correct the error. The situation was resolved when editors Koenig and Noiret renounced all publication rights to the works and Hausmann wrote to Iliazd granting him rights for five years. This incident occurred in spring 1958. By August 1958, Iliazd had pulled a number of proofs from the woodblocks and was predicting the book might be finished by winter.

A year later the book was still not done. Hausmann had his own historical rectifications to make; he wanted the priority of his phonetic verse to be recognized. In late November 1959, he urged Iliazd to complete the book as quickly as possible, but it was not finished until April 1961. Hausmann invited Iliazd to Limoges, where he was living by that time, for an opening to celebrate the book. He asked Iliazd which wines he preferred and promised to show him works that were rarely shown, or known, including some of Hausmann's gouaches and paintings.

A study of the layout of the book and the typographic organization of its pages makes clear what took so long. Aside from the fact that Iliazd was involved in several other productions (*Tale of the North, The Wandering Friar,* and some other proposals), the sheer conceptual and technical complexity of the layouts would have made for slow progress. Iliazd copied features of the woodcuts as the way to structure the layout of the type, rendering each line with architectonic emphasis. The letter spacing and justification posed their own technical challenge, but the conceptual orchestration was also complex. Figuring out which features of each print should provide the graphic armature for the layout and then making the poems and images talk to each other effectively took time and care. The texts of the 1947 works became transformed into elemental features of the page. This was Iliazd at his most virtuosic, inventing technical solutions that were aesthetically innovative and specific to each project.

The dismantled poem, taken apart into skeletal elements, was arranged with structural rigor that reinforced (rather than copied) the visual structures in the woodcuts. The strict vertical, horizontal, or diagonal alignment of textual elements became the verbal tracing of the lines of force, vectors of energy, to be perceived within the images. It was as though Iliazd had dissected the body of the woodblock and found the structuring elements, the bones, within it. The resulting correspondence between the shapes in the blocks and arrangements of type was so close that the skill of the work was almost effaced. The poems were spare, the blocks, though vivid and dynamic, were simple. Iliazd had them printed against solid blocks of color to add definition and density.

Iliazd wrote a short preface to the work, "An Unlettered Homage" (or, alternatively, "An Illiterate Homage"—"*Un Hommage illettré*") dedicated to Hausmann:

I'm proud to render homage to you
In arranging your poems and wood cuts
And in holding the paper knife like a pen

Poems and Woodcuts, text and images by Raoul Hausmann (Paris: Forty-One Degrees, 1961). © 2020 Artists Rights Society (ARS), New York / ADAGP, Paris

Don't reproach me for this professional
Attitude—remember that in 1913
I began my work
With a book dedicated to modern painting

Admit, nonetheless, that criticism
Has become insufferable

Ignorance and pretention have taken over,
Asserting rights over art

What nonsense is to be found in these prefaces
And these texts
The dead weight of illustrated tomes

Art didn't change in order to be talked about
And having lost its anecdotes
Has gotten itself stuck in criticism

So please accept my *illiterate* homage.[50]

Iliazd refused to make his productions academic, even if some, like *The Wandering Friar,* were scholarly. He insisted that his work as a publisher and editor was the work of an artist. The *"illettré"* in his preface title voiced his refusal to write about either art or literature from the outside as a critic. Instead, he always wrote as a poet. His contribution was not a gloss on the work of others; it was an artistic contribution equivalent to that of his collaborators. On the most literal level, Iliazd's treatment of Hausmann's texts demonstrated this fact dramatically. He gave them their form in a manner that was more transformation than publication. *Poems and Woodcuts* is a fully mature expression of Iliazd's vision of the book as a complete work of art, one that he brought into being.

Sentence without Words (*Sentence sans Paroles*) (1961) and *The Twelve Portraits of the Celebrated Orbandale* (*Les Douze Portraits du Célèbre Orbandale*) (1962)

These two books were intimately related to each other. The first was a "crown" of sonnets, written in Russian, and the second a collection of portraits that were versions of the frontispiece for the first.

Sentence was published with an engraving by Braque on its parchment cover and a frontispiece portrait of Iliazd by Giacometti. Neither Braque nor Giacometti were figures with whom a social connection with Iliazd remained—unlike Picasso, whose connection with Iliazd Hélène frequently referred to for its familiarity and warmth. Braque's connection was minimal. The engraving suggests a crown or a wandering wreath of lines that composed themselves into floral motifs that are just on the verge of dissolving back into abstraction. The device suggested a memorial wreath without overdetermining the image. Since the poems made up a cycle of sonnets in which the fifteenth was composed of the final line of the preceding (each of which was begun with the final line of the one before), the interlocking suggestiveness of the graphic motif announced the form of the text. The sonnet sequence had been written over a ten-year period, and according to Annick Lionel-Marie, it was "elegiac in tone . . . the song of an impossible love."[51] Later translated by André Markowicz and published, the cycle was inaccessible to either me or Hélène at the time, and as in many instances, we relied on André's critical and poetic insights to appreciate the virtuosic achievement. Reading it in French, one feels the melancholy tone. Iliazd was in his early sixties at this point, and the fact that he would produce a work in Russian to express emotions speaks to the costs of many displacements and losses. But, again, the remove of language and the absence of clear referents make it difficult to link to biographical specifics.

The interlocking sequence was echoed by the portrait cycle by Giacometti that constituted the second book. Giacometti had engraved thirteen plates in the process of making the frontispiece. Each was scratched with the burin into the dry surface of the metal, an effort to catch the essential quality of Iliazd in a portrait. One of these did serve that purpose, and the other twelve became *The Twelve Portaits of the Celebrated Orbandale*. The portraits were of Iliazd, and when asked why he used the name Orbandale, he said he couldn't very well use the title "The celebrated *Iliazd*." This kind of displacement was part whimsy and part a game of hide-and-seek, like the play of names used by Monluc and Roch Grey. Such ploys were part of that ongoing paradoxical opposition between "falling into oblivion" and "being brought to light" that was such an important aspect of Iliazd's editorial attitude.

The twelve portraits were in varying degrees of completion—eyes filled out or blank, sketched, more detailed, and so on. The series became the portrait of a portrait, the intersubjective play between two artists, each one shifting and changing through the interaction.[52] As a pair, the two books emphasize repetition and variation. The *Twelve Portraits* had no words at all beyond the title. The *Sentence* had no images besides the frontispiece and cover motif. Each were works of enchained production, one without words, the other without images.

The Twelve Portraits of the Celebrated Orbandale, image by Alberto Giacometti (Paris: Forty-One Degrees, 1962). © 2020 Alberto Giacometti Estate/VAGA at Artists Rights Society (ARS), New York/ADAGP, Paris

65 Maximiliana, the Illegal Practice of Astronomy
(*65 Maximiliana, ou l'Exercice Illégal de l'Astronomie*) and
The Art of Seeing (*L'Art de Voir*) (1964)

By contrast with the allusive and private character of *Sentence without Words*, *Maximiliana* is graphically vivid and conceptually clear. Of the mature works, nothing quite compares in scope and ambition to this project—finally achieved with Max Ernst. Finally, because the book had been initiated about fifteen years earlier, as was often the case for these elaborate productions within friendships of long standing. While each of Iliazd's editions displays some feature of his talents for design, typography, research, scholarship, and collaboration, the graphical range in *Maximiliana* is a virtuosic demonstration of Iliazd's capacity to engineer a book through a well-organized collaboration of all of its parts.

Iliazd and Ernst had been friends since the early 1920s. In 1924, Iliazd stayed with Ernst while recuperating from an ear operation. In sympathy, Ernst and Éluard had offered Iliazd a text they had authored collaboratively, "The Unhappiness of Immortals." A long-standing agreement existed between Ernst and Iliazd to collaborate on a project.

In the course of some research, Iliazd discovered that a star designated Maximiliana had been named by the nineteenth-century astronomer Guillaume Tempel (1821–1889).[53] Tempel's itinerant life had been complicated by tangles with the law, as the term "illegal" in the title implies. The coincidence of the name of the star and of his friend (Max) became the motivation for the book's content and design.

Once in pursuit of Tempel, Iliazd became obsessive, tracking his movements and activities through texts and landscapes the same way he had tracked those of Monluc. The result was *The Art of Seeing* (1964), a small booklet written to accompany the deluxe edition composed of scraps written by Tempel and facts about his life culled from Iliazd's research:

> It is a hundred years since the art of seeing which precedes the art of painting was sketched by the lithographer and amateur astronomer Guillaume Tempel.
>
> Native of Haute Lusace, he left his village to learn his new trade at Meissen on Elbe, then across Europe. Attracted by astronomy, he installed his telescope at the top of the Bolovo staircase in Venice, and began with the discovery of the comet of 1859 and the famous nebula of Merope in the constellation of the Pleiades. Valz, the director of the observatory there, helped him get to Marseilles,

where, in poverty, he lived nine years in the Rue Pythagore, high up and well oriented, beneath a sky moistened by damp wind, finding new comets, planets, and nebulae without number.

Obliged to leave Marseilles at the end of the Franco-German war, he went to Milan to hide, and from there he went to the Arcetri Observatory in Florence which had remained empty after the death of Donati.

Wrongly accused of lying by the official astronomers, charged with stupidity, deprived of the right of baptizing his discoveries, and of the right to even make observations, Tempel bequeathed to us his periodic comets as a persistent reproach, recorded in all the almanacs.

It was not mere visual acuity which accounted for his success. Along with it went a certain skill of observation and a corrective reflection which contributed to his art of seeing. Preoccupied with the future of vision, which was falsified by the inventions of optical instruments of optics and photography, a paradox for an astronomer, he pushed himself to use the arbitration of painting. Having measured the impact of these inventions on the future of painting, he nevertheless took refuge in the eye.[54]

Iliazd appreciated Tempel's prose for its lapidary sense of language, so aptly suited to extraction in the fragments he used for *Maximiliana*. He felt a sympathy with Tempel as a writer whose striving spirit had been beset by adverse circumstances. The plates and sketches of nebulae and star patterns he had observed in Tempel's work gave him a basis for the layout of the texts and the instructions to Ernst about the variety of forms—all part of Ernst's own graphic language—he wished to see in the images.

Iliazd's correspondence with various experts in the history of astronomy began in the early 1960s. He found out that Tempel had begun his professional life as a lithographer, but that his passion for astronomy had led him to an itinerant existence as he went from one observatory to another in Germany, Denmark, France, and Italy. According to Iliazd, he "died of sadness, having been forced to sell his telescope. Among the injustices which had made him suffer particularly was that which touched upon his discovery in 1861 of planet # 65. He named it Maximiliana in honor of Maximilian, King of Bavaria. But his discovery was not officially recognized, and the planet was later re-baptized 'Cybele' by German astronomers."[55] This "injustice" was the kind of historical oversight that pained Iliazd with respect to his own accomplishments. The personal identification was clear.

Subtle questions about vision, visuality, text, and textuality were posed

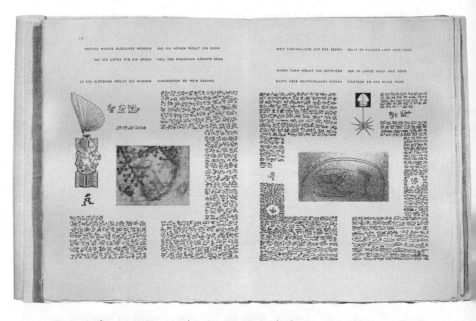

65 *Maximiliana*, interior page showing Max Ernst glyphs, imaginary writing, collages, and Iliazd's typography and design (Paris: Forty-One Degrees, 1964). © 2020 Artists Rights Society (ARS), New York / ADAGP, Paris

throughout the completed book. In fact, *Maximiliana* constitutes an engagement with *writing* in all of its various forms as a pictorial mode of communication. The book contains glyphs, symbols, type, scribbles, small signs, and motifs combined with typographic "constellations" of Tempel's words. Ernst's inventive graphical style fit with the questions posed by the text, and he produced a wide array of beautifully designed plates. Iliazd organized the page layouts and sent the already cut and sized plates to Ernst with their roles and placement designated. The book's graphics posed the question: At what point does writing become image, not language? And how long can it occupy the indeterminate space where it resists final definition as either one or the other? Iliazd directed Ernst to embody these questions in his drawings, and the result is an elegant inventory of inscriptions, including an imaginative pseudo-writing invented by Ernst.

The structure of *Maximiliana* incorporated Iliazd's understanding of the book as a spatial whole, rather than only as a linear sequence. Three balanced sections, whose divisions are punctuated by the same device, consti-

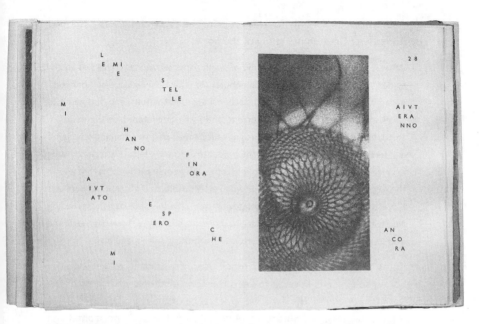

65 *Maximiliana*, interior page showing Max Ernst aquatints and Iliazd's constellation-ary typography and design (Paris: Forty-One Degrees, 1964). © 2020 Artists Rights Society (ARS), New York / ADAGP, Paris

tuted the sum of thirty folded sheets. Of these, only the first, the title page, was not mirrored by a sheet at the end. The second folded sheet contained only a column of text, also mirrored by the colophon. Working forward from the beginning and backward from the end, the book was symmetrical in structure—a design approach used in *Skinnybones* (1952) as well. The third and twenty-ninth sheets were completely composed of images, and five folded sheets followed (again, repeated from both beginning and end). These symmetries and repetitions were carried out through the book, so that the sequences of folded pages combine the dynamism of their images and text with an overall stability of organization and layout. To see this structure as a whole, the reader has to stand outside the experience of turning the pages and reading/viewing the work—in essence, occupying the omnipotent position of the designer.

Many more graphic and linguistic elements appeared in this book than any of the earlier editions. The texts are in French and German and were printed in what Iliazd termed *"typographie carrée"*—a way of setting the type that he designed expressly for this project. The typography was described by Anne Hyde Greet in her study of the book:

> What is "le carré"? On the same kind of graph paper where he [Iliazd] was accustomed to map out an old Byzantine church or a new dance step, he now composed his make-up; he chose as his schema a geometric form and outlined it in small squares. The schema is recurrent, and it is not centered on the page. Instead, shapes are tilted and the design is off center; part of a rectangle or spiral is missing, as if it sloped off into the void. Furthermore, letters are placed only in certain of the squares. Thus not only is the design only partly contained within the page, but what is on the page is only partly visible, as if glimmering here and there through the texture of the Japan paper. This invisible design, spreading across the page and beyond its margins, corresponds to the sky as we see it and also to mystical ideas of a cosmic structure, arbitrary, secret, and divine.[56]

Translating these graph-paper mock-ups into printing forms required elaborate setting and spacing to keep the constellationary patterns of the letters in place. For all the dynamic appearance of the type, however, Iliazd maintained a classical foundation, never altering the basic horizontal and vertical squareness of the type. Though the pages give the illusion of diagonals, spirals, and moving forms, they are actually set within the constraints of a letterpress grid—which explains the term *"carré,"* or square. Iliazd understood the mechanics of the square forms of metal type and also knew how to exploit the possibilities inherent in the medium to sustain these dynamic illusions.

Ernst's "secret" writing glyphs appeared at various scales. Some of the glyphs escaped and became full-sized figures, enigmatically bordering on the explicitly figurative, but never so fixed that they detached from the swarming mass of written forms with whom their genetic relation remained explicit. Organic and swarming, they were engraved to fit the shaped plates cut by Iliazd. Other figurative elements were present as well. Ernst made small collages, with bits of fan, material, faces, and costumes, and also included frottage techniques that cast starlike images in patterns of nets and lines of lace-like patterns made by putting fabrics onto the aquatint ground. Simultaneously material and celestial, these patterns represented the micro and macro scales of the cosmos. While all the visual elements bordered on the readable, they also maintained their character as lines and glyphs.

A small amount of red and black overprinting occurs in this book, generally working with the same image at different scales. Iliazd used photographic methods to reduce and enlarge the images before having them made into relief plates. The text fragments were often poignant, and the beautifully set passages stood in unrelieved isolation as if to indicate that no mitigating circumstances would soften the difficulties of the astronomer. Here is a fragment from Tempel's text: "Memory is no longer cultivated and exercised as it used to be, owing to the masses of printed matter accumulated over the course of the centuries-and the art of seeing is on its way to being lost on account of the invention of all sorts of optical instruments." And another: "Since Easter I have carried in my pocket the announcement that my telescope is for sale." Or: "In Marseilles, during the period when the mistral blows, I was obliged to set myself up at the window of my bedroom with the window opposite the terrace closed—because the wind blew so violently against my window, trying to break it with grains of sand."[57]

The themes of difficulty and artistic struggle, vision and integrity, attempts to survive against real difficulties were all present. So was the poetry that Iliazd recognized in these apparently ordinary statements, jottings in a notebook, haphazard, but direct, immediate. Iliazd tracked the locations in which many of these statements had been written and entered into Tempel's notebooks. Photographs taken by Iliazd at the tower of Bovolo in Venice show where the astronomer had set up his telescope. In one photograph, an empty, isolated doorframe stood alone. The building into which it once led had been demolished. In the next photograph, taken by Hélène, who had accompanied him on that voyage,[58] Iliazd occupied that doorframe, walking through it to the phantom space of Tempel's vanished life.

Maximiliana is a comprehensive statement of Iliazd's aesthetics. Every element of what contributes to a book has been carefully considered so that the connections of image and text, the location of the line between them, and the spatial organization and structure of the whole are all engaged.[59] The material sensibility is also fully developed. Under the parchment wrappers, no less than three different folded guard sheets, in increasing degrees of delicacy, lead the reader into the work: a heavy white pulp sheet (Auvergne), a gray rag paper, and then, thinnest of all, an "ochre" sheet that anticipates the antique Japon on which the interior is printed.[60] The theatrical sequence—the series of veils and curtains, turnings and gradual revelation—was never surpassed in Iliazd's work.

The project was not easily realized. Tensions emerged in the course of the collaboration that almost threatened the outcome. Iliazd had to remind Ernst several times of his long-standing commitment to do the project. In

1961, Iliazd sent this note to Ernst: "The world is full of rumors these days that books illustrated by you are about to appear which are not mine. Let me remind you of your promise that your next illustrated book would be by me and no one else. I continue to believe that you will hold to your promise."[61]

Then Ernst questioned the terms of the project, apparently quibbling with Iliazd over business matters. Iliazd was offended, and in a letter on October 19, 1961, he wrote:

> We are not dealing with a commercial project. This is an expression of friendship and that's all and if you do not wish to do a book with me in spite of all our preparations, the plates, the changes in the text, etc., then there is nothing I can do. Neither am I attempting to profit from our friendship. I am not sure exactly how the book will turn out, but in offering you fifteen examples out of forty-five, which will be placed on the market at 4000 francs each, I did not think I had attempted to rob you.[62]

The exchange provides insight into Iliazd's collaborative processes and the way he conceived of each partner's contribution. Money was not exchanged, at least not apparently. Fortunately, the difficulties were worked out, and the book was produced. The text was printed at the Imprimerie Union during the "full moon" of March 1964. The finished work was exhibited at the venue Point Cardinal from April 29 to May 31 and was well subscribed, with half of the edition subscribed at the time of publication.[63] Even among the many expertly designed works in Iliazd's complete oeuvre, *Maximiliana* stands out. The compositional repetition and variety of motif, shape, type of image and text relationship, and all other conceptual issues and design considerations reached a height in this work whose complexity posed daunting design challenges. Iliazd was close to seventy years old when the book appeared, and yet several more books lay ahead.

The Georgian Itinerary of Ruy Gonzales de Clavijo and the Churches in the Vicinity of Atabegat (L'Itinéraire Géorgien de Ruy Gonzales de Clavijo et les Eglises aux confins de l'Atabégat) (1966)

This publication was not a deluxe edition, but a pamphlet printed for the XIIIth Congress of Byzantine Studies at Oxford University. It showcased Iliazd's interests in the architecture of Orthodox churches and is cited in scholarly literature on the topic.[64] As we have seen, his earliest trips into the Caucasus had been as a teenager with his father, and his brother Kirill recalled that Iliazd was even then taking dimensions of the Byzantine churches. His skills had been honed in 1917 on the trip with the archaeologist Takaishvili, when he had been hired as an assistant to draw plans based on observations of Byzantine monuments.

In 1931 an exhibition of the materials prepared in Takaishvili's expedition was mounted in Paris. Iliazd had renewed contact with the archaeologist, and he remained in communication with him intermittently through the 1930s. They exchanged notes for an eventual article. Contact with other scholars working on Armenian or Byzantine architecture also followed.[65] Between July 27 and August 2, 1948, Iliazd attended a Byzantine Studies conference in Brussels and delivered a paper on "A Little-Known Church, Neighbor to St. Sophia," and later that summer and fall, other papers on "Urbain de Bolzano" and Byzantine architecture. He presented eight such papers, written between 1948 and 1961, in scholarly conferences.[66] Iliazd was an educated and intellectual man, but his persistence in these pursuits, without any institutional support or position, was exceptional.

The research that formed the basis of *The Georgian Itinerary of Ruy Gonzales de Clavijo* tracked the itinerary of a traveler through an area of the Caucasus that was familiar to Iliazd from his own expeditions. Using his linguistic skills to identify points on which the itinerary had been misread, he was able to pinpoint locations on a trail where Gonzales had passed between September 5 and 17, 1405. Iliazd had retained detailed accounts of his own mountaineering expeditions, noting the dates of his movement on maps. The scholarly reengagement allowed him to renew his acquaintance with a landscape he knew well.

The itinerary of the fifteenth-century Spanish diplomat, Clavijo, read like a diary, with great immediacy and detail in its first-person narrative. The publication included the reproduction of a carefully drawn map, compiled from exhaustive research, marking Clavijo's courses through areas Iliazd had traversed in 1916-17.[67] A path through this area of northern Turkey led to Trebizond on the Black Sea—again, familiar territory from his youth.

Iliazd's investment in the *Itinerary* led to his delivering the text as a scholarly paper and also printing up a booklet in five hundred copies for distribution at the conference. Photographs, drawings, plans, and architectural studies of medieval churches in the region traversed by Clavijo corresponded to notecards and research materials. In addition to making use of scholarly resources, Iliazd followed his research interests to Yugoslavia to trace the course taken by Simon Begnius (Simun Benja). In 1964 he took another trip by boat along the Greek coastline to repeat the journey of Cyriacus of Ancona, and in 1965, he went to Crete explicitly to measure the church at Kissamos.

No large-scale editioned book resulted from this work, though Iliazd clearly drew on similar research methods in seeking out the texts for his books.

Roger Lacourière, Fisher of Plates (Rogelio Lacourière, Pêcheur de Cuivres) (1968)

In 1966 Roger Lacourière died. His atelier was the place where the plates for Iliazd's books, and those of many other publishers and artists, had been printed. Iliazd designed this book as a memorial tribute. Again, the work is as much a testimony to community as to individual artists or works. The title loses its elegance when translated into English. The simple image of the printer leaning over the acid bath with the careful attention of a fisherman, engaged and distracted simultaneously, tuned with perfect patience to his task, sounds either too whimsical or too satirical in English.

The book was designed to allow the many artists who had benefited from Lacourière's careful craftsmanship to pay homage to the value of artisanal skill and its crucial role in producing *livres d'artistes*. Iliazd had a deep and reciprocal appreciation of the collaborative role of the professionals with whom he worked.

The format is landscape, with parchment wrappers. The guard sheets in heavy printmaking paper are followed by the ochre paper Iliazd had used in *Maximiliana*. The works were printed on antique Japon, with extra copies of the images printed on Chine and parchment. Thirteen images appear in the volume. The artists who contributed were Nicolas Beauduin, Camille Bryen, André Derain, André Dunoyer de Segonzac, Max Ernst, Alberto Giacometti, Alberto Magnelli, Louis Marcoussis, André Masson, Joan Miró, Jules Pascin, Pablo Picasso, and Léopold Survage.[68] These were presented simply, as images on folded sheets facing the name of the artist.

But the typographic treatment of the page donated by Picasso deserves special mention. The artist had written a poem on an etching plate, and the lines sloped down from left to right, spanning out into a wider and wider fan. This autographic image took liberties with the straight lines and quadrature (squareness) that are part of letterpress technology. Imitating it in print form, which Iliazd did for the facing page, was a remarkable achievement. The result is an image of gentle dissolution, as the text moves out of its tight

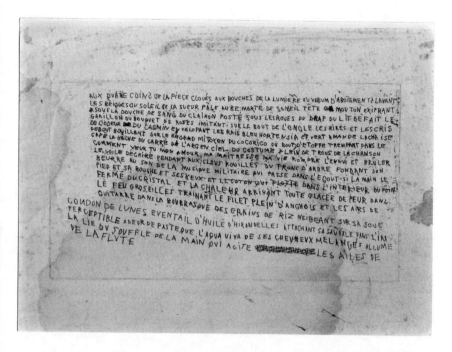

Hand-drawn etching by Picasso from the homage to *Roger Lacourière* (Paris: Forty-One Degrees, 1968). © 2020 Estate of Pablo Picasso/Artists Rights Society (ARS), New York

setting and drops down the page in a slow dissipation of order. The form for this page—the lockup of the letterpress, leading between lines, and spacing material in a chase—still exists, interestingly: someone in the shop found it unusual enough to be worth keeping the type from redistribution for further use.[69]

Iliazd had formed a strong bond with Lacourière based on their respect for technical craft skill. Lacourière's widow said of Iliazd: "We came to appreciate the poet's understanding of manual and artisanal techniques. He never hesitated to participate in the work, and when we printed on parchment, he was there all day working with the printer to help prepare the skins."[70]

The cover of the book contained signatures of all the artists involved, ordered in the same sequence as their prints appeared in the book. Iliazd cut a template to be sure the positioning of the signatures was consistent, and each artist signed through a window cut in its surface. A long memorial

AUX QUATRE COINS DE LA PIÈCE CLOUÉS AUX BOUCHES DE LA LUMIÈRE DU VELUM D'ABOIEMENTS LAVANT LES BRIQUES DU SOLEIL DE LA SUEUR PALE AUBE MORTE DE SOMMEIL TÊTE DU MOUTON EXPIRANT SOUS LA DOUCHE DE SANG DU CLAIRON POSTÉ SOUS LES ROUES DU DRAP DU LIT DÉFAIT LE GRAILLON DU BOUQUET DE ROSES IMITANT SUR LE BOUT DE L'ONGLE LES RIRES ET LES CRIS DE L'ODEUR DU JASMIN ENVELOPPANT LES RAIES BLEU HORTENSIA ET VERT AMANDE LA CHAISE DEBOUT BOUILLANT SUR LE REGARD MITOYEN DU COCORICO DU BOUT D'ÉTOFFE TREMPANT DANS LE CAFÉ LA HACHE DU CARRÉ DE L'ARC EN CIEL DU COSTUME PLEIN DE TROUS DE LA CHANSON COMMENT VEUX TU MON AMOUR MA MAITRESSE MA VIE ROMPRE L'ENNUI ET BRULER LE VOILE DÉCHIRÉ PENDANT AUX CLOUS ROUILLÉS DU TRONC D'ARBRE FONDANT SON BEURRE AU SON DE LA MUSIQUE MILITAIRE QUI PASSE DANS L'ÉGOUT SI LA MAIN LE PIED ET SA BOUCHE ET SES YEUX ET LE COTON QUI FLOTTE DANS L'INTÉRIEUR DU POING FERMÉ DU CRISTAL ET LA CHALEUR ARRIVANT TOUTE GLACÉE DE PEUR DANS LE FEU GROSEILLES TRAINANT LE FILET PLEIN D'ANCHOIS ET LES AIRS DE GUITARE DANS LA BOURRASQUE DES GRAINS DE RIZ NEIGEANT SUR SA JOUE CONDOM DE LUNES ÉVENTAIL D'HUILE D'HIRONDELLES ATTACHANT SA SANDALE DANS L'IMPERCEPTIBLE ODEUR DE PASTÈQUE L'ACQUA VIVA DE SES CHEVEUX MÉLANGÉS ALLUME LA LIE DU SOUFFLE DE LA MAIN QUI AGITE LES AILES DE LA FLUTE

The same text, printed by Iliazd from metal type, in homage to *Roger Lacourière* (Paris: Forty-One Degrees, 1968). © 2020 Estate of Pablo Picasso/Artists Rights Society (ARS), New York

poem, written by Iliazd, accompanied the pages. His poem was a riddle, containing a small textual portrait of each artist in turn, cleverly disguised, and it was composed in a dynamic layout so that the words floated on the page. The publication date was 1968, but the opening was held on the 12th of December 1969, at the Galerie Dina Vierny. A chapter in Iliazd's life had closed, and the portrait of Lacourière we get through Iliazd's eyes suggests a strong sense of identification:

> He was always bending toward the troubled liquid
> Scrutinizing the depth in which the plate had plunged
> Invisible to others
> Who could never even imagine the risks
> Of his occupation . . .[71]

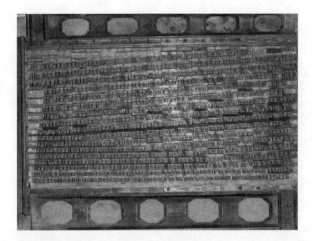

The type used for printing the Picasso text, saved for posterity. Courtesy of François Mairé and the Fonds Iliazd

The reference to risk is that of breathing fumes from the acid baths in which plates are immersed for etching. Though it included the work of more than a dozen artists, *Lacourière* is almost hermetic. Iliazd's poem was less esoteric than many works he had already produced. Much information and many subtexts were concealed in *Lacourière,* and the social context in which the printer functioned was obscured by the renown of the artists whose names appeared in print.

Milestones

In 1968, Iliazd married Hélène Douard in Vallauris. They had been acquainted for more than twenty years. Iliazd was seventy-four years old. The witnesses at the wedding were Jacqueline Picasso and Georges Ribemont-Dessaignes. The wedding announcement had been engraved by Picasso, with typography by Iliazd. This was a point of great pride for Iliazd, and for Hélène, though with typical discretion she barely dwelt on the matter. Picasso had been meant to attend the wedding as well but was ill.

In 1967 Iliazd had tried to visit the Soviet Union to see his brother Kirill, but the trip never took place. Kirill died in 1969. The brothers had not seen each other for more than forty years.

These personal milestones are enormous in scale but do not register in the work, or notes, or records—but they were fulcrum points that shifted

Iliazd and Hélène Douard Zdanevich on their wedding day, October 31, 1968. Courtesy of François Mairé and the Fonds Iliazd

all kinds of conditions and alignments in the personal realm. Iliazd said little of the emotional costs of his lifelong displacement, though the melancholy in the *Sentence without Words* and the work of his final publications provided some indication of these things. Iliazd lived his life in exile, as an émigré, though his cosmopolitan spirit resisted such characterization. The loss of his brother and of all the connections and memories shared had an irrevocable finality to it.

The Grotesque Courtesan (*Le Courtisan Grotesque*) (1974)

Though this work bears the latest publication date of any of Iliazd's works, it is not the "final" work in the same conceptual sense as *Boustrophedon* and *Pirosmanachvili*, both of which are works of recapitulation.

For *Courtesan*, Iliazd turned again to a text by Monluc. His interest in the writing of the Comte de Cramail had not diminished, and traces of other projects that might have come into publication were also present in his notes. This was to be a project with Joan Miró, another companion of earlier years. In January 1951, Iliazd had written to the artist describing the text: "I have a text for your book, and I am certain that you will approve of the choice—it is an ancient text, extraordinary, extravagant, very fine and very beautiful, sufficiently known, and never published with a Spanish preface before . . ."[72]

Following this message was a thirteen-year gap in the correspondence with Miró, and not until 1964 was there another trace of the project, at which point Miró wrote to say that he would study the mock-up Iliazd had sent to him, so the project must have been underway. As usual, other projects were underway at the same time, including the complex *Maximiliana*. Iliazd always began his projects with a detailed design to give an idea of layout, scale, size, and the artist's place in the scheme.

A note dated January 1965 expressed Iliazd's frustrated impatience with the slow rate of progress, comparing the whole exchange to a litigation with endless delays and negotiations.[73] Contact continued, but only in 1971 did the production work begin. Iliazd had secured materials for the book, solicited subscriptions, and began to establish a schedule for printing the plates. The work dragged on. The engraver had difficulty completing the production on schedule. The atelier of Lacourière had passed into the hands of Jacques Frélaut, and they had to relocate the studio during this period.

By the end of April 1974, Iliazd wrote to tell Miró that the work was done. Though the date, May 10, was named as the day of the vernissage, Iliazd wrote to Miró on May 30: "The text of *The Courtesan Grotesque* is printed! The plates are in the hands of the engraver; everything is turning out for the best. I congratulate you. Bravo. This has taken fifteen years, but the paper has held up well, and so have we. Once again, thank you!"[74]

A letter dated June 24, 1974, contained this response by Iliazd to the printed images: "I have seen all the black plates. They are marvelous. The brachycephalic heads appear solitary and menacing among the other fearful and numerous creatures . . ."[75]

A letter from Miró, dated December 29, 1974, written after completion, must have gratified Iliazd: "I find the book more and more beautiful, and I am very proud to have done it with you."[76] The book was luxurious. The materials were sumptuous, and Miró noted his delight with the paper, the layout, the overall effect. The dense and surreal image of the courtesan makes its appearance in the engravings balanced by the solid form of the regular field of the type. The letterpress grid feels absolutely stable. The re-

AMIS & LE COURTISAN PRENANT CONGÉ
SE RETIRA COMME VN NERF GRILLÉ DANS
SON CHASTEAU THIERRY IL ARRIUE A LA
PORTE ☐ш ┘ O∝-∽OZ MONTE EN
SA CHAMBRE ☐ш∽ ∪OΣ∂├ш∽
ENTRE DANS LE CABINET ☐ш Σ-Zш∝⊃ш
IL PRIT DE L ANCRE ☐ш Z<⊃-∝ш VNE
PLUME ☐ш ∪O♂ & FIT DES VERS <
∽O├ш PROPOSA ┘< ∪┘O∽ш
☐ O∝┘ш<Z∽ SUR VN PARCHEMIN
>-ш∝∪ш DONNA SA LETTRE
☐OΣ-Z-∪<┘ш FERMÉE DE
SOYE ☐ш ∂O⊃∝∪ш<⊃ & CACHETÉE
AVEC CIRE ∂-ш∝∝ш LA DONNA A
VN POSTILLON ☐ шO┘ш LUY PROMET
MONNOIE ☐ш ∽>Z∪ш & QUANTITÉ
D OR POTABLE DONT IL LUY BAILLA QUELQUE
POIGNÉE ☐ш∽∂ш POUR L OBLIGER 8

A FAIRE DILIGENCE AFIN QUIL REUINT EN
ALLANT LE COURRIER MONTÉ SUR LE CHEUAL
☐ш ├∝O>ш BOTTÉ DE FOIN IUSQUES AU
JARRET ☐ш >ш<⊃ AUEC ESPERONS
☐ш ∪<┘┘ш∝ш VNE CHAMBRIERE
☐ ΣO∽├ш┘┘ш∝-ш EN LA MAIN LE
CORNET ☐ <∂O├-∪<-∝ш
EN ESCHARPE EMPOIGNE LES RENNES шZ
∝ш├<∪Zш MET LE PIED EN
L ESTRIER ☐ш ∽<-Z∪├ ∪∝ш∽∂-Z
SE MET A FENDRE LE VENT VOLE COMME
LA PENSÉE QUELQUE FOIS PREND LE GALLOP
D VN CHASSEUR LE TROT D VN CHASSE MARÉE
L EMBLE D VN MARCHAND LE PAS D VN
MEDECIN PASSE DEUANT L HUIS ☐ >Z
∂<├-∪-ш∝ TROUUE LE BAC
DE SON COSTÉ & COURT EN FIN COMME
VN LEURIER ARRIUÉ FAIT SA CHARGE

Typography of *The Grotesque Courtesan*, text by Adrian de Monluc, showing the balanced setting of letters turned on their sides (Paris: Forty-One Degrees, 1974). Courtesy of François Mairé and the Fonds Iliazd

ality of the balancing act that provided that illusion of stability was far more complex. As often happens, the work that looks most simple hides its own difficulties of composition. The typesetting in *Courtesan* is masterful in many ways, most of which only a printer would have seen or appreciated. To a reader, the idea of turning type on its side seems like a minor decision. To a typesetter, it is a monumental challenge.

As with the earlier text by Monluc, *Skinnybones,* the text was full of puns, and Iliazd turned the letters of these words on their sides to indicate their double meaning. The technical labor was considerable. All metal letters are cast on variable-width bodies. By this time, Iliazd was unable to do the actual composing work on account of his deteriorating health (he had been diagnosed with Parkinson's disease some time earlier). The optical difficulty of balancing the letters in the midst of the lines was compounded by the effort required to pack them individually with copper and brass spacers. Visually, they appear to be balanced on an imaginary center line which runs through them at a point midway above the baseline of the letters in normal position. The variable width of letters (the dimensions of the pieces of type) would require tedious work to create the effect of balancing among their upright companions.

The color images were printed using two different black inks. Ilizad had seen the original gouaches and said what was needed was "one warm, the other cold, two blacks of distinct and different character."[77]

The layout was opulent. Even the parchment covers had Miró's calligraphy, and the counters (open spaces) of the letters were filled with color. For this project, Hélène made frequent trips to take plates, proofs, and signature pages back and forth between the two artists. The book had been in production off and on for twelve years and had been longer in conception. But even with the long delays, Iliazd's optimism, expressed in 1965, was fulfilled: "In spite of everything, I believe we will finish by making a veritable firework of form, colors, and materials."[78]

The first copies of the book were finished in time for Iliazd's eightieth birthday, April 21, 1974, celebrated at the Galerie Darial. Each of the artists who came to the opening brought a canvas to hang in celebration and those who could not be there simply sent the work in their stead. The walls were hung with pieces by François Arnal, Hugo Ball, Jean Beauduin, Georges Braque, Camille Bryen, Serge Charchoune, Marc Chagall, Max Ernst, Hélène Zdanevich, Cecil Michaelis, André Masson, Grégoire Michonze, Joan Miró, Pablo Picasso, Kirill Zdanevich, Fernand Léger, Robert Delaunay, and many others.[79] The book was done, but so were books. This was the last work Iliazd completed before his death in 1975. But we have still to address *Boustrophedon* (1971) and *Pirosmanachvili 1914* (1972) for their place in Iliazd's life and conception of his own work.

Work in the Form of a Constellation

In her title for the 1984 Iliazd exhibit, Françoise Le Gris-Bergmann used the descriptive phrase "work in the form of a constellation." The phrase is apt, since it allows a spatial distribution of the artist's work across a field of topics and notions. The constellationary image suggests times and places, starts and stops, rather than requiring the works to be read in a single linear chronology. Similarly, the apparent proximity of stars has no correlation with their relative positions in space, but creates a figure made by our perception. Thus the sense that Iliazd's books or projects appeared one after another needs to be tempered by the realization that each work took its own time. Some projects were decades in the making, like the *Maximiliana* with

Ernst, which was published in 1964 as the outcome of a promise made decades earlier. As we have seen, the same was true of *The Grotesque Courtesan* (1974) and *A Hint* (1965), works whose gestation was of long duration. The speed with which *Poetry of Unknown Words* was produced is remarkable by contrast, and the sense of urgency with which it appeared in response to the provocations of Isou and the Lettrists is notable.

But the concept of constellationary reading extends to a topographical approach to study of historical materials and biographical details, shifting the reading of evidence away from causal logic. Many events in the course of a life are accidents of proximity or sequence. Iliazd's arrival in Paris had certain immediate causes, many of which have disappeared. The documents and other evidence are still available witnesses to these events. The configuration of Iliazd's activities emerges from the evidence. This can be read without speculation on his interior state or decision-making processes. The apparent justifications for actions are just that—apparent. But to suggest that the evidence is a surface behind which or below which is an actuality to be revealed misses the critical point. Even in a lived life—an inhabited actuality of psychic presence and social engagement—no coherent, holistic, complete phenomenon of a reality waits to be revealed. The evidence does not cover the truth, does not hint at its repleteness. The evidence makes the best and strongest argument for the radical incompleteness of any presentation of a life, a persona, a character, a circumstance.

The idea of connections at a distance, the aggregation of evidence across disparate moments in time, and the formation of a figure as an image projected from discrete points of information are all aspects of the constellation metaphor. Any one of Iliazd's projects can be read this way, with the initial notes, correspondence, production drawings, proofs, more correspondence, acquired reference texts, and paper mock-ups all assembling into a whole. The parts do not lose their specificity. The necessity to see each piece of evidence as discrete does not go away, but rather comes to the fore in recognizing the different kinds of distances and space between that still allow each element to be read within the configuration of the whole. I have read the evidence in one particular way. From another direction or perspective these pieces of evidence might configure very differently.

A Life in Reverse

Recapitulation

As Iliazd came to the end of his life he returned to one of his earliest projects and also composed a work that embodied the process of reflection in reverse. *Boustrophedon* and *Pirosmanachvili* are both works of recapitulation. They reference a life engaged with poetry as fundamental to experience and representation of that life. With *Pirosmanachvili*, Iliazd returned to his earliest work, an essay written in 1914 on the Georgian painter, and presented it among his last. This same movement, forward and back in a cycle of return and review, was what motivated the structure of *Boustrophedon*. Individually, these two books each played a specific role in Iliazd's larger plan of work. Each is a closing parenthetical bracket within the entire span of his production from the earliest moments of his engagement with arts and literature to the end of his life. The deliberateness of this gesture and the design of closure it embodies is poignant as well as admirable. The care with which Iliazd thought about his work as an entire oeuvre shows how intimately his identity was bound up with the editions, the essays, the design and typography, and every other aspect of aesthetic expression in these books.

Boustrophedon (Boustrophédon) (1971)

The text of *Boustrophedon* consisted of a series of palindromes—texts whose sequence of letters mirror each other from a midpoint to both the start and the finish. This kind of assignment for writing under a constraint had great appeal to Iliazd, and it had featured in many other of his works as well as texts like those of Monluc that he had chosen to publish.

In *Boustrophedon* (the term refers to early writing that follows the track

of an ox pulling a plow, reversing direction with each line) Iliazd's poems
were spelled out in conventional order, reading left to right. Beneath these,
the letter sequence was reversed, ordered right to left. This text is set in a
smaller font size, almost like an echo. This was the *zaum* rendering, a kind
of esoteric reading of the original French poems. Not quite comprehensible,
the reversed lines are suggestive rather than explicit, and play with sound
pattern and its potential to reveal hidden value through playful manipulation and allusive qualities of language.

The initial poems were spare, distilled, and intensely personal. Each referred to an intimate connection to a person who mattered to Iliazd. The
reversed phrases did not repeat the line, or continue it, but echoed it in
pronounceable nonsense syllables, an instance of *zaum* created by reversing
the letters in the poetic line. They did not make "sense" but made sound: "It
is not enough to spell out the inverse of the sentence, it is necessary to also
regroup the fragments in order to make them readable, and beyond that,
perceptible."[1]

One feature of Iliazd's work as a poet had been the belief that sound (not
sense) held the essence of language. Taking the poems, carefully wrought,
that described important figures and moments from his life, he had inverted
them as a revelation of their phonetic value. The evident right-reading statements were only part of the search for poetic understanding. Only the ob-
verse, the return to the raw material of the words, could satisfy the impulse
to understand poetry as sound.

Iliazd had been fascinated with palindromes. On three-by-five cards he
kept a collection of examples he had encountered or created himself. He
had used the same bilateral symmetry in many of his book designs (a form
also present in the Byzantine churches he so admired), and the seeming perfection of the mirror phrases clearly appealed to his aesthetic. The aptness
of the structure for reviewing a life in language is clear.

The text of the poems was set in Gill Sans, a face so familiar to Iliazd by
this time that he could set it with accuracy and precision for any purpose or
text. The optical weight of each letter in relation to the next was elegantly
integrated into the composition. The *zaum* echoes were printed in the same
Gill, but in a smaller point size. The pages had the dynamic stability of a mo-
bile. Each phrase was suspended, not hung on the rigid edge of a margin, but
balanced above the next at a critical point of weight and counterweight.

This was the most personal book that Iliazd ever produced. The ten
poems were each written in memory or celebration of persons who had

figured prominently or symbolically in his life. The first poem was written for Hélène, who had broken her leg skiing in December 1967, the winter before their marriage. Visiting her in Chamonix during her recuperation he had written:

Elena
the covers of the bed
extend
in glaciers
your green eyes
in astrophysics.[2]

The reverse setting of the French version of this poem, slightly modified to serve Iliazd's sense of the sounds, read:

Anele
tele d spard sel
tnegno lorpes
srei calgne
strev xueys el
eu
qisyhportsa ne[3]

Nine other people figure by name in the remaining poems. Each had personal significance for Iliazd: Kirill, his brother, who had died in 1969; Ledentu, the companion of his early futurist activities for whom *Ledentu as Beacon* (1923) had been titled; Pirosmani; and Monluc. These were obvious choices. From among his many friends and collaborators, Iliazd chose only one, Marie-Laure de Noailles, of whom he wrote, "mute poetry/painting speaks/in celestial voice."[4] One poem was a verse to Claude Garnier, author of an unrealized project that Iliazd had proposed to Picasso, *The Heartbreak of an Old Soldier* (*Crève-Coeur d'un Vieux Soldat*). The commemorative tone of the verse made clear that now the work would never be undertaken. The final three choices were slightly more obscure: Mario Nuti, an Italian painter who had shown his modern work in Venice in an ancient museum whose wall paintings had nearly been washed away. A friend of Michel Guino, he had shown Iliazd his work, and the impact of the incident remained, perhaps an image of the power of art to remain in the face of change. Next was Anne Rosli Zyrd, a Swiss skier whose name had attracted Iliazd by its *zaum* quality. And last was a soldier, Henri-François Maillot, whose peculiar fate

ÉLÉNA
ANELE

LES DRAPS DE LIT
TIL ED SPARD SEL

SE PROLONGENT
TNEGNO LORPES

EN GLACIERS
SREI CALGNE

LES YEUX VERTS
STREV XUEYS EL

EN ASTROPHYSIQUE
EUQISYHPORTSA NE

ANNEROSLI ZRYD
DYRZIL SORENNA

FLOCON DE NEIGE
EGIEN ED NOCOLF

CHAUSSÉE DE SKIS
SIKS ED E ESSUAHC

MESURE LE TEMPS
SPMET EL ERUSEM

AUTOUR DU MONDE
EDNOMUD RUO TUA

VAL GARDENA
ANEDRAGLAV

Boustrophedon, poems by Iiazd, typeset forward and in reverse (Paris: Forty-One Degrees, 1971). Courtesy of François Mairé and the Fonds Iliazd

in the Algerian war (he had deserted the French army to fight on the side of Algerian independence and died in combat in 1956) had caught Iliazd's attention.[5]

The book is recollective in tone, reflective, and poignant, even melancholic:

Pirosmani
my painter
my mountains
my forests
my courage
all evaporate[6]

Iliazd had solicited from Georges Ribemont-Dessaignes a series of etchings that were to work with the theme of doubling and mirroring. By February 1971 the work was underway, but Iliazd was finding it rough going, and he wrote to him: "I have done nothing the whole of 1970, not even any taxes to pay—but since the arrival of Hélène in Paris I have found some strength and resolve to continue the work toward the publication of our book—the paper for the engravings is at Lacourière and I have finished the composition of the text of which I send you proofs which have just been done."[7] The etchings by Ribemont-Dessaignes contained strange hybrid beasts, odd sutured images that sketched the visual equivalent of palindromes in delicate, almost tentative, lines. Another of Iliazd's long friendships, the one with Ribemont-Dessaignes had long ago resulted in the preface to *Ledentu* in 1923. He wrote a short article on this last collaboration: "Poetry goes in a direction which is the same as that of life—it runs towards death. Oh river Archeron! And everyone in their own fashion on the barge—some signing, some broken hearted to see the remnants of their youth disappear in the wake. But imagine, all of you, that life unrolled in the other direction! That time passed . . . in such a way that you were compelled to decipher the effect that produced the cause. Do you understand? . . . Finally, in short, imagine that life was a vast palindrome . . ."[8]

Iliazd had taken this image and rendered *Boustrophedon* as the palindromic inscription of his life at once written and unwritten, stated and inverted, lived out and lived again in language, in a circularity of meaning and material, figure and form. The book was finished on March 23, 1971, in an edition of fifty-five copies, signed by the author and artist. In keeping with his mode of production, Iliazd had printed the work on antique Japon, wrapped it in parchment, added heavy printmaking paper guard sheets and blue textured *dragée* sheets, which had become one of his favorite elements of color and texture. The work was a deliberate gesture toward closing an aesthetic life.

Pirosmanachvili (*Pirosmanachvili 1914*) (1972)

Iliazd had wanted to end his large editions as he had begun them, with a collaboration with Picasso. This would have made closure on only one of his beginnings, that of the cycle of books that had begun with *Afat* (1940). Another, longer cycle had begun in 1912 with the discovery of Pirosmani and subsequent publication in 1914 of an article in the *Vostok* journal in Tbilisi that marked the debut of Iliazd's creative and critical work. In 1969, an exhibit of Pirosmani's work had been mounted in Paris by the Soviet government, with no mention of Kirill and Ilia Zdanevich or Mikhail Ledentu. Nor was there any mention of their ownership of the works, dozens of which had been confiscated by the state museum.

Iliazd had had the project in mind for some time when an illness in winter 1971-72 had given the work a certain urgency. He had written to Picasso: "I am preparing to publish the article which I wrote years ago on the Georgian painter. Since you have always loved his work, I hope you will not refuse to take part in this publication by providing a frontispiece. Certain of your positive reception of this proposal, I am taking the liberty of including a small plate. I am giving Hélène this letter to bring to you and I am sorry to not see you myself . . ."[9] Iliazd had been hospitalized in Cannes in the winter 1971-72 and Picasso sent his own physician to Iliazd's beside during the critical illness, a severe grippe or flu. When Iliazd was released, Picasso engraved the plate in a few hours. The image is striking. The figure is an old man, a painter, a common theme in Picasso's late work. But it is also an image of Iliazd, the artist as an old man—not the old man Iliazd had become, in any literal sense, but the old man he had imagined himself to be as a young man, identifying with Pirosmani. The Georgian painter had presented the very essence of the artist to Iliazd. He had personified the life of authenticity and difficulty, of a refusal to compromise, which, finally, had come to be the very terms according to which Iliazd lived his life. In the features of Pirosmani, standing in a frenetic field of activity before the canvas, there is a suggestive trace of the face of Iliazd in the mass of lines that define the high round cheeks, deep eyes, and short mustache.

The work served as a testimonial to the friendship Picasso and Iliazd had kept over almost fifty years. They had collaborated on many projects, and only one of the proposed collaborations had failed to materialize, the *Heartbreak of an Old Solider,* a text written by a soldier whose sufferings in the civil wars of Louis XIII Iliazd thought would provoke Picasso's sympathetic engagement, reminiscent as it was of the horrors depicted in *Guernica.* Iliazd had been persistent: "The wind and rain seek to extinguish the flame which you lit when you decided, as you said, to finish the plates for the *Heartbreak of an Old Solider* which wait to be completed. I beg you to think how many years I have lived with the uncertainty that this book will be done and I have always known that I could depend on the vigor and strength of your engravings . . ."[10]

The epitaph for *Heartbreak* had been written in *Boustrophedon* with the

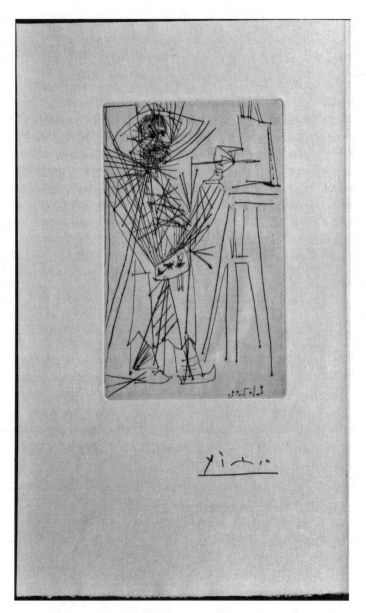

Pirosmanachvili 1914, text by Iliazd, image by Picasso (Paris: Forty-One Degrees, 1972). © 2020 Estate of Pablo Picasso / Artists Rights Society (ARS), New York

finality of the phrase *"à jamais"* (now never). But by completing the work on *Pirosmanachvili* Iliazd and Picasso had celebrated their friendship *"à toujours"* (forever). Iliazd had even, at one point, begun a text on Picasso, a *"Préface Imaginaire,"* in which he presented Picasso's aesthetic positions:

> Picasso is a painter of reality. He always begins with a visual sensation, interpreting it in this or that manner in order to render reality in a free and non-conventional manner as Cezanne did before him. Using the real as the point of departure is either done directly or else through unexpected and distant associations—thus the paradox of his statement: "I never travel because I don't see a thing." . . . With Picasso the version of nature which appears is not the version of his eye. One could even say the artist doubts his eye, as if he works to remedy the defects of his eye. It is not his vision of reality which he seeks to represent, but his comprehension of it.[11]

The most vivid images of their friendship are the photographs of the men together on the beach in the South of France, in fraternal intimacy. Picasso is cutting Iliazd's hair in one, and in another, the two men stand side by side, the similarity of their stance overwhelming differences in their appearance.

A recollection by Iliazd's daughter-in-law, Claude Zdanevich, portrays an incident in 1955:

> The two men shook hands and with mock seriousness addressed each other:
>> Salut my colonel!
>> Salut my general!
> They wore almost the same exact thing: sandals, shorts, Tahitian shirts—red with white flowers for Iliazd, yellow with black flowers for Picasso—as if by prior arrangement.[12]

Work on *Pirosmanachvili* continued. In the summer of 1972, Iliazd had the original Russian text translated into French by Andrée Robel and André du Bouchet. Iliazd wrote a brief preface to link the discovery of Pirosmani to futurism. It began: "It is now sixty years since the afternoon of our first encounter with Pirosmanachvili in December 1912."

Iliazd had brought his work full cycle. The book was finished in January 1973 and Hélène took two copies to Picasso at Mougins. Iliazd went to Golfe-Juan in April, having fixed the morning of April 9 for a meeting with Picasso, but Picasso died the day before, April 8, 1973. The two men were ending more than a friendship.

Unfinished and planned projects still existed, but these books were the

Iliazd with Picasso in the late 1950s. Courtesy of François Mairé and the Fonds Iliazd

final ones. Iliazd died at home on Christmas Day, 1975, at the age of eighty-one. He had lived according to his own words:

I am not a slave,
I am not a functionary
and I am not obliged to know what I am supposed to know
or what I am supposed to say or not say
I am a poet.[13]

A Place in History

In 1986, I traveled with Hélène to see the enormous *Futurismo!* exhibit in the newly renovated Palazzo Grassi in Venice. I had finished my doctoral dissertation at University of California, Berkeley, received my degree, and secured an academic, tenure-track position. I returned to Paris in the summer of 1986 to finish some details in the research on the biography. As to my change in stature, Hélène responded with disbelief, *"Mais, pas un vrai prof?"* ("Not a *real* professor?"). Assuring her that I was indeed appointed to a full-time academic position did not fully convince her. I assume it was my youth, perhaps my gender, that did not fit her notion of a real professor; but also, in the French university system the title of professor was reserved for more senior scholars.

Venice was cold that year in May-June. The details of dates are obscured by distance, but the experience of European springtime—wet, gray, chilly, damp—remains. I met Hélène in Paris and we took the train together. Someone else was with us, her niece perhaps. Our *pensione* was minimal. We ate in cafeterias, and the *salade carrote* featured largely in our diets in a desperate search for vegetables in the pasta-based environment. Odd that these are the recollections still vivid.

Hélène was imperious on that trip. She had come on a mission, determined to see how the installation of Iliazd's work did justice to his legacy. But her expectations were out of scale with the realities, and the disappointment she experienced was visceral. I was pained as well, witnessing her reaction. But the gap between reality and her expectations was useful in considering the project we had worked on together. The importance of any individual's work is always determined in relation to the position from which it is viewed.

On arrival, we went to the Palazzo. She explained to the museum ticket takers who she was, the wife of Zdanevich. She spoke French. They were

Italian. She was tall, strong looking, and with her fully upswept silver-gray hair, wide forehead, and grand manner she was imposing. Her conviction persuaded them of her importance, across the barriers of custom and protocol. They let us in. She demanded a catalogue. The publication was enormous, heavy as bricks, beautifully designed and printed.

"Where is Zdanevich?" she asked as we came into the entry of the exhibit. The guard had no idea, shook his head, puzzled. "Zdanevich!?" she repeated. The exhibit hall was filled with treasures. The sculpture and paintings of Umberto Boccioni, heavy, strident, iconic, the dynamic canvases of Giacomo Balla, Carlo Carrà, and Gino Severini. Everywhere, the canonical works of Italian futurism were displayed in all their vital presence. Seeing them together, all caveats about the politics of their militarism and masculinist aesthetics aside, they were overwhelming in their sheer energy. Among the major objects, dozens of smaller cases displayed photographs, publications, a pristine copy of *Zang Tumb Tumb* and the *Mots en Liberté*. The 1909 Futurist Manifesto, from the front page of *Le Figaro*, and the many other declarations of aesthetic principles and propositions were woven into the leitmotif of the exhibition. Among these documents were photographs of Filippo Marinetti and his colleagues, improbably attired in their fully bourgeois bowler hats and overcoats, bow ties, foulards, formal collars, and polished shoes—all accoutrements of their class. The historical specificity of it congealed into images of a now fully codified past.

Not surprisingly, for the Italian curators, *futurismo* was Italian.

Hélène strode through the rooms. The spaces were large, the collections vivid, the exhibit broad in scope and scale. Marinetti's intersections with dispersed communities of European artists were also documented. But where was Zdanevich?

The trajectory of that walk at high speed through the galleries compressed the emotional conflicts of the project into a single swift arc of expectation and disappointment. When we finally located a case with Russian futurist books, among them those of Iliazd from the 1910s and early 1920s, Hélène came to rest. Driven by an impulse to attend to the memory of her lost spouse, perform her duty as the guardian to his monumentalization within the historical record, she could not rest until she found his spot. The place he occupied was modest, inconspicuous even, within the large expanse of the futurist project. But he was there. He was present. His name appeared within the vast scope of the exhibit. His spot in history was marked.

Watching her adjust her expectations, recalibrate her idea that the exhibit would have placed him in a central role, was painful. This was not an intellectual matter. Rewriting the script on site was difficult. She said they had missed the point, did not understand, had misrepresented the role of Zdanevich. He *was* futurism. In her understanding, he was the key and principal figure within the movement. Even allowing for the Italian rather than a Russian focus, how could they have missed this? At the same time, she celebrated his presence, hovering by that small bit of real estate within the glass case, to make a declaration of its significance in this presentation of the history of futurism.

Whatever his role in Russian futurism, Iliazd's connection to the Italian movement had been minimal. But when others had deserted Marinetti for his political views and withdrawn their support, Iliazd had remained loyal. This commitment was evident in the notes written in the 1960s when he revisited his engagement with the movement. Iliazd had maintained the affiliation while distancing his own work and its claims to originality from any sense of subordination to the "master" figure, Marinetti. He needed to feel his achievements had been *sui generis*, entirely his own, but he wanted to claim a peer connection to the prominent figure. These appear as conflicts but were not.

As Hélène processed the discrepancy between the place she thought Iliazd would occupy and her satisfaction in knowing he had been recognized, she held several different emotional states in mind simultaneously. Disappointed, angry at what she perceived as a slight, but proudly standing by the case with a justified fierceness, she could barely look at the paintings and sculptures, the rich array of futurist works assembled after nearly seven decades to celebrate one of Italy's major contributions to modernism. Our perception of that movement and its values had changed in recognition of its assertion of nationalism; it had come to be seen as an aesthetics of destruction and aggression, with masculinist and fascist qualities and debased affiliations. But in that late twentieth-century moment, as the work to anchor the newly renovated Palazzo Grassi within one of the most archetypical of Italian cities, it was one of the few modern movements with sufficient stature to elevate the profile and originality of Italian art beyond its celebrated Renaissance and baroque past. Complexities abound.

Hélène struggled to counter her deflation. She kept looking for external signs of recognition of the importance of Iliazd, his work, his influence, his achievements. In the hours and days that followed our dash through the galleries, her need to compensate for the experience, to pull evidence forward to cover the wound in her psyche, was painfully clear. I had no role to play beyond careful support, kindness, and sympathy. But I had known, long before we had arrived, when planning for our trip, that Iliazd was not a significant figure within Italian futurism. His accomplishments were unique. But I understood in advance of our experience at the Palazzo Grassi that we would not find Iliazd enthroned as the shining center of futurism, certainly not in Italy, where his contribution barely registered except as a small part of a distant reflection of the Italian movement.

Iliazd had met Hélène in his fifties, when the futurist period was already long behind him, and they married late. The tenderness between them was evident in Hélène's gentle recollections, the few hints she gave, and in the eloquence of the poem in *Boustrophedon*. But she was also clearly the posthumous guardian of his legacy, a role she embraced with dignity and perseverance. She believed in Iliazd and in the value of his work, but her understanding of his early years, in particular those futurist activities, was entirely according to his narrative. She had no counterevidence with which to gauge the scope and scale of his place in those histories.

Hélène's Iliazd was not mine. I could not construct the mythic image she desired. I could appreciate his accomplishments—the editions, the typography, the *zaum* work and lectures on poetry—in relation to other work I knew and studied. I had tried to understand those accomplishments by replacing them in the field of their original production. My relation to that field had shifted as well from unqualified celebration of the avant-garde and the larger undertakings of modernism into a view that historicized their claims and ambitions. The work remained, but the field against which it registered included many more terms—such as OuLiPo (a group of experimental writers founded in 1960), conceptual art, concrete poetry, work of a diverse range of artists in a global context.

I felt a deep sympathy as I watched her struggle to reconcile the centrality of Iliazd within her life, and within his version of his life and its relation to twentieth century art and literature, to what she had seen. I felt some anger toward Iliazd, toward his self-mythologizing in her eyes, since it had left her vulnerable to this confrontation with the inflated value of his claims.

In this condition of conflict, I drafted the first version of the biography, somewhat resentful toward the subject of my work, but with a loyalty to Hélène and the project. I was then, and always, reading his identity through the imprint it had made on the living, as well as the evidence of documents left behind. The traces of tone and demeanor were present in the notes and

Hélène Zdanevich at the print shop helping facilitate production. Courtesy of
François Mairé and the Fonds Iliazd

correspondence with which he frequently asserted the need to rectify
misperceptions of the past. Does character matter? Should I care whether
Iliazd was a kind man, generous, domineering, or egotistical? Could I tell
from any of what I researched what his temperament was like? He was meticulous in his designs and persevering in his work, and the evidence for that

was everywhere. A biography cannot be limited to a study of the work of an artist. A biography presumes a human being. That presumption was always problematic, and I wrestled, after the Venice trip, with my own conflicting feelings toward this figure and my imagined character of his projected persona.

When I sent the draft of the biography to Hélène in 1989, she responded by saying that it "was not a novel." Her disappointment was palpable. I understood what I had not realized in the years of working with her—that what she had wanted from the biography was a vivid, living hologram of the man and his life that she could walk into in order to live again the experiences they had shared—and also participate in those chapters in which she had not been able to be present.

Postscript

Recovering the Project

Modernism is now so fully historicized that it appears remote, a set of figured tropes and canonical works that have been lauded, critiqued, praised, and denigrated from every possible point of view. But the works remain. Though the debates about modernism have subsided somewhat, and biases and blind spots have been acknowledged to some extent, the fact of its historical existence cannot be contravened. The biases that most immediately came under critical scrutiny included the aspirations to a universal language of form. The Eurocentrism of this position, as well as the colonial aspect of a conception of "primitivism," began to unravel the ideology of Modernism (writ large) by the 1970s and early 1980s. Feminist work in critical art history, both the tasks of recovery (forgotten women pulled into the canon) and of revalidation on rethought terms of assessment (intimacy, personal work, domestic scenes and decorative work revisited), had opened the canon to revision. The masculinist terms of mastery and absolute abstraction also came under scrutiny, though acceptance for the unique vision of a figure like Florine Stettheimer, with her highly precise observations and depictions, or of Hilma af Klint, steeped in mystical thought, or Marie Laurencin, with her lightness and humor, all took time. The Russian avant-garde had had more women artists in it than the European movements, and Iliazd had connections with one of the most significant and influential among them, Natalia Goncharova.

But the eclipse of modernism's aesthetic investment in formal innovation, and its aspirations to universal values and qualities, were not matched by similar doubts about the belief that aesthetic work could bring about social change. Utopian transformation and the notion of a political aesthetics were (in some ways still are) a legacy of the avant-garde. That idea persisted, even persists, within the post- and post-post conditions of the current twenty-first century, a topic for a different discussion. But for Iliazd, whatever idea he had about the social efficacy or culturally transformative power of *zaum*, if he ever did, his engagement with a classical mode of elegant, highly orchestrated and balanced production dominated his last decades. Attention to history, to individual artists or texts, and to the full realization of a project—these were the motivations for his editions.

Now, at the start of the 2020s, more than three decades after the moment of meeting Hélène, that 1980s era feels remote, part of my own youth, precious in the best sense, preserved and thus accessible in memory. The corridor by which I access that moment is much longer now. The number of points of reference I pass to make my way, virtually, metaphorically, mnemonically to the door of her apartment, knock, and am welcomed are more numerous, and mark my own distance from beliefs I held in that time. The narratives are embellished by the combination of forgetting and remembering, research done and impressions kept.

Iliazd made a contribution to futurism and to the intellectual life of Paris in the 1920s, but the impact of *zaum* remains as a unique intervention in modern poetics, important to study as a specific formation and expression. The *dras* are a singular accomplishment by their length and connection with each other and a group of poets operating in this period of historical transformation. The editions, by which I mean the works from 1940 onward, have their own place in the history of *livres d'artistes* and printing. That Iliazd used the book as his primary mode of artistic expression seems incontrovertible: the evidence supports this. But the extent to which such a legacy has an influence or impact is less clear. Luxury objects do not circulate widely, and though entirely legitimate on their own terms, they occupy a particular niche in the social world and economies of consumption. The 1949 *Poetry of Unknown Words* retains its importance as an anthology, a major compendium that declared the significance of a particular body of experimental work in visual and sound poetry of the first half of the twentieth century, and that gave it definition. After the fact, this seems obvious. But before the editorial compilation, nothing is obvious. Had Iliazd done nothing else after that project, he would still deserve recognition on its account for the way it gave definition to the work of an entire generation. Across "movements" and styles, nations and factions, that anthology made an argument for the value of visual poetry and sound work as a distinct aspect of modern literature. Like the encounter with Iliazd, with Madame, and with modern art through my relationship with this project, that work re-

Hélène Zdanevich sketching. Courtesy of François Mairé and the Fonds Iliazd

mains available to be accessed, opened, enjoyed. The sheer pleasure of engagement with poetics and aesthetics feels like a luxury now. What felt like an urgency at the time seems so rarefied that any reflection on its worth seems to borrow the values of another time. What a privilege it was to have had these experiences, to enter into that living relation with the history of an era through the investigation of an individual artist.

I let this project go for many years. I could not find a way to engage with it directly. The question was not whether Iliazd mattered, was important,

Portrait of Iliazd by Hélène Zdanevich, 1966. Courtesy of François Mairé and the Fonds Iliazd

but whether a biography could be written that did not take its subject for granted. I had ceased to believe in the object of the study in any unequivocal way. I would not work on a "biography" of "an artist" as I had once imagined without reflecting on the circumstances of the encounter. Only when I realized I could reflect on the process of the biographical project could I begin to see a way forward. I encountered Iliazd in all the many forms of surrogacy that were available, through documents and evidence, anecdotes, notes in his own hand, and correspondence in the hands of others. I was able to speak with witnesses, to see the impact and impressions he had made and left behind. The biography remains a record of that process, a memoir of the encounters with evidence, and the memories of others, not with the man. I never met Iliazd, and I did not know who he was when I began. I came to know him through the biographical project. He was both subject and object of the research. I have looked so long at the books, the projects, spent so many hours in his studio and room, sat at his desk, and read his notes, that I feel I would immediately recognize the man in the photographs with his cap, his salt-and-pepper beard, and his sturdy presence. But even if I did, he would not recognize me. The lack of reciprocity is remarkable, and even noting it registers the asymmetries on which a biographical encounter is based. Hélène gave me access, and charged me with the tasks and responsibilities, but however rich and full her presence was, the absence at the center of the biography remains: Iliazd. The encounter with the project *was* and also *was not* an encounter with the man. And yet, how much depth the experience provided in understanding who he was, what he did, and how one comes to know someone through a biographical project. Hélène is not a shadow figure here, some mere auxiliary to the major project, but the living person I came to know. No portrait of her is adequate to communicate the grace, dignity, generosity, and kindness of her spirit.

Appendix

A Note on Recent Scholarship about Iliazd

When I began this project, published material on Iliazd was scarce. Work on the catalogues for the Museum of Modern Art in New York and the Musée d'Art Moderne in Paris, and the excellent scholarship of Françoise Le Gris (then -Bergmann) in *Iliazd* (1984) provided material that has been cited throughout my study. In addition, Régis Gayraud shared his work generously so that I could access the concepts of Iliazd's *conférences* in Paris, and other matters for which Russian language was essential. André Markowicz's valuable contributions have also been noted in the text. The purpose of this appendix is not to repeat what has been cited within the body of this biography, but to point the interested reader toward other recent materials relevant to the subject.

Standard references for Russian futurism, artists' books, *zaum* poetics, and typographic innovation have increased since the early 1990s, and so has research focused directly on Iliazd. Some of that material is in Russian and some in French, which determines its readership.

One of the most fruitful realms from which to understand Iliazd's contribution is the work on artists' books in the Russian context. For this material Margit Rowell and Deborah Wye's catalogue for New York's Museum of Modern Art exhibit in 2002, *The Russian Avant-Garde Book 1910-1934,* is the best starting point. It includes essays by Gerald Janecek and Nina Gurianova, among others. Margarita Tupitsyn's edited volume, *Russian Dada* (Cambridge: MIT Press, 2018) adds depth to the understanding of typography and graphic arts as the intersection with literary and visual art. The website from the 2008-09 Getty Center exhibition, *Tango with Cows: Book Art of the Russian Avant-Garde, 1910-1917,* contains digitized versions of several important avant-garde books. Daniel Mellis and Eugene Ostashevsky's translation and typographic reconstruction of Vasily Kamensky's *Tango with Cows*

(Brooklyn, NY: Ugly Duckling Presse, 2020) brings another classic work of the period back into print. Likewise, Thomas Kitson's superb translation of Iliazd's *The Rapture* has made that work accessible beyond the French translation of the Russian original (New York: Columbia University Press, 2017). Susan Compton's *Russian Avant-Garde Books 1917–34* (Cambridge: MIT Press, 2006) is an essential reference work.

For those interested in Russian poetics and language theory, Gerald Janecek remains an essential resource: *Zaum: The Transrational Poetry of Russian Futurism*, 2nd ed. (San Diego: San Diego State University Press, 1996). Marjorie Perloff, *21st-Century Modernism: The "New" Poetics* (Malden, MA: Blackwell, 2002) contains a discussion of *zaum*, particularly that of Velimir Khlebnikov, situated within an insightful understanding of modernism and its complexity. Nancy Perloff's *Explodity: Sound, Image, and Word in Russian Futurist Book Art* (Los Angeles: Getty Research Institute, 2016) connects this early work to that of later innovators. Christina Lodder, "The Transrational in Painting: Kazimir Malevich, Alogism and *Zaum*," *Forum for Modern Language Studies* 32, no. 2 (April 1996): 119–136, extends *zaum* concepts to the visual arts.[1]

Under the leadership of François Mairé, the Iliazd Club has produced a series of publications (the *Carnets*) that contain previously unavailable manuscript materials from the Iliazd archive that are invaluable for anyone studying Iliazd's work.[2] Thanks to the efforts of Boris Fridman, a major exhibition was mounted from December 2015 to February 2016 at Moscow's Pushkin Museum of Fine Arts titled *Iliazd: The 20th Century of Ilia Zdanevich*. Natella Voiskunksi's review of the exhibit, "The 'Everyfeelingism' of Iliazd," contains interesting information.[3] The catalogue of that exhibit contains multiple essays relevant to the book works. Between May and September 2016 the Georgian National Museum hosted an exhibit dedicated to the memory of Iliazd, *Avant-Garde 1900-1937*.[4] In spring 2019, an exhibition at Columbia University's Rare Book & Manuscript Library was accompanied by a symposium on Iliazd as Transnational Artist. One of the organizers of that symposium and Iliazd translator, Thomas Kitson, posted an entry on his blog: Ilia Zdanevich: The Tbilisi Years.[5] In April 2019, The Fundación Pablo Ruiz Picasso Museo Casa Natal hosted *Iliazd & Picasso: Paginas de Arte y Vida*. Numerous publications by Régis Gayraud should be consulted by anyone serious about research on Iliazd, beginning with his 1984 D.E.A. thesis, "Il'ja Zdanevic Theoricien et Promoteur du *zaum'* dans ses conferences parisiennes," *Slavic and East European Arts* 10, no. 1 and 2 (Winter 2002): 45–100.

Additional material was contained in his unpublished doctoral work, a summary of which was published as *Il'ja Zdanevič (1894-1975): l'homme et l'oeuvre; compte rendu de thèse,* in *Revue des études slaves,* t. LXIII/4, 1991, 863-867. Gayraud is also responsible for the translation and presentation of *Record de tendresse: hagiographie d'Ilia Zdanevitch écrite par son ami Terentiev* (Paris: Hiver, 1990), and numerous titles in Russian. In 1989 the Tbilisi museum mounted an exhibit of *Kirill Zdanevich, Ilia Zdanevich,* Katalog vystavki (Tbilisi: Gos. muzei iskusstv Gruzii, 1989).

The two-day colloquium held in June 2019 in Paris, at Reid Hall and the Bibliothèque Nationale, provided a useful sense of new scholarship on Iliazd. Various research projects that draw on previously unavailable archives have made it possible to know much more about the work Iliazd did in the Caucasus Mountains and the relationship between this early work and his lifelong interest in church architecture. "Pilgrimage amidst Maps and Territory," by Nana Shervashidze, conservator at the Musée National des Beaux-Arts in Tbilisi, Georgia, showed hand-drawn maps by Iliazd and detailed information about his ascents in the late 1910s and early 1920s that have never been published. Tatiana Nikolskaia, a historian from St. Petersburg, presented research on the linguistic structure of Iliazd's *zaum* plays in greater detail than earlier scholars. Sergey Kudriavtsev's work on the events that occurred in Iliazd's life in Constantinople in 1920-21, including a possible political plot (in which he was not involved), made a link to his *Philosophia,* which is a pseudo-autobiographical novel about that year. Thomas Kitson, who is finishing the translation of that novel, commented on the contrast between this account and that of the other pseudo-autobiographical text, *Letters to Morgan Philips Price,* also written in the 1920s. Valentina Izmirlieva situated Iliazd's experience within the larger cultural flux and milieu of Constantinople in this period and its symbolic identity within Russian imagination and reality. These in-depth studies add considerable new insight into the way each phase of Iliazd's early life and work is being understood. Régis Gayraud has continued to work on Iliazd in fine-grained detail, and his current analysis of *toutisme* or "Everythingism" offers a critical framework for understanding the way Iliazd conceived of his individual—and individuated— practice within a network of other aesthetic activities and movements.

Much more is now known about the work Iliazd did for Coco Chanel, both the extensive design activity for textiles and the technical contribution to the knitting machine on which jersey was made. Marika Genty, who works in the Chanel archives, gave a detailed and extensive presentation on this material. Iliazd's performance work (his plays) and the performative aspect of his work were the focus of Liana Dimitrieva, an early-career Russian scholar, while André Markowicz demonstrated the complex structures of Iliazd's poetic compositions. Likewise, David Sume's studies of the architectural form of Iliazd's books and Boris Fridman's interest in Iliazd as a publisher brought forward analyses of these aspects of his career. The very complete study by Antoine Perriol, French scholar, on the unfinished book by Adrian de Monluc, envisioned with images by François Arnal, added a speculative chapter to the work under examination. Françoise Le Gris summarized her analysis of the *Poetry of Unknown Words* with an argument that brought many of the structural features of the work into view, and, in a similar vein, Sophie Lesiewicz's study of the struggles between poet André du Bouchet and Iliazd over the construction of white space in the setting of the poems provides a close-up engagement with the details of typographic and poetic interactions on the page.

These carefully focused and detailed studies greatly extend engagement with the archival and material record of Iliazd's work and life, and more scholarship can be expected as Iliazd becomes known for his specific contributions to twentieth-century art and letters. The general conclusion of these scholars, however, aligns with arguments that emerged from (and recognize) my 1988 article, "Iliazd and the Book as a Form of Art"—arguments that Iliazd worked with the book within a modern sensibility in ways that parallel the work of visual artists and poets working with the properties of their media as material.[6] The emphasis on Iliazd as an international figure is also growing, along with interest in his status as a "stateless" person in the postrevolutionary period.

Other scholarship exists, often embedded in other scholarship, but the discussion above will serve to guide interested readers to many materials.

Notes

Preface

1. That "book" can still be found referenced online. The title, *Iliazd: Ilia Zdanevich and the Modern Art of the Book*, is listed with Northwestern University Press, 1994, as its publication information, but the book does not exist and never did.

2. Among the most recent: *Iliazd. The 20th Century of Ilia Zdanevich*, Moscow, Pushkin Museum 2016; *Iliazd and Picasso*, Picasso House Museum, Málaga, Spain, March-June 2019; *Ilia Zdanevich: The Tbilisi Years*, Columbia University, Rare Book & Manuscript Library, April-July 2019.

3. *La Rencontre Iliazd-Picasso*, Musée d'Art Moderne de la Ville de Paris, May-June 1976; *Iliazd*, Centre Georges Pompidou, Musée d'Art Moderne, Paris, May-June 1978; *Iliazd, Maître d'Oeuvre du livre Moderne*, Université de Montréal Art Gallery, Montréal, September 1984; *Iliazd and the Illustrated Book*, Museum of Modern Art, New York, June-August 1987.

4. The *Carnets,* small-format (four by six inches) publications in French, contain texts by and about Iliazd. The earlier issues focused on bringing materials from the archives into publication. The most recent issue was published to coincide with a June 2019 colloquium in Paris and contains a study by Antoine Perriol of an unfinished project, analysis of a film excerpt in which Salvador Dali discusses "Zdanevich," and an in-depth analysis of Iliazd's typography by Mikhaïl Karassik, among other works. The *Carnets* are an invaluable resource for study of Iliazd and his work.

Chapter 1. Encountering Iliazd: The Biographical Project

1. Ilia Zdanevich is mentioned in the excellent reference *Russian Futurism,* by Vladimir Markov (Berkeley: University of California Press, 1968) and other texts, but not discussed at great length. If I had known to look, I could have found some notes and materials in other sources as well.

2. Christopher Hewett is the person referenced.

3. Materials for the books, including maquettes, designs, and other documents had been acquired by the Bibliothèque Nationale for their archives. Antoine Coron, then curator, refused to allow access to the materials, saying they were not processed and that he would need to address them before they could be used. The collection is now available, and description of its contents is here: https://archivesetmanuscrits.bnf.fr/ark:/12148/cc908753.

4. I had been the recipient of a 1984-85 Fulbright Fellowship to support research for my dissertation on Dada and futurist typography, and the opportunity changed the course of my life and work.

5. Iliazd's probably romantic friendship with Olga Djordjadze, for instance, which occurred between the death of his second wife and his connection with Hélène, is documented in letters to which I did not have access. According to Boris Fridman, in conversation in 2019, the letters reveal intimacy and tenderness between the two.

Chapter 2. 1894-1916: Childhood and Formative Years

1. These had been created with the assistance of Françoise Woimant and Annick Lionel-Marie. But we also relied on Lionel-Marie's *Iliazd 1894-1985 Chronologie Summaire (Summary Chronology)* (Paris: 1984), published by Hélène Zdanevich to accompany the exhibition in Montréal in 1984.

2. Iliazd, "Letter to Soffici / Fifty Years After," written in 1962 to Ardengo Soffici in response to his request for information on the history of Russian futurism; published in *Carnet* 2 (Paris: L'Iliazd Club, 1992), with an excellent introduction by Régis Gayraud, 15-54; translated from the French by Johanna Drucker. (Unless otherwise noted, all translations are by Johanna Drucker.)

3. Valentina Kirillovna Zdanevich, *Journal*, translated from Russian to French by Hélène Flamant, in *Carnet* 1 (Paris, 1990): 91-92. The journal is about fifty manuscript pages and goes from late 1902 through 1903. Poignantly, she added an appendix in August 1925, in response to Iliazd's queries to his mother, that contains an account of the armoire in their nursery, still present in her home, and reminding her of his absence.

4. Valentina Kirillovna Zdanevich, *Journal*, 92-93.

5. Olga Djordjadze [*sic*, as per note on orthography], "Ilia Zdanevitch [*sic*] et le Futurisme Russe," *Iliazd*, exhibit catalogue (Paris: Centre Georges Pompidou, 1978), 16.

6. Konstantin Paustovsky, *Story of a Life* (New York: Pantheon, 1964); Paustovsky was nominated for the Nobel Prize in 1965.

7. The version cited here was from a manuscript translation by Olga Djordjadze.

Excerpts were translated from Russian to French by Hélène Flamant and published in *Carnet* 1 (Paris, 1990). Unpublished manuscript. A version of these two passages, slightly different, was published in *Carnet* 2 (Paris, 1992): 107.

8. Iliazd, unpublished manuscript.

9. Iliazd, "Fifty Years After."

10. Iliazd, "Fifty Years After." At the time I was working with Hélène, these manuscripts were unpublished.

11. The letter must have been written in the 1960s between the draft and publication of the book.

12. Marinetti was born in 1876; Larionov and Goncharova in 1881; Mayakovsky in 1893; Iliazd in 1894.

13. Iliazd, "Fifty Years After," 18–20.

14. See Vladimir Markov, *Russian Futurism* (Berkeley: University of California Press, 1968), 27, for a discussion of the term *budetlyane*.

15. According to art historian John Bowlt, ed., *Russian Art of the Avant-Garde* (New York: Viking, 1976).

16. Iliazd, undated manuscript.

17. Solomon Volkov and Antonia Bouis, *St. Petersburg: A Cultural History* (New York: Simon and Schuster, 1997), 272.

18. The translations were by the poet Vadim Shershenevich.

19. Tim Harte, *Fast Forward: The Aesthetics and Ideology of Speed in Russian Avant-Garde* (Madison: University of Wisconsin Press, 2009).

20. Iliazd, "Fifty Years After." The establishment of Vkhutemas and INKhUK in Moscow helped institutionalize a role for avant-garde art in the early years of post-revolutionary Russia.

21. Iliazd, "Fifty Years After," 31.

22. Iliazd, "Fifty Years After," 5.

23. Iliazd, undated letter to Georges Hugnet.

24. Letter from Soffici, January 28, 1964.

25. We have no evidence that Marinetti actually designed the graphic format of his visual works, and it would be even more unlikely, given class distinctions and biases, that he would have been willing to work in a print shop.

26. Vladimir Markov, *Russian Futurism,* and Benedikt Livshits, *The One and a Half-Eyed Archer* (Newtonville, MA: Oriental Research Partners, 1977).

27. In 1971 Iliazd responded with some reservation to an inquiry from Tatiana Longuin for information about Goncharova and Larionov. He indicated that he had felt "obliged to break with them," though precisely why was unclear. He and Larionov may have quarreled about the ownership of some canvases by Georgi Yakulov that had been left in Iliazd's care as a long-term gift. Neither was included in the long list of contributors to *Poetry of Unknown Words* (1949), which is indicative that

there had already been a break. Iliazd's final memories of Goncharova painted a sad portrait of her decayed condition, living the life of an émigrée with some hardship in her last years in Paris.

28. The catalogue essay, "Natalia Goncharova and Mikhail Larionov," and "Why We Paint Our Faces" were published in French, translated by Olga Djordjadze, in *Iliazd: Maître d'oeuvre du livre modern,* ed. Françoise Le Gris-Bergmann (Montréal: Université du Québec à Montréal, 1984), 85-100; Ledentu's preface was in manuscript form in the archive.

29. Iliazd, unpublished notes.

30. Markov, 183.

31. When Iliazd goes to Paris and begins to present these ideas, he refers to "New Schools of *Russian* poetry," so if he felt an identification with Georgian literary traditions, he did not make that explicit.

32. Iliazd, "Natalia Goncharova and Mikhail Larionov," 85-98.

33. Nina Gurianova, *The Russian Futurists and Their Books* (Paris: La Hune, Libraire Éditeur, 1993).

34. Iliazd, "Natalia Goncharova and Mikhail Larionov," 92.

35. Iliazd, "Natalia Goncharova and Mikhail Larionov," 95.

36. Iliazd, "Natalia Goncharova and Mikhail Larionov," 98.

37. Bowlt, *Russian Art of the Avant-Garde,* 98.

38. Mikhail Larionov, "Rayonist Painting," in *Une Avant-Garde Explosive*, trans. Michel Hoog and Solina de Vigneral (Paris: L'age d'Homme, 1976), 111.

39. See note on spelling of Olga Djordjadze's name to conform to references.

40. Djordjadze, "Ilia Zdanevitch [*sic*] et le Futurisme Russe," 10.

41. Katarina Clark, *Petersburg, Crucible of Cultural Revolution* (Cambridge: Harvard University Press, 1995), 47, describes the ambitions of the journal, which aimed at a general audience even as it published some of the work from the radical avant-garde. See also Bowlt, *Russian Art of the Avant-Garde,* 79.

42. Ilia Zdanevich and Mikhail Larionov, "Why We Paint Our Faces," in *Russian Art of the Avant-Garde*, 82.

43. The manuscript account of her first encounter with Ilia Zdanevich was recorded in 1984 by Régis Gayraud and is in the archive.

44. Gayraud, manuscript account, 1984.

45. Ledentu manuscript, Iliazd archive.

46. Djordjadze, "Ilia Zdanevitch [*sic*] et le Futurisme Russe," 12.

47. Correct orthography in English of the painter's name is Pirosmanashvili; as Iliazd uses the alternate spelling in the title of his work, I preserve it here for consistency, but reserve use of it mainly for the title.

48. Iliazd, *Pirosmanachvili 1914* (Paris: Forty-One Degrees, 1972), translated by Andrée Robel into French from the 1914 original, preface.

49. Annick Lionel-Marie, "Iliazd, facettes d'une vie," in *Iliazd*, ed. Annick Lionel-

Marie, Germain Viatte, and Laure de Buzon-Vallet (Paris: Centre Georges Pompidou, 1978), 46-47, citing Iliazd's journal.

50. Kirill Zdanevich, *Pirosmani* (Paris: Gallimard, 1970), 87.

51. I have not been able to locate Pirosmani paintings by these specific titles, though the first might refer to *The Beauty of Ortachala.*

52. Iliazd, manuscript, 1968, 76.

53. The note in my chronology says *Vostok (Orient)* of Tiflis [*sic*] (no. 1, 1914).

54. Iliazd, *Pirosmanachvili* (Paris: Forty-One Degrees, 1972).

55. Iliazd, *Pirosmanachvili.*

56. Iliazd, *Pirosmanachvili.*

57. Iliazd, *Pirosmanachvili.*

58. Kirill Zdanevich, *Pirosmani*, 143.

59. Kirill Zdanevich, *Pirosmani*, 155.

60. Konstantin Paustovsky, *Incursions dans le Sud* (Paris: Gallimard, 1966), 196. The collection amassed by Kirill and Ilia Zdanevich is now in the Art Museum of Georgia; an independent Nikos Pirosmani Museum dedicated to his work exists in Mirzaani, Georgia.

61. Lionel-Marie, "Iliazd, facettes d'une vie," 47, citing Iliazd.

Chapter 3. 1916-1920: Futurist Poetics

1. The four *dras* of his *zaum* cycle, a work titled *Milliork,* a single issue of the *40 Degrees Journal*, the anthology for Sofia Melnikova, and Igor Terentiev's *Record of Tenderness* (1919) and *Fakt* (1919).

2. Benedikt Livshits, *One and a Half-Eyed Archer*, trans. John Bowlt (Newtonville, MA: Oriental Research Partners, 1977); Vladimir Markov's comprehensive *Russian Futurism* (Berkeley: University of California Press, 1968); John Bowlt, ed., *Russian Art of the Avant-Garde* (New York: Viking, 1976); and Viktor Shklovsky's *Mayakovsky and His Circle,* trans. Lily Feiler (London: Pluto Press, 1975).

3. Gerald Janecek, *The Look of Russian Literature* (Princeton: Princeton University Press, 1984); Susan Compton, *Worldbackwards: Russian Futurist Books 1912-16* (London: British Library, 1978).

4. Note in the chronology for 1919, no source.

5. Published in *Carnet* 5 (Paris: L'Iliazd Club, 2000), with an introduction by Régis Gayraud.

6. The chronology suggests they went to Mount Kloukorsk, but I have been unable to track this.

7. Ilia Zdanevich, "Two Attempts to Climb Tbilisis-tseri (4419 meters) in Uilpaty Mountains," *Bulletin of Caucasus Department of Russian Geographical Society*, 1917.

8. A cyclostyle is a desktop printing machine that can be used to reproduce handwriting with stencils.

9. The chronology gives the location of this production as the studio of "Stéphanie Essen," which I have not been able to track or cross-reference unless it is a misspelling of Sergei Essenine.

10. "Words in liberty" is Marinetti's phrase, the poem for Roland Garros, *Carnet* 5 (Paris, 2000).

11. Iliazd, "Letter to Soffici / Fifty Years After," *Carnet* 2 (Paris, 1992): 21–54. Written in 1962, the letter references the conflict that Iliazd had had with the Lettrists in the 1940s, a conflict discussed in chapter 7.

12. Iliazd, "Fifty Years After," 31.

13. Willem G. Weststeijn, "Another Language, Another World: The Linguistic Experiments of Velimir Khlebnikov," *L'Esprit Créateur* 38, no. 4, Altérités dans la langue (Alterities in Language) (Winter 1998): 27–37, https://www.jstor.org/stable/pdf/26288139.pdf.

14. Iliazd, "Fifty Years After," 31; "Dyr bul shchyl," considered one of the most famous *zaum* poems, is credited as the first, appearing in 1912.

15. Iliazd manuscript, dated 1968, 17.

16. Iliazd manuscript, dated 1968, 17.

17. The chronology identifies this as Mount Katchar, but I cannot locate the geographical reference with that spelling.

18. Iliazd, *Letters to Price,* 1929 manuscript, subsequently published as *Lettres à Morgan Philips Price,* translated from Russian by Régis Gayraud (Paris: Clemence Hiver, 1989), contains descriptions of incidents that turned him against the Russians and also recorded some of the political complexities of the Turkish capital.

19. Unable to verify this name or any individual identified with it.

20. Iliazd, "Letter to Marinetti," written at the beginning of 1922, reproduced in facsimile and transcription in *Iliazd: Maître d'oeuvre du livre moderne,* ed. Françoise Le Gris-Bergmann (Montréal: Université du Québec à Montréal, 1984), 102–104.

21. Tatiana Nikolskaya, *Ardis Anthology of Russian Futurism* (Ann Arbor, MI: Ardis, 1980), 295–326 (297).

22. Nikolskaya, in *Ardis Anthology*, gives her source for this: G. Robak'idze, *Phalestra kartuli mts'erloba*, no. 4, 1928.

23. *Kuranty* 2 (1919), cited by Nikolskaya in *Ardis Anthology*. I have not been able to find cross-references for S. Koron or Degen.

24. Markov, *Russian Futurism*, 338–339.

25. Cited by Raymond Cogniat, *Comoedia*, November 1921.

26. The version translated here from French was published in Paris in 1921, but Columbia University's Rare Book & Manuscript Library has acquired a copy of the first version that was shown in the 2019 exhibition *Ilia Zdanevich: The Tbilisi Years.*

27. Annick Lionel-Marie, Germain Viatte, and Laure de Buzon-Vallet, eds., *Iliazd* (Paris: Centre Georges Pompidou, 1978), 94, translated from French by Johanna

Drucker, but there is no indication in the publication of who did the French translation from Russian.

28. The cyclostyle technique described earlier was ideal for reproducing handwriting.

29. The full list appears as "Appendix I" in *Iliazd*, ed. Lionel-Marie, Viatte, and Buzon-Vallet, 92.

30. Lionel-Marie, Viatte, and Buzon-Vallet, "Appendix I," 92.

31. Lionel-Marie, Viatte, and Buzon-Vallet, "Appendix I," 92; "Dody" is likely a nickname for David Burliuk. The names Tioutchev and Brioussov refer to Fyodor Tyutchev and Valery Bryusov.

32. Iliazd, "Letter to Marinetti," 103.

33. Olga Djordjadze, "Ilia Zdanevitch [*sic*]," in *Iliazd*, ed. Lionel-Marie, Viatte, and Buzon-Vallet, 14.

34. Appears in the manuscript version of the text prepared by Olga Djordjadze, but not in the published version.

35. Lionel-Marie, Viatte, and Buzon-Vallet, eds., *Iliazd*, 52. The journal contains Igor Terentiev's "A record of tenderness."

36. Tatiana Nikolskaya, "Russian Writers," in *Ardis Anthology of Russian Futurism*, 303, citing the only issue of *Journal of 41 Degrees* 1 (July 1919): 1.

37. Nikolskaya, "Russian Writers," 309. I can find no trace of "Ginna Matignoni."

38. Iliazd, manuscript, "50 Years of Forty-One Degrees," 1968.

39. These were abilities I could understand from my own firsthand experience in the print shop since I had played with the possibilities of typographic combination in the 1970s and early 1980s.

40. Iliazd, "50 Years of Forty-One Degrees."

41. The futurist scholar, Vasily Katanyan, cited by Gerald Janecek in *The Look of Russian Literature*, 165.

42. Markov, *Russian Futurism*, 340.

43. See *Ilia Zdanevich: The Tbilisi Years*, https://blogs.cul.columbia.edu/global -studies/2019/04/24/ilia-zdanevich-the-tbilisi-years-an-exhibit-at-columbias-rare -book-manuscript-library-through-july-12-2019/.

44. Nikolskaya, "Russian Writers," 313. See an image of the anthology with Iliazd's page displayed: https://blogs.cul.columbia.edu/global-studies/2019/04/24 /ilia-zdanevich-the-tbilisi-years-an-exhibit-at-columbias-rare-book-manuscript -library-through-july-12-2019/.

45. Gerald Janecek, *Zaum: The Transrational Poetry of Russian Futurism* (San Diego: San Diego State University Press, 1996), 256.

46. Janecek, *Zaum*, 49.

47. Janecek, *Zaum*, 50.

48. Inspirations for *zaum* came from many sources, including the celebration of emotion over reason that was a persistent element in romanticism. By the late

nineteenth century, this sensibility had been reformulated in the symbolist poetics of Andrei Bely. Bely ascribed magical properties to language, and considered the invention of words as an innovative breakthrough essential to imaginative life. Attention to sound as a fundamental element of sensation is always a central feature of poetics, but the *zaum* poets took this as the means by which to get beyond the limits of reason and literal imagery and work with the affective potential of language. If symbolists believed that the resonances of the word offered access to a plane beyond the literal, one that revealed the higher meaning or symbolic value of language, then the *zaum*niks differed in their belief that poetic language had a direct effect, embodying sensation and emotion, rather than pointing to its existence in a symbolic form. This insistence on the immanent quality of language, on its material force and effect as the site and instrument of poetics, made futurism modern and marked the radical break with symbolist aesthetics. But other features of *zaum*, in particular the attention to affect and emotion, stressed continuity with a long tradition in which non-rational thought was associated with poetics.

The *zaum* confederates drew on a synthesis of other sources that were much debated in artistic circles in the preceding years. These included the philosophy of Henri Bergson and his interest in change, flux, and instability, the work of Sigmund Freud, translated into Russian and a source through which to justify eroticism in many forms, and works of Russian linguists interested in sound symbolism, folk etymology, and the affective impact of language in communication that had been fostered by the highly influential nineteenth-century figure, Alexander von Humboldt. Other theoretical insights arose as the group of young linguists who identified themselves as "The Society for the Study of Poetic Language," or Opayaz, formed in St. Petersburg around Viktor Shklovsky in 1914, and a group with different sensibilities but equal seriousness formed as the Moscow Linguistics Circle at about the same time. (A letter received by Iliazd in Paris confirmed his acquaintance with Shklovsky.) Linguistics, formalism, and aesthetics shared themes and sources, but also, the communities of intellectuals involved overlapped in their activities so that the study of sound and meaning, of sense and affect, of politics and meaning, moved through these scenes with fluidity.

49. Janecek, *Zaum*, 256.
50. Janecek, *Zaum*, 263.
51. Janecek's studies in *Zaum,* as well as his work in *The Look of Russian Literature,* provide the most complete examination of this aspect of Russian poetics to date and are invaluable.
52. Markov, *Russian Futurism*, 341-342.
53. Markov, *Russian Futurism*, 342.
54. Markov, *Russian Futurism,* 348.
55. Markov, *Russian Futurism,* 358.

56. Johanna Drucker, "The Futurist Work of Ilia Zdanevich," "Back to Futurism," ed. Nicholas Rzhevsky, *Slavic and East European Arts* 10, no. 1 & 2 (Winter 2002): 13-43; also in the same issue, my translation of Régis Gayraud, "Ilia Zdanevich: *Zaum* and the Parisian Lectures (1921)," 45-100.

57. Nina Gurianova, *The Russian Futurists and Their Books* (Paris: La Hune, 1993).

58. "The Future of the Book," a theoretical text about books by Lazar El Lissitzky, was published in the 1926-27 issue of *Gutenberg-Jahrbuch* (Mainz). It proclaims that books are instruments for mass communication of ideas, meant for broad circulation. The year 1923 was when Lissitzky published the strikingly designed edition of Mayakovsky's *For the Voice*. It was also the year that Iliazd produced *Ledentu,* the fifth and final volume of his series of *zaum* plays. The two works bear comparison for their difference in approach as well as the features they have in common, http://monoskop.org/images/6/6a/Lissitzky_El_1926_1967_The _Future_of_the_Book.pdf.

59. Olga Djordjadze, "Ilia Zdanevitch [*sic*] et le Futurisme Russe," in *Iliazd,* ed. Lionel-Marie, Viatte, and Buzon-Vallet, 16. See also Régis Gayraud, "Iliazd et le Degré 41," in *Iliazd,* ed. Le Gris-Bergmann, 9-16. Gayraud's discussion of the *dras* uses Djordjadze as its source.

60. Iliazd, "Fifty Years After," 26; the coincidence of Yanko and the surname of Marcel Janco, the Dadaist whose piece "L'Amiral Cherche une Maison à Louer" was also set in orchestral verse in 1916, is merely that. Iliazd did not know what the Dadaists were doing at that moment and did not learn of the existence of that piece until 1920. (See Markov, *Russian Futurism,* 417, n.136.)

61. Iliazd, unpublished notes on the death of Mané-Katz.

62. Iliazd, "Fifty Years After," 26; see Markov, *Russian Futurism,* 417, n.136.

63. Iliazd, unpublished notes on the death of Mané-Katz.

64. Markov, *Russian Futurism,* 358.

65. Djordjadze, "Ilia Zdanevitch [*sic*] et le Futurisme Russe," 18.

66. Terentiev, "Record of Tenderness," *Journal of 41 Degrees* 1, cited by Nikolskaya, "Russian Writers," 303.

67. Djordjadze, "Ilia Zdanevitch [*sic*] et le Futurisme Russe," 18; André Marko-wicz, "Ilia Zdanevitch [*sic*]," unpublished manuscript, undated (before 1985), 7.

68. Terentiev, "Record of Tenderness," cited by Nikolskaya, 306.

69. Terentiev, "Record of Tenderness," cited by Nikolskaya, 306.

70. All details in this paragraph are from Djordjadze, "Ilia Zdanevitch [*sic*] et le Futurisme Russe."

71. Terentiev, *Journal of 41 Degrees* 1, and from Nikolskaya, 303.

72. Djordjadze, "Ilia Zdanevitch [sic] et le Futurisme Russe," 19.

73. Nikolskaya, "Russian Writers," 303-304.

74. Nikolskaya, "Russian Writers," 303.

75. Djordjazde, "Ilia Zdanevitch [*sic*] et le Futurisme Russe," 20; Markowicz, "Ilia Zdanevitch [*sic*]," undated manuscript. 9-10.

76. Djordjazde, "Ilia Zdanevitch [*sic*] et le Futurisme Russe," 20. Her source is unpublished notes that I have not seen.

77. See Museum of Modern Art's online gallery, https://www.moma.org /collection/works/11650?artist_id=12660&locale=en&page=1&sov_referrer=artist.

78. Janecek, *The Look of Russian Literature,* 167. Janecek's discussion explores the orthography and language in detail.

79. Mzia Chikhradze, "Futurist Books: Tbilisi 1917-1919" (2018), http:// kunsthallezurich.ch/en/articles/futurist-books-tbilisi-1917%E2%80%931919.

80. Markov, *Russian Futurism,* 354.

81. Recent scholarship on Iliazd's futurist typography and writings can be found in Robert Leach, *Russian Futurist Theater: Theory and Practice* (Edinburgh: Edinburgh University Press, 2018), and Alan Bartram, *Futurist Typography and the Liberated Text* (New Haven: Yale University Press, 2005); both depend on and stay close to Markov and Djordjadze. The best and most imaginative treatment of the typography of the *dras* is Mikhaïl Karassik, "Les Cinq Pièces Typographiques d'Ilia Zdanevich," *Carnet* 9 (Paris, 2019): 17-48.

Chapter 4. 1920-1921: Transition: Tbilisi, Constantinople, Paris

1. Hélène never signaled that these were anything other than actual letters, so I took their mode as that of actual correspondence, not a work composed in a conceit of communication.

2. Iliazd, "Declaration to the Arts Commission of the Georgian Assembly by Elie Zdanevitch [*sic*], Fifth of October, 1920, Tiflis," Fonds Iliazd.

3. Iliazd, *Letters to Price,* 1929 manuscript, subsequently published as *Lettres à Morgan Philips Price,* translated from Russian by Régis Gayraud (Paris: Clemence Hiver, 1989), 47.

4. Iliazd, *Letters to Price*, 18.

5. Iliazd, *Letters to Price*.

6. Iliazd, *Letters to Price*.

7. Iliazd, *Letters to Price,* 52.

8. Iliazd, *Letters to Price,* 24.

9. Iliazd, *Letters to Price*, 33-34.

10. Letter to M. G. Deny, December 1932, Iliazd archive.

11. Iliazd, *Letters to Price*, 38.

12. Iliazd archive manuscript.

13. A copy remained in the Iliazd archive.

14. Thomas Kitson is in the process of translating this novel.

15. Iliazd archive manuscript.

16. Iliazd, *Letters to Price*, 38. Pera and Galata refer to districts of the city.

17. Régis Gayraud, Préface, in Iliazd, *Lettres*, 16.

18. The notes suggest that this was someone related to his mother's stepfather, a woman named Jeanne Mojnevsky, but he had little if any contact with her once he was in France.

19. Iliazd, *Letters to Price*. The first letter in particular but also *Carnet* 2 (Paris: L'Iliazd Club, 1992) contains a section on letters and articles from 1915-1916, a dossier put together by Luigi Magarotto with translations by Régis Gayraud, 79-100. This contains letters to editors of various Caucasian journals as well as other documents about the treatment of the Laz people and others.

20. The fourth letter is dated June 24, 1929.

Chapter 5. 1921-1926: Paris

1. Chronology for 1921, established with the help of Hélène Zdanevich; Iliazd manuscript, letter to Ali Bey dated February 9, 1922.

2. Florence Calle, *Robert et Sonia Delaunay* (catalogue) (Paris: Bibliothèque Nationale, 1977), 44.

3. All of these figures are identifiable as part of an émigré community of artists, intellectuals, dancers, and writers.

4. Lucien Scheler, "Le Magicien du Mont Caucase," *Bulletin du Bibliophile* 2, special issue, "Hommage à Iliazd" (Paris, 1974).

5. Vladimir Pozner, *Het Overzicht* 20, Anvers (January 1924).

6. Serge Rafalovich, "Presentation of Ilia Zdanevich to the Paris Public on the Occasion of His First Lecture in Paris," November 27, 1921, manuscript, Iliazd archive.

7. Rafalovich, "Presentation of Ilia Zdanevich."

8. The text of Iliazd's "New Schools of Russian Poetry" is translated from the French version in Régis Gayraud's thesis, "Il'ja Zdanevic, Theoricien et Promoteur du *zaum'* dans ses conferences parisiennes (1921-1923)," Mémoire de D.E.A. sous l direction de M. Michel Aucouturier (Université de Paris-Sorbonne, 1984). Translated by Johanna Drucker and eventually published in *Slavic and East European Arts* 10, no. 1 and 2 (Winter 2002): 45-100. With permission of Gayraud.

9. Iliazd, "Conference at the Studio of Olénine d'Alheim," November 1922 manuscript, translated by Vitaly Kerdimun.

10. Iliazd, "Conference at the Studio of Olénine d'Alheim."

11. Raymond Cogniat, "The University of 41 Degrees, A Laboratory of Poetry," *Comoedia*.

12. Cogniat, "The University of 41 Degrees."

13. Gayraud's 1984 thesis notes that the French translation was done by Mikhail Tamanscheff and that the Russian manuscript is only partially extant.

14. Gayraud, "Il'ja Zdanevic, Theoricien et Promoteur," provided a window into

the Russian-language lectures Iliazd delivered on Russian poetics and theoretical issues central to his own thinking.

15. Gayraud, "Il'ja Zdanevic, Theoricien et Promoteur," 14.

16. Iliazd, "New Schools of Russian Poetry," Paris, November 27, 1921.

17. Iliazd manuscript, reproduced in facsimile and transcription in *Iliazd: Maître d'oeuvre du livre moderne*, ed. Françoise Le Gris-Bergmann (Montréal: Université du Québec à Montréal, 1984), 102–104.

18. Iliazd, manuscript letter to Ali Bey, February 9, 1922.

19. Iliazd, poster text, "The Praise of Iliazd," May 12, 1922.

20. André Germain, *Créer* 1 (January-February 1923).

21. Régis Gayraud, manuscript translation of the lecture at the studio of Olénine d'Alheim, November 28, 1922.

22. Iliazd, "Letter to Soffici/Fifty Years After," *Carnet* 2 (Paris: L'Iliazd Club, 1992).

23. Iliazd, "Fifty Years After," 16.

24. The date of this adoption is not consistent in Iliazd's notes.

25. The letter addressed to Romoff, the director of the Union of Russian Artists (OUDAR), was signed by various artists and was in partial response to an article that had appeared in *Le Messager Russe*, entitled, "The Artistic Life of Russian Artists and Painters in Montparnasse from 1921-1924," written by L. Volguine, Iliazd archive.

26. The letter addressed to Romoff.

27. Notes on the 1923 chronology, from the announcement.

28. From archive notes.

29. What the objection to Herrand was is unclear; he apparently played swashbuckler parts on stage.

30. Iliazd, "En Approachant Éluard," published in *Carnet* 1 (Paris, 1990) in a version edited and with an excellent introduction by Régis Gayraud, and including various related documents.

31. Scheler, "Le Magicien du Mont Caucase," 181-184.

32. Iliazd, "En Approchant Éluard."

33. Iliazd, "En Approchant Éluard."

34. From the Éluard account sworn with witnesses before the lawyer, Maitre Boulard, July 1923, manuscript preserved in the Iliazd archive.

35. Éluard account.

36. Letter from Iliazd to Tzara, 1937.

37. Iliazd, "En Approchant Éluard."

38. The sale was presided over by Leonce Rosenberg; the collection included works by Braque, de Chirico, Derain, Vlaminck, Ernst, Gris, Laguet, Klee, Modigliani, Masson, Metzinger, Picasso, Picabia, Redon, Renoir, Man Ray, Survage, and others. Iliazd, "En Approchant Éluard." This section also cited in Annick Lionel-Marie, Germain Viatte, and Laure de Buzon-Vallet, eds., *Iliazd* (Paris: Centre Georges

Pompidou, 1978) in the chronology established by Hélène Zdanevich and Annick Lionel-Marie, 60.

39. Iliazd, Subscription announcement for *Ledentu* (1923).

40. Iliazd, "En Approachant Éluard," 45.

41. Markowicz offered this observation in his analysis of the play. Unpublished manuscript, "Ilia Zdanevitch [*sic*]," 10.

42. Olga Djordjadze, "Iliazd," in *Iliazd*, ed. Lionel-Marie, Viatte, and Buson-Vallet (1978), 22.

43. Gerald Janecek, *The Look of Russian Literature* (Princeton: Princeton University Press, 1984), 180.

44. Iliazd, "New Schools of Russian Poetry."

45. Djordjazde, "Iliazd," 21.

46. Djordjazde, "Iliazd," 21.

47. Iliazd, "New Schools of Russian Poetry."

48. Markowicz, unpublished manuscript, "Ilia Zdanevitch [*sic*]," 12.

49. A transcription from the notes in the archive has *Humanité* scribbled onto it. The source of this information is unclear.

50. Vladimir Pozner, notes in the archive.

51. De Massot, transcribed from a note in the archive, source unclear.

52. Viktor Shklovsky, archive manuscript written around 1923-24.

53. By contrast, Lazar El Lissitzky's treatment of Vladimir Mayakovsky's *For the Voice*, also published in 1923, had been regularly reproduced in histories of graphic design.

54. Text of the announcement. The book was dedicated to Vera Choukaïeff.

55. Iliazd, unpublished manuscript in the archive.

Chapter 6. 1927-1946: Family, Fabric, and Fiction

1. Shari Benstock, *Women of the Left Bank* (Austin: University of Texas Press, 1986).

2. Unpublished letter to Axel, 1926, Iliazd archive.

3. Unpublished manuscript, Iliazd archive.

4. Unpublished manuscript, Iliazd archive.

5. Notes in the archive.

6. Legal deposit for this design, a loom named "Rachel," was made on May 9, 1928, which "would give to knits the strength of woven fabric while keeping them soft and supple."

7. Iliazd, *Letters to Price*, 1929 manuscript, subsequently published as *Lettres à Morgan Philips Price*, translated from Russian by Régis Gayraud (Paris: Clemence Hiver, 1989), 1.

8. Elizabeth Klosty Beaujour, "Iliazd Romancier," in *Iliazd: Maître d'oeuvre du livre*

moderne, ed. Françoise Le Gris-Bergmann (Montréal: Université du Québec à Montréal, 1984), 17–19.

9. Beaujour, "Iliazd Romancier," 17–19. I cannot say I share her enthusiasm for this book.

10. The complete list includes these additional names: Price (England); Jakobson (Czechoslovakia); Wederkorp, Nanaba (Germany); Feldstein, Blacke, Soudekin, Tarsadize (Russia) Kirill Zdanevich, Terentiev, Brik, Mayakovsky, Tretiakov, Tyutchev, Svidersky, Gorky (Moscow); Lechkova, Ermolaeva, Lapchine, Kouzmine, Kharms, Vvedensky, Vaguinov, Lourkoun, Malevich (Leningrad). The list does not include people in Paris.

11. A year later, Mirsky requested permission to return to the Soviet Union; he was arrested soon after and died.

12. D. S. Mirsky, *Nouvelle Revue Française,* December 1931, from text reprinted in *Iliazd,* ed. Lionel-Marie, Viatte, and Buzon-Vallet (1978).

13. The assessment paraphrased here is Beaujour's, "Iliazd Romancier," 17.

14. The book was reprinted in Russian, with the title *Voskhishchenie,* by the *Berkeley Slavic Specialties,* 1983. The book was translated into French by Régis Gayraud, published as *Le Ravissement* (Paris: Alinea, 1986).

15. An inventory of notebook texts assembled by Régis Gayraud and François Mairé and published in *Carnet* 7 includes an entry for the account of this journey, 189.

16. Letter to Axel, August 31, 1929, when he was in Sixt at the Hotel des Alpes.

17. "Cercle de Cervantes," unpublished manuscript, Iliazd archive.

18. Iliazd archive manuscript.

19. Unpublished notes, Iliazd archive. My own notes include the statement that the portrait by Spencer was in Hélène's possession.

20. Unpublished manuscript, Iliazd archive. The date is unclear, as it suggests the note was written on November 9, 1937, but that would be nineteen years after Apollinaire's death. Perhaps the event was honored yearly.

21. Iliazd was adamant on this point, Hélène said, and he refused to have Axel visit the children, who were then about eleven and twelve.

22. André Markowicz's French translations are presented in *Carnet* 2 (Paris: L'Iliazd Club, 1992), 7–12.

23. Printed announcement for *Afat,* 1940.

24. Le Gris-Bergmann, ed., *Iliazd: Maître d'oeuvre du livre moderne* (1984), 44.

25. Unpublished notes dated 1965, cited in *Iliazd,* ed. Lionel-Marie, Viatte, and Buzon-Vallet (1978).

26. A note dated February 14, 1977, from J.-P. Breitling is the source for this information in the Iliazd archive.

27. I am unsure what the source of this information was, except Hélène.

28. Also cited in *Iliazd,* ed. Lionel-Marie, Viatte, and Buzon-Vallet (1978), 64.

29. April 11, 1984, is the date on the transcript, a year before I knew Hélène. Eristoff said that he had returned the manuscript to Hélène after the death of Iliazd. Ania Starisky, a Russian painter and friend of Iliazd, had created a layout and engravings for the book, but she died in 1982 before it was published. In 1983, Hélène published the book with the text translated by André Markowicz and Guillevic.

30. Archive notes.

Chapter 7. 1947-1950: Lettrist Provocations and *Poetry of Unknown Words* (*Poésie de Mots Inconnus*)

1. Jean Leymarie, *La Rencontre Iliazd-Picasso, Hommage à Iliazd* (Paris: Musée d'Art Moderne, 1976), cited in *Iliazd*, ed. Annick Lionel-Marie, Germain Viatte, and Laure de Buzon-Vallet (Paris: Centre Georges Pompidou, 1978), 67.

2. From Iliazd, *The Letter*, trans. André Markowicz, in *Poésie Russe, La Decouverte* (Paris: Maspero, 1983), 469, reissued as a bilingual Russian-French edition, *La Lettre: Pismo [L'Epistolaire]* trans. André Markowicz (Paris: Clemence Hiver, 1990).

3. Iliazd, *The Letter*.

4. Raymond Cogniat, *Arts*, July 9, 1948.

5. For a detailed analysis of the book's structure, see David Sume, *The Architectural Nature of the Illustrated Books of Iliazd*, dissertation, Université de Montréal, 2018, 76-88. Sume's work is invaluable for its attention to structural detail and its bibliography, https://papyrus.bib.umontreal.ca/xmlui/bitstream/handle/1866/21735/Sume_David_2018_these.pdf.

6. See François Chapon, "Bibliographie des livres imprimés édités par Iliazd," in *Iliazd*, ed. Lionel-Marie, Viatte, and Buzon-Vallet (1978), 111.

7. The dossier for *Poésie de Mots Inconnus & Le Débat Lettriste* was published as *Carnet* 8 (Paris: L'Iliazd Club, 2014) and contains analysis by Françoise Le Gris, Régis Gayraud, and much useful information about the conflicts leading to the book and the profiles of the artists involved.

8. Many of these are at the Beinecke Library at Yale; others are at the Bibliothèque Nationale in Paris, and show the kind of careful, detailed, even obsessive design that characterized his work. All decisions are worked through carefully, down to the detail of every letter's placement in relation to the folded sheets, the sketched images, and organization of the whole. Proofs and page dummies also exist, as well as models for the cover and its pleats and folds.

9. The reference to "La tour du Pin" remains obscure as does "Emmanuel," but the sense is clear.

10. "La Danse du Scalp à La Mode Lettriste," *Arts,* August 30, 1946.

11. "La Danse du Scalp à La Mode Lettriste." A very similar report by Colin-Simard appeared in print on November 28, 1946.

12. *Combat*, June 20, 1947, unsigned.

13. June 20, 1947.

14. *Arts*, December 12, 1947.

15. Letters from Iliazd to *La Libération* dated November and December 1947.

16. Isidore Isou, *Traité d'économie nucléaire. I. Le soulèvement de la jeunesse* (Paris: Aux Escaliers de Lausanne, 1949).

17. If there are others, I have not seen them. The next major anthologies of visual poetry were issued in the 1960s, edited by Emmett Williams, *An Anthology of Concrete Poetry* (New York: Something Else Press, 1967); Mary Ellen Solt, *Concrete Poetry: A World View* (Bloomington: Indiana University Press, 1968); and Stephen Bann, *Concrete Poetry: An International Anthology* (London: Mag Editions, 1967). *The Dada Anthology of Poets and Painters*, edited by Robert Motherwell, was another milestone publication, and appeared in 1951.

18. Absent were Guillaume Apollinaire, Pierre Reverdy, and Stéphane Mallarmé, two of whom Iliazd had never known personally.

19. Françoise Le Gris includes a useful analysis of these pairings in her study in *Carnet* 8.

20. Unpublished notes, Iliazd archive.

21. Woodblocks were printed at the Imprimerie Union by Pierre Breuillet from May 5 to June 23, 1949; etchings by Emile Gontharet on the press of Paul Haasen, May 24, 1949; engravings and drypoint by Guy Aner and Georges Chertuite at the studio of Roger Lacourière from April 1 to May 6, 1949; and the lithographs by Pierre Derue, Joseph Legras, Emile Rapp, and Georges Sagourin under the supervision of Jean Celestin at the studio of Mourlot Frères. See Chapon, "Bibliographie des livres imprimés édités par Iliazd," in *Iliazd* (1978), 107–117.

22. Unclear to whom this letter was addressed, possibly Herta Hausmann, who may have helped him with the pages of *The Letter* a year earlier, or perhaps more likely, Olga Djordjadze.

23. Iliazd archive, notebook with information about *Poésie de Mots Inconnus*.

24. The pairings are as follows: Akinsemoyin/Matisse, Albert-Birot/Picasso, Arp/Bryen, Artaud/Braque, Audiberti/Metzinger, Ball/Taeuber-Arp, Beaudin/Gleizes, Dermee/Laurens, Huidobro/Magnelli, Iliazd/Léger, Iliazd/Wols, Jolas/Masson, Khlebnikov/Chagall, Kruchenykh/Giacometti, Poplavsky/Férat, Schwitters/Hausmann, Seuphor/Survage, Terentiev/Tytgat, Tzara/Miró. A certain amount of alphabetical order appears, but it is not strictly adhered to and neither are there evident connections of prior relationships.

25. The "friends" were Paul Éluard, Jaime Sabartes, Françoise Gilot, Lydia Delectorskaya (Matisse's companion), and Louis Broder.

26. In spring 2019, a much overdue exhibit at the Pompidou brought attention to Isou's work (to a mixed critical reception).

Chapter 8. 1951-1975: The Editions: Collaborations and Projects

1. See Françoise Le Gris-Bergmann, "Iliazd and the Constellation of His Oeuvre," in *Iliazd and the Illustrated Book* (New York: Museum of Modern Art, 1987). This essay is a condensed version of the French text in the catalogue of the 1985 exhibit she curated. She reads the books through her own set of useful frameworks.

2. A living artist can be commissioned to do new images, but not a dead one, obviously, while contemporary writers were a risky business since their commercial viability was harder to gauge than that of a well-established painter. The marketing model depended on a certain amount of celebrity status to guarantee sales.

3. Beatrice Warde, "The Crystal Goblet, or Printing Should Be Invisible" (London, 1932), originally published under the pseudonym Paul Beaujon. http://very interactive.net/content/2-library/52-the-crystal-goblet/warde-thecrystalgoblet.pdf.

4. Anne Moeglin-Delcroix is the French critic most attached to this definition of the artist's book. *Esthétique du livre d'artiste: 1960-1980* (Paris: Bibliothèque Nationale, 1997). The date range of her subtitle indicates her focus on conceptual artists' books from this period.

5. The bibliography established by François Chapon, "Bibliographie des livres imprimés édités par Iliazd," in *Iliazd,* ed. Annick Lionel-Marie, Germain Viatte, and Laure de Buzon-Vallet (Paris: Centre Georges Pompidou, 1978), 107-117, provides detailed information on these features, the specific papers, edition sections, and sizes.

6. Iliazd, unpublished notes, archive. The original edition, which appears to be the only possible source for Iliazd's work, was published in 1630 under the title *Les iuex de l'incognv.* (Paris, Chez T. del al Ruel). This must be the volume in which the text of *La Maigre* is bound.

7. This work was put into print after his death through the joint efforts of Antoine Coron and Hélène Zdanevich.

8. Iliazd, unpublished notes, archive.

9. Adrian de Monluc, *La Maigre* (Paris: Forty-One Degrees, 1952).

10. The observation is cited in Jean Leymarie's "Introduction" to *La Rencontre Iliazd-Picasso, Hommage à Iliazd* (Paris: Musée d'Art Moderne, 1976), unnumbered pages.

11. Iliazd, unpublished notes, archive.

12. Letter from Iliazd to Alexander Loewy dated December 11, 1956, describing the proofs and printing details. Iliazd archive.

13. *Carnet 7* (Paris: L'Iliazd Club, 2010): 11-92, contains an extensive dossier on the Imprimerie Union with reminiscences and commentary.

14. Alfred Jarry, *Exploits and Opinions of Doctor Faustroll, Pataphysician: A Neo-Scientific Novel* (Boston: Exact Change, 1996).

15. Louis Barnier, "Iliazd, notre compagnon," in *Iliazd,* ed. Lionel-Marie, Viatte, and Buzon-Vallet (1978), 23–31.

16. Cited by Françoise Le Gris-Bergmann, ed., *Iliazd: Maître d'oeuvre du livre moderne* (Montréal: Université du Québec à Montréal, 1984), 62.

17. Le Gris-Bergmann, ed., *Iliazd* (1984), 62.

18. Iliazd, unpublished notes, 1969; he communicated in 1952–53 with M. Caillet, head librarian at the Bibliothèque de la Ville de Toulouse about a possible exhibition of the work.

19. Lionel-Marie, Viatte, and Buzon-Vallet, eds., *Iliazd* (1978), 119–120.

20. Iliazd, unpublished notes, dated August 8, 1948.

21. Pierre Minet, "Le poete et dramaturge, Iliazd," *Combat,* July 18, 1947. The article described Iliazd as the "veritable founder of Lettrism." Published when the battles with the Lettrists were highly visible, it discussed Iliazd's *zaum* at some length and his proposals for using it as a ballet score. His aesthetic goals were to foster the rejuvenation of language through poetic invention—familiar themes of Iliazd's work and vision.

22. Iliazd, unpublished notes. Iliazd suggests he had begun collaboration with Matisse on this project in the summer, at Cannes, and further notes that when he visited Chauviré in her studio he "found" Lifar there as well.

23. Iliazd, unpublished notes dated January 29, 1970, at the time of her death.

24. Iliazd, unpublished notes on ballet. Balthazar Baro and Pierre Goudelin were poets, and Jean Chalette was a seventeenth-century portrait painter.

25. A page of my own notes from the 1980s lists works by Boissière and others, presumably in the Bibliothèque Nationale (they have call numbers), that extends the lists Iliazd put together in his page listing desired publications for which he was looking.

26. Ilizad, *Traité de Balet* (Paris: Forty-One Degrees, 1956).

27. Cited by Lionel-Marie, Viatte, and Buzon-Vallet, eds., *Iliazd* (1978), from a long text by Pierre Albert-Birot written as the introduction to a posthumous exhibition of her paintings.

28. Iliazd correspondence dated January 31, 1962, with a Madame Rousseau, who was the manager of Roch Grey's estate. Some confusion arose with regard to this project, and Madame Rousseau tried to extract payment from Ilizad for having used the manuscript. Earlier correspondence with Férat (in 1955) makes the terms of the arrangement explicit. Férat was to pay for production costs in exchange for 10 percent of the edition, which consisted of fifty-two numbered copies, plus sixteen examples given Roman numerals, reserved for friends and the *dépôt légal.*

29. For a more detailed discussion of the various communities of Russian émigré artists among whom Iliazd moved, see François Chapon, "Itinéraire d'Ilia Zdanevitch [sic] de Tiflis à la rue Mazarine," in *Iliazd,* ed. Lionel-Marie, Viatte, and Buzon-Vallet (1978), 33–41. Chapon characterizes Iliazd's disposition as inclined

toward those individuals who had been drawn *to* Paris for its artistic milieu, rather than those who had arrived simply to escape *from* their circumstances.

30. Roch Grey, *Chevaux de Minuit* (Paris: Forty-One Degrees, 1956).

31. Roch Grey, *Chevaux de Minuit*, 15.

32. Original publications by René Bordier on the subject of balls and ballets are readily located in WorldCat, and unlike Monluc, Bordier is not an entirely obscure or elusive figure.

33. This information is all from Iliazd's notes, cited in Lionel-Marie, Viatte, and Buzon-Vallet, eds., *Iliazd* (1978), 71.

34. Iliazd, cited in Le Gris-Bergmann, ed., *Iliazd* (1984), 43.

35. René Bordier, *Récit du Nord* (Paris: Forty-One Degrees, 1956).

36. François Chapon, "Bibliographie," in *Iliazd*, ed. Lionel-Marie, Viatte, and Buzon-Vallet (1978), 114. Georges Leblanc at the Atelier de l'Ermitage is named as the printer of the etching, while the text was produced, as usual, at the Imprimerie Union.

37. Iliazd, "En Approchant Éluard," unpublished notes dated 1965. Published in *Carnet 1* (Paris, 1990).

38. Lionel-Marie, Viatte, and Buzon-Vallet, eds., *Iliazd* (1978), 73.

39. Iliazd, "En Approchant Éluard."

40. Chapon, in the entry "Sillage intangible," *La Rencontre Iliazd-Picasso* (1976), n.p.

41. Chapon, "Sillage intangible," *La Rencontre Iliazd-Picasso* (1976), n.p. The reference is to Siegfried Bing's store, *Maison de L'Art Nouveau,* and Edouard Pelletan, publisher of deluxe editions in Paris.

42. Iliazd, "En Approchant Éluard."

43. Cited by Lionel-Marie, Viatte, and Buzon-Vallet, eds., *Iliazd* (1978), 83.

44. Cited by Lionel-Marie, Viatte, and Buzon-Vallet, eds., *Iliazd* (1978), 83.

45. Guino blamed his own lack of stature as an artist for this perceived failure.

46. The testimonials were in the Iliazd archive. The statement by Pierre Verger is a bit odd and describes Iliazd this way: "This sympathetic creature was dressed in winter in the curious coat of many overlapping skirts sworn by dandys of the last century or coach drivers of the pre-war era. He generally wore a black felt hat with floppy brim. Recently, he has taken to wearing the costume of a fisherman of Concarneau and the hat of a fresh water fisherman in the summer."

47. The signature of the Secretary of the Société Africaine de Culture is unreadable, but the letter is dated 1959.

48. Unpublished Hausmann-Iliazd correspondence, Iliazd archive.

49. Excerpt dated October 15, 1957, from Hausmann-Iliazd correspondence in the Iliazd archive.

50. Iliazd, *Poèmes et Bois* (Paris: Forty-One Degrees, 1961).

51. Lionel-Marie, Viatte, and Buzon-Vallet, eds., *Iliazd* (1978), 77. The crown of

sonnets is rarely found in Russian poetry, owing to the difficulty of completing the full cycle while retaining poetic language.

52. Hélène's explanation of the choice of name was very unclear, with a suggestion that the name combined features of "Alberto" and "Iliazd" in a sort of anagram.

53. The "planet" Maximiliana was first mentioned in the Éluard/Ernst collaboration in 1947, *A L'Interieur de la Vue.*

54. Iliazd, *L'Art de Voir de Guillaume Tempel* (Paris: Forty-One Degrees, 1964).

55. Iliazd manuscript, archive.

56. Anne Hyde Greet, "Iliazd and Max Ernst," *World Literature Today* 56 (Winter 1982).

57. All quotes from *Maximiliana* (Paris: Forty-One Degrees, 1962).

58. I believe this is true, though I may be misremembering her comments.

59. Antoine Coron, for some reason, disparages this work as a purely commercial undertaking meant to please the gallerists and dealers, according to comments in the May 2019 symposium at the Bibliothèque Nationale. Françoise Le Gris and I, both present, were equally surprised by this assessment as we share an appreciation of this remarkable book.

60. Chapon, "Bibliographie," in *Iliazd,* ed. Le Gris-Bergmann (1984), 130.

61. Annick Lionel-Marie, "Iliazd, facettes d'une vie," in *Iliazd,* ed. Lionel-Marie, Viatte, and Buzon-Vallet (1978), 78.

62. Iliazd archive, unpublished correspondence.

63. Notes in the archive indicate the following subscribers: Berggruen 3, Blaizot 6, Hughes 13, Loewy 6, Nicaize 3, Loeb 1, Hartug 1, with Ernst receiving 15. That totals 48, and in actuality the edition, according to Chapon, was 65 copies in the regular edition and 10 more, numbered in Roman numerals, on antique Japon. Chapon, "Bibliographie," in *Iliazd,* ed. Le Gris-Bergmann (1984), 130.

64. Mine Kadiroglu, "Islamic Features in the Architecture of Tao-Klardjet," in *Islamic Art and Architecture in the European Periphery*, ed. Barbara Kellner-Heinkele, Joachim Gierlichs, and Brigitte Heuer (Wiesbaden: Otto Harrassowitz Verlag, 2008), 189, fn.20.

65. The names H. Berberian, M. Izzet, M. Whittmore, and M. Salia appear in his correspondence.

66. The full list includes "Geometric Construction of a Byzantine Plan," Palermo, April 3–10, 1951, VIII Byzantine Congress; "Ruy Gonzales de Clavijo," Ochride-Belgrade, September 10–16, 1961, XII Byzantine Congress; "The Cathedral of Kissamos in Crete," Oxford, September 5–9, 1966, XIII Byzantine Congress; "The Georgians in the War of the Grand Seigneur," July 1–4, 1968, First International Congress in the History of Venetian Civilization; and notes for a paper projected for a conference in Bucharest in 1971 on "The Problem of the Asiatic Frontier of

the Seventh through Seventeenth Empires," which his health prevented him from delivering.

67. The place names are difficult to track: Avnik, Trevizond, Ekek, Tortum, and Kachkar are mentioned.

68. Iliazd, *Rogelio Lacourière* (Paris: Forty-One Degrees, 1968).

69. Boris Fridman presented a slide image of this form in a conference at Columbia University, March 7, 2019.

70. Madeleine Lacourière and Jacques Frélaut, *Bulletin de Bibliophile* 2 (Paris, 1974): 159-160.

71. Iliazd, *Rogelio Lacourière* (Paris: Forty-One Degrees, 1968).

72. Iliazd to Miró, January 25, 1951, unpublished correspondence; no trace of the Spanish preface exists.

73. "This lengthy business is not without resemblance to that of a lawsuit." January 20, 1965, unpublished notes. Iliazd had experienced certain difficulties in working with each of his collaborators. Miró, Ernst, Picasso, and Braque had been laggardly in their correspondence, needing continual reminders to send plates, or, in the case of Picasso, requiring replacements.

74. Unpublished correspondence, Iliazd archive. Which "fifteen years" are being referenced is unclear given the various starts and stops along the way.

75. Correspondence, Iliazd archive, published in Le Gris-Bergmann, ed., *Iliazd* (1984), 118-119.

76. Correspondence, Iliazd archive, published in Le Gris-Bergmann, ed., *Iliazd* (1984), 118-119.

77. Undated letter to Miró, Iliazd archive, published in Le Gris-Bergmann, ed., *Iliazd* (1984), 118-119.

78. Letter from Iliazd to Miró, dated January 20, 1965, published in Le Gris-Bergmann, ed., *Iliazd* (1984), 118-119.

79. Lionel-Marie, Viatte, and Buzon-Vallet, eds., *Iliazd* (1978), 90.

Chapter 9. 1971-1972: A Life in Reverse

1. Iliazd, in the invitation to the opening for *Boustrophédon*.

2. Iliazd, *Boustrophédon* (Paris: Forty-One Degrees, 1971). Elena/les draps de lit/se prolongent/en glaciers/les yeux verts/en astrophysique.

3. Iliazd, *Boustrophédon*. An equivalent of the English translation rendered this way would be: Anela/eht srevoc fo eht/dnetxe/ni sreicalg/ruoy neerg seye/scisyhportsa ni.

4. Iliazd, *Boustrophédon*.

5. Apparently the soldier had blacked his face and red hair for camouflage, but the hair had shone through the dye and given him away, causing his death.

6. Iliazd, *Boustrophédon*.

7. Iliazd, unpublished correspondence, February 2, 1971, Iliazd archive.

8. Georges Ribemont-Dessaignes, Preface, Iliazd, *Boustrophédon*.

9. Unpublished correspondence, Iliazd archive.

10. Cited by Louis Barnier in his introduction to the posthumously published edition of *Crève-Coeur* (Paris: Imprimerie Union, 1977). The book was published without images, but with the text laid out following Iliazd's design leaving empty the areas blocked for the plates.

11. Unedited notes of Iliazd, Iliazd archive. Other unpublished notes in Iliazd's papers described Picasso's place as a political artist and his relationship with the Communist party. Iliazd denigrated "party line" painting in general and praised the authentic politics of Picasso's work.

12. Claude Zdanevich, 1955, Iliazd archive.

13. Iliazd, "Letter to Soffici / Fifty Years After," *Carnet* 2 (Paris: L'Iliazd Club, 1992): 37.

Appendix. A Note on Recent Scholarship about Iliazd

1. https://doi.org/10.1093/fmls/XXXII.2.119.

2. The *Carnets* include many useful primary documents and critical studies. The full list can be found here: https://fr.wikipedia.org/wiki/Carnets_de_l%27Iliazd -Club.

3. Natella Voiskunski, "The 'Everyfeelingism' of Iliazd," *The Tretyakov Gallery Magazine* 1 no. 50 (2016), https://www.tretyakovgallerymagazine.com/articles/1 -2016-50/everyfeelingism-liiazd.

4. http://museum/ge/index.php?lang_id=ENG&sec_id=69&info_id=13900.

5. https://blogs.cul.columbia.edu/global-studies/2019/04/24/ilia-zdanevich-the -tbilisi-years-an-exhibit-at-columbias-rare-book-manuscript-library-through-july -12-2019/.

6. Johanna Drucker, "Iliazd and the Book as a Form of Art," *Journal of Decorative and Propaganda Arts* 7 (Winter 1988): 36–51.

Bibliography

Listed here are the chief sources of information about Iliazd on which I drew in the initial study, finished in the early 1990s. More recent sources are listed in the appendix and in the notes. The bulk of sources were manuscripts in the Iliazd archive, now in Marseilles.

Compton, Susan. *Russian Avant-Garde Books 1917-34*. Cambridge: MIT Press, 2006.

Isselbacher, Audrey. *Iliazd and the Illustrated Book*. New York: Museum of Modern Art, 1987.

Janecek, Gerald. *The Look of Russian Literature*. Princeton: Princeton University Press, 1984.

Le Gris-Bergmann, Françoise, ed. *Iliazd: Maître d'oeuvre du livre moderne*. Montréal: Université du Québec à Montréal, 1984. Contributions in this volume by Le Gris-Bergmann, Olga Djordjazde, Régis Gayraud, François Chapon, and primary documents reprinted have been cited throughout my study.

Leymarie, Jean. *La Rencontre Iliazd-Picasso: Hommage à Iliazd*. Paris: Musée d'Art Moderne, 1976. Includes: "Catalogue" by François Chapon and "Éléments pour une biographie," by Françoise Woimant.

Lionel-Marie, Annick. *Iliazd 1894-1985 Chronologie Sommaire*. Paris, 1984.

Lionel-Marie, Annick, Germain Viatte, and Laure de Buzon-Vallet, eds. *Iliazd*. Paris: Centre Georges Pompidou, 1978 (exhibition catalogue). Contributions by Olga Djordjadze, François Chapon, and Louis Barnier are invaluable resources, as are the chronology and appendices.

Livshits, Benedikt. *The One and a Half-Eyed Archer*. Newtonville, MA: Oriental Research Partners, 1977.

Markov, Vladimir. *Russian Futurism*. Berkeley: University of California Press, 1968.

Index

Page references to photographs and illustrations are in *italic* type.